PENGUIN CANADA

THE PENGUIN TREASURY OF POPULAR CANADIAN POEMS AND SONGS

John Robert Colombo is known as the Master Gatherer for his compilations of Canadiana. He is the author, editor, or translator of more than 130 books, which range from collections of science fiction and anthologies of ghost stories to *Colombo's Canadian Quotations* and *The Penguin Book of Canadian Jokes*.

THE PENGUIN TREASURY of Popular CANADIAN Poems  SONGS

EDITED BY

JOHN ROBERT COLOMBO

PENGUIN
CANADA

PENGUIN CANADA

Published by the Penguin Group

Penguin Books, a division of Pearson Canada, 10 Alcorn Avenue, Toronto,
Ontario, Canada M4V 3B2

Penguin Books Ltd, 80 Strand, London WC2R 0RL, England

Penguin Putnam Inc., 375 Hudson Street, New York, New York 10014, U.S.A.

Penguin Books Australia Ltd, 250 Camberwell Road, Camberwell, Victoria 3124,
Australia

Penguin Books India (P) Ltd, 11, Community Centre, Panchsheel Park,
New Delhi – 110 017, India

Penguin Books (NZ) Ltd, cnr Rosedale and Airborne Roads, Albany,
Auckland 1310, New Zealand

Penguin Books (South Africa) (Pty) Ltd, 24 Sturdee Avenue, Rosebank 2196,
South Africa

Penguin Books Ltd, Registered Offices: 80 Strand, London WC2R 0RL, England

First published 2002

10 9 8 7 6 5 4 3 2 1

Manufactured in Canada.

Pages 293–312 constitute an extension of the copyright page.

NATIONAL LIBRARY OF CANADA CATALOGUING IN PUBLICATION DATA

Main entry under title:

    The Penguin treasury of popular Canadian poems and songs / edited by
John Robert Colombo.

ISBN 0-14-301326-2

1. Canadian poetry (English). 2. Songs, English—Canada—Texts.
3. Songs, French—Canada—Texts. 4. Canada—Poetry.
5. Canada—Songs and music—Texts. I. Colombo, John Robert, 1936–

PS8273.P45 2002   C811.008   C2002-901944-3
PR9195.25.P45 2002

British Library Cataloguing in Publication Data Available
American Library of Congress Cataloguing in Publication Data Available

Visit Penguin Books' website at **www.penguin.ca**

For
Raymond Souster
and
William Toye

Contents

La Belle Province

Nature and Weather

People on the Land

Work and Labour

Stuff and Nonsense

Our Home and Native Land

Preface

This treasury consists of more than 150 popular poems, verses, songs, and rhymes that were composed by Canadians over the last century and a half. The collection exists because I feel that it is worthwhile to preserve these lyrics and to bring them to the attention of readers today and tomorrow.

One day it occurred to me that if, following some unforeseen catastrophe, all the volumes of Canadian poetry vanished from the face of the earth, only those poems, verses, songs, and rhymes that Canadians had learned by heart would remain in circulation. Using familiarity as a criterion, I asked myself, "What poems or titles of poems or lines of poems do I remember?" Then I asked relatives, friends, acquaintances, and colleagues to recall the compositions that they could remember. To these compositions, whether familiar to some or familiar to all, I have added other poems, verses, songs, and rhymes that I assume will become part of the canon of popular culture.

The coverage is broad. I have mingled major compositions and minor compositions, mainstream poems and marginal verses, as well as semi-literary compositions that are familiar to some degree to a great many English-Canadian readers. Hence the reader will find in these pages the still-eloquent lines of John McCrae's "In Flanders Fields," Rudyard Kipling's moving Great War inscriptions, the celebrated limerick that begins "There was a young lady named Bright," plus all the words of the monologue "I Am Canadian."

There are thirteen sections, and the arrangement of the contents is chronological within each section.

"With Glowing Hearts" offers the texts of our anthems in the two official languages, English and French.

"The True North" begins with two Native lyrics of great beauty and then recalls events in the country's past.

"Cries of Battle" pays homage to peace, bravery, sacrifice, and the war dead.

"Seas and Ships" takes a nautical turn and invites the reader aboard some vessels that ride the waves.

"Places Far and Near" moves briskly from Newfoundland to the Maritime provinces, crosses Quebec and Ontario before moving into the Western provinces, and then comes to rest in the Yukon and Northwest Territories.

"La Belle Province" begins with some folk songs identified with French Canadians and ends with some nationalistic pop songs of *les Québécois*.

"Nature and Weather" takes a look at the seasons and the weather and the climates we take for granted.

"Longing for Love" reprints the lyrics of old-fashioned songs, moving love poems, and a contemporary song of enchantment.

"Devotion and Remembrance" establishes a contemplative mood of awe and wonder.

"People on the Land" consists of portraits of men and women from many walks of life.

"Work and Labour" moves along briskly with songs that reflect the spirit of effort and endeavour.

"Stuff and Nonsense" takes delight in verbal oddities and curiosities, including limericks and satires.

"Our Home and Native Land" envisages the country as a whole and ends with a poem that offers a rich condensation of its culture and history.

The poetry of the twentieth century is better represented than the poetry of the nineteenth century. "So far as I am aware, there has been no single piece of verse that has spoken with so sure an accent as to become current among the Canadian people," Duncan Campbell Scott wrote in 1901 in a survey of the poetry of his day. As well, Northrop Frye observed in his study of E. J. Pratt, "There are no Canadian lyrics of any account before about 1880." In the absence of lyrics, Frye noted the presence of narrative forms. I have reprinted a number of narrative poems written by Duncan Campbell Scott, whose poetry remains of enduring worth. In our own time, contemporary poets are at an obvious disadvantage as their work has yet to withstand the so-called test of time and meet the criterion of familiarity.

The reader will find a handful of song lyrics composed by Canadians in the past that were publicly performed, privately sung, and deeply loved. I am thinking of such sentimental favourites as "When You and I Were Young, Maggie" and "In the Shade of the Old Apple Tree." The reader will also find a few pop songs composed by Canadians over the last few decades that have reached the ears of an appreciative public that far outnumbers the readership of popular poetry. A song like "Northwest Passage" is deeply rooted in the country's history. A lyric like "Suzanne Takes You Down" is recognizable around the world and identified as the work of a Canadian singer-songwriter-poet.

Longer works go unrepresented. (Yet I did include one excerpt from a longer work. I will allow the reader the pleasure of identifying it!) Older readers with good memories are probably able to recite the rhythmical lines of two narrative poems with early Canadian settings written by Henry Wadsworth Longfellow. The first is *Evangeline: A Tale of Acadie* (1847), which begins in a stately fashion:

> *This is the forest primeval. The mourning pines and the*
> *   hemlocks,*
> *Bearded with moss, and in garments green, indistinct in the*
> *   twilight,*
> *Stand like Druids of old. . . .*

The second is *The Song of Hiawatha* (1855), which starts with a rhetorical question:

> *Should you ask me, whence these stories?*
> *Whence these legends and traditions,*
> *With the odours of the forest,*
> *With the dew and damp of meadows.* . . .

Fewer readers will recall passages from the longer compositions of Archibald Lampman ("City at the End of Things," "At the Long Sault"), E. J. Pratt ("Brébeuf and His Brethren," "Towards the Last Spike"), and Earle Birney ("David"). I would dearly love to have included these works, but they are lengthy and suffer in excerpt.

Also unrepresented are verses and songs of protest. These range from "rhymes of rebellion" (which are occasionally recalled today at political gatherings) to "songs of labour" (among them Joe Hill's song "Where the Fraser River Flows"). The reader will find that these lyrics have been collected by N. Brian Davis and included in his two-volume anthology *The Poetry of the Canadian People* (1976, 1978). This anthology represents individual writers (Dawn Fraser, Edna Jaques, Joe Wallace, etc.), but it also contains the work of unknown bards and singers as well as anonymously written songs of work, labour, and protest.

Finally, I was glad to give short shrift to patriotic poems and verses, not so much to avoid the charge of jingoism as to spare the reader embarrassment. For instance, "Canada," the once-popular poem by Sir Charles G. D. Roberts, begins with the following memorable comparison of the country to a semi-intelligent giant:

> *O Child of Nations, giant-limbed,*
> *Who stand'st among the nations now*
> *Unheeded, unadorned, unhymned,*
> *With unanointed brow.* . . .

Twelve more stanzas follow before the poem's conclusion:

> But thou, my Country, dream not thou!
>   Wake, and behold how night is done,—
> How on thy breast, and o'er thy brow,
>   Bursts the uprising sun!

Well, maybe. Roberts wrote other poems in this vein, including "An Ode for the Canadian Confederacy" (which begins "Awake, my country, the hour is great with change!" and concludes thirty-four lines later: "Till earth shall know the Child of Nations by her name!") and "Collect for Dominion Day" (notable line: "Father of nations . . . banish old feud in our young nation's name"). The rhetorical flag-waving brings to mind Dennis Lee's observation in *Alligator Pie* (1974): "Wherever a poem comes from, it's not from good intentions." Verses written to be inspiring are generally dispiriting to read.

There are many types of anthologies: literary, historical, critical, thematic, regional, etc. Ezra Pound described as "active" those collections that concentrate on the work of writers who form a circle, group, or movement. There is another notable type of anthology, however, a type that is encountered less often in Canada than in other countries: the anthology as treasury.

The purpose of the treasury is to preserve the heritage and make it available to a wide range of readers, especially those of the next generation. There have been treasuries of Canadian prose and verse in the past. I have in mind Margaret Fairley's *Spirit of Canadian Democracy* (1945), John D. Robins's *A Pocketful of Canada* (1946), William Toye's *A Book of Canada* (1962), *Colombo's Book of Canada* (1978), Desmond Morton and Morton Weinfeld's *Who Speaks for Canada* (1998), and Barbara Hehner's *The Spirit of Canada* (1999). These books take a broad approach to cultural history. There is much that is public about them but also much that is personal. (No two anthologists—or treasurers—could be expected to make identical selections.) *The Penguin Treasury of Popular Canadian Poems and Songs* is the first such treasury to concentrate on popular Canadian poetry. The Modernist movement in literature belittled these "gatherings" (with their implied canons of taste), and such collections fared no better under Postmodernism (which derided popularity itself). Yet there is a place for these collections on the shelves of bookcases and in the hearts and minds of readers. I hope there will be more treasuries in the future because I know full well that there are treasures yet to come!

These poems, verses, songs, and rhymes shed light on our past, our history, and our heritage. These treasures tell us something about the popular taste of their time and place. They inform us about common assumptions and cultural concerns. They entertain and occasionally edify us. They bring gaiety and variety to our lives. But most of all, they entertain us as only wonderfully chosen words are able to do.

Acknowledgements

Many people contributed to the conception and compilation of this collection. First and foremost, I wish to acknowledge the advice and assistance that I received from William Toye, editor and friend, who has enjoyed a long and productive career in Canadian publishing and whose judgement is certain and whose experience is vast.

I found an excuse in the preparation of the present work to devote many pleasant hours to turning the pages of the standard textbooks and anthologies of Canadian poetry. Many of these volumes are identified in the notes to the texts. Three books that occupy positions of importance on my bookshelf are the popular compilations edited by Ralph L. Woods and issued by the Macmillan Company: *A Treasury of the Familiar* (1942), *A Second Treasury of the Familiar* (1950), and *A Third Treasury of the Familiar* (1970). On the same shelf may be found a copy of *The Best Loved Poems of the American People* (New York: Doubleday, 1936, 1939, 1974) edited by Hazel Felleman. The present work may be considered a Canadian version of these volumes.

Over the last four decades I had many an occasion to consult the most influential Canadian literary anthologies that have appeared over the last century and a half. I would need a bibliography to list all of them. Instead I offer here a limited number of the most accessible anthologies.

Selections from Canadian Poets: With Occasional Critical and Biographical Notes and an Introductory Essay on Canadian Poetry (Montreal: J. Lovell, 1864) edited by Edward Hartley Dewart.

Songs of the Great Dominion: Voices from the Forests and Waters, the Settlements and Cities of Canada (London: Walter Scott, 1889) edited by William Douw Lighthall.

Canadian Poets (Toronto: McClelland, Goodchild & Stewart, 1916) edited by John W. Garvin.

The Canadian Poetry Book: A Book of Modern Verse (Toronto and London: J. M. Dent & Sons Limited, 1922) edited by D. J. Dickie.

The Book of Canadian Poetry: A Critical and Historical Anthology (Toronto: W. J. Gage and Company, Limited, 1943; rev. ed., 1948) edited by A. J. M. Smith.

Canadian Poetry in English (Toronto: The Ryerson Press, 1922; rev. ed., 1954) edited by Bliss Carman, Lorne Pierce, and V. B. Rhodenizer.

The Blasted Pine: An Anthology of Satire, Invective and Disrespectful Verse Chiefly by Canadian Writers (Toronto: The Macmillan Company, 1957; revised edition, 1967) edited by F. R. Scott and A. J. M. Smith.

The Penguin Book of Canadian Verse (Harmondsworth: Penguin Books, 1958; rev. ed., 1967) edited by Ralph Gustafson.

Singing Our History: Canada's Story in Song (Toronto: W. J. Gage Ltd., 1960) by Edith Fowke and Alan Mills.

The Oxford Book of Canadian Verse in English and French (Toronto: Oxford University Press, 1960) chosen by A. J. M. Smith.

Colombo's Book of Canada (Edmonton: Hurtig Publishers, 1978; 1998) edited by John Robert Colombo.

The Poets of Canada (Edmonton: Hurtig Publishers, 1978) edited by John Robert Colombo.

Songs from the Front and Rear: Canadian Servicemen's Songs of the Second World War (Edmonton: Hurtig Publishers, 1979) by Anthony Hopkins.

The New Oxford Book of Canadian Verse in English (Toronto: Oxford University Press, 1982) edited by Margaret Atwood.

Another influence on the present work has been the Favourite Poem Project. This was initiated by Robert Pinsky, U.S. Poet

Laureate (1997–2000), with the support of the New England Foundation for the Arts, Boston University, the Library of Congress, and the National Endowment for the Arts. That undertaking resulted in the publication of the book *Americans' Favorite Poems: The Favorite Poem Project Anthology* (New York: W. W. Norton, 1999) edited by Pinsky and Maggie Dietz. It includes 200 poems, with personal commentaries on the selections made by Americans from all walks of life. Billy Collins, who succeeded Pinsky to the office of Poet Laureate in 2001, arranged for the Library of Congress to post on its Web site the full texts of the 180 poems that every American should know, along with teaching aids and suggestions for the reading or the study of these poems in primary and secondary schools across the United States. Perhaps the Canada Council or the National Library of Canada will follow suit and make the texts of the poems in this volume available to everyone with a computer and access to the Internet.

One other initiative drew my attention to the desirability of an anthology of this sort: Poems on the Underground. Patrons of public transit systems in the largest Canadian cities, including Ottawa, Montreal, Vancouver, and Toronto, are no doubt pleasantly surprised—and perhaps even puzzled—to see posters and placards that feature poems written by past and contemporary Canadian poets displayed in buses, trolleys, subway cars, and waiting stations. The original initiative was taken in 1986 by the London Underground authority with the backing of the Poetry Society, the London Arts Council, and the British Council. The first posters appeared in the Tube that year, and since then such posters and placards have been displayed in the transit systems of major cities throughout the Western world. In the London system, two million transit passengers have the opportunity to read a newly posted poem every day. Annual collections of the posters appear as *Poems on the Underground*. The accumulative effect of such viewings and readings has been to increase public interest in the poetry of the past and the present.

To prod my memory for "old favourites," "gems," and even "chestnuts," I queried the subscribers to the Internet's Can-Lit Discussion Group, and about ten percent of its 376 academic subscribers posted their choices. Poems and poets were also drawn to my attention by avid readers, writers, poets, editors, educators, and publishers. Among my benefactors are Marc Côté, Mary Lou Fallis, Tony Hawke, Barbara Howard, Carol Malyon, Richard Outram, James Reaney, Stephen Roney, Gayle and John Smallbridge, Fraser Sutherland, and William Toye. Especially helpful were George Whipple and Sandy Shreve.

My researcher, M. Alice Neal, made use of the facilities of the Toronto Reference Library, where librarian Norman McMullen was particularly helpful. Research librarian Philip Singer was as resourceful as ever with obscure queries. I am also indebted to the librarians of the CBC Reference Library, the John P. Robarts Research Library of the University of Toronto, and the Library of Parliament in Ottawa.

At Penguin Books Canada I am once again in the debt of publisher Cynthia Good, editor Michael Schellenberg, copy editor Edward O'Connor, and proofreader Kathleen Richards.

This treasury is dedicated to William Toye, fellow editor and friend, whose critical standards remain a source of wonder to me; and to Raymond Souster, fellow poet and friend, whose passion for poetry and whose own moving poems remain a considerable joy and delight.

With Glowing Hearts

GOD SAVE THE KING (QUEEN)

God save our gracious King (Queen),
Long live our noble King (Queen),
God save the King (Queen);
Send him (her) victorious,
Happy and glorious,
Long to reign over us;
God save the King (Queen).

DIEU PROTÈGE NOTRE REINE (ROI)

Dieu protège la reine (le roi)
De sa main souveraine!
Vive la reine (le roi)!
Qu'un règne glorieux,
Long et victorieux
Rende son peuple heureux.
Vive la reine (le roi)!

"This must be the best-known tune in the word," suggested Percy A. Scholes in *The Oxford Companion to Music* (ninth edition, 1956). "If any attribution is necessary in song-books, the word 'traditional' seems to be the only one possible, or, perhaps, 'Traditional; earliest known version by John Bull, 1563–1628.'" In their present form, the words and music of Great Britain's national anthem go back to 1744. It is truly an inspired anthem. Beethoven, for instance, regarded it as "a blessing."

The national anthem has been sung in Canada for centuries. Yet the Parliament of Canada did not proclaim "God Save the Queen (King)" to be the Royal Anthem of Canada until February 16, 1968.

O CANADA
English

O Canada! Our home and native land!
True patriot love in all thy sons command!
With glowing hearts we see thee rise,
The True North strong and free!
From far and wide, O Canada,
We stand on guard for thee.
God keep our land glorious and free!
O Canada, we stand on guard for thee!
O Canada, we stand on guard for thee!

O CANADA
French

O Canada! Terre de nos aïeux,
Ton front est ceint de fleurons glorieux!
Car ton bras sait porter l'épée,
Il sait porter la croix!
Ton histoire est une épopée
Des plus brillants exploits.
Et ta valeur, de fois trempée,
Protégera nos foyers et nos droits.
Protégera nos foyers et nos droits.

The words and music of "O Canada" were declared to be the National Anthem of Canada—*Hymne national du Canada*—by *An Act Respecting the National Anthem of Canada,* which received Royal Assent on June 27, 1980, and was proclaimed on July 1, 1980.

The history of "O Canada" illustrates the bonding of French and English influences. Sir Adolphe-Basile Routhier (1839–1920) wrote an original French poem that he called "Chant National" and included in a volume of his verse titled *Les Echoes* (1882). The four-verse poem celebrates valour, glorious exploits, faith, honour, liberty, Christ, and the King. With the musical setting of Calixa Lavallée (1842–1891), the patriotic composition was first heard in Quebec City on St Jean Baptiste Day, June 24, 1880. That accounts for the French lyrics and the music.

The familiar English words express sincerity and nobility. They were composed by R. Stanley Weir (1856–1926), who prepared what is essentially a new composition in English for a performance at the Tercentenary of Quebec in 1908. His four verses of lyrics celebrate patriotism, loyalty, geography, and hope. His version met with approval and was performed on official occasions, yet sixty years would pass before Parliament would give official recognition to the words.

It is a sad comment on our educational standards and our lack of patriotism that so few youngsters know the words of "O Canada" in either of the official languages.

—

O CANADA!

R. Stanley Weir

"That True North."—Tennyson

O Canada! Our Home and Native Land!
True patriot-love in all thy sons command;
With glowing hearts we see thee rise,
The True North, strong and free,
And stand on guard, O Canada,
 We stand on guard for thee.
 O Canada, glorious and free!
 We stand on guard for thee!

O Canada! Where pines and maples grow,
Great prairies spread and lordly rivers flow,
How dear to us thy broad domain,
From East to Western Sea;
Thou land of hope for all who toil!
 Thou True North, strong and free!
 O Canada, glorious and free!
 We stand on guard for thee!

O Canada! Beneath thy shining skies
May stalwart sons and gentle maidens rise,
To keep thee steadfast through the years,
From East to Western Sea.
Our Fatherland, our Motherland!
 Our True North, strong and free!
 O Canada, glorious and free!
 We stand on guard for thee!

Ruler Supreme, Who hearest humble prayer,
Hold our dominion in Thy loving care.
Help us to find, O God, in Thee,
A lasting, rich reward,
As waiting for the Better Day
  We ever stand on guard.
  O Canada, glorious and free!
  We stand on guard for thee!

This is the text of "O Canada!" written by R. Stanley Weir and published in his collection *After Ypres and Other Verse* (Toronto: The Musson Book Co., Limited, 1917). The three-word epigraph is taken from Alfred Lord Tennyson's poetic narrative *Idylls of the King* (1873). The Poet Laureate wrote specifically about the Dominion of Canada as "that true North, whereof we lately heard," the word "true" being understood to mean "loyal," as in the phrase "true blue."

THE MAPLE LEAF FOR EVER
Alexander Muir

In days of yore, from Britain's shore,
Wolfe the dauntless hero came,
And planted firm Britannia's flag,
On Canada's fair domain.
Here may it wave, our boast, our pride,
And joined in love together,
The Thistle, Shamrock, Rose entwine
The Maple Leaf for ever!

The Maple Leaf, our emblem dear,
The Maple Leaf for ever!
God Save our Queen and Heaven bless
The Maple Leaf for ever!

At Queenston Heights and Lundy's Lane,
Our brave fathers, side by side,
For freedom, homes, and loved ones dear,
Firmly stood and nobly died;
And those dear rights which they maintained,
We swear to yield them never!
Our watchword ever more shall be,
The Maple Leaf for ever!

The Maple Leaf, our emblem dear,
The Maple Leaf for ever!
God Save our Queen and Heaven bless
The Maple Leaf for ever!

Our fair Domain now extends
From Cape Race to Nootka Sound;
May peace for ever be our lot,
And plenteous store abound:
And may those ties of love be ours
Which discord cannot sever,
And flourish green o'er Freedom's home,
The Maple Leaf for ever!

The Maple Leaf, our emblem dear,
The Maple Leaf for ever!
God Save our Queen and Heaven bless
The Maple Leaf for ever!

On merry England's far-famed land
May kind Heaven sweetly smile;
God bless Old Scotland evermore,
And Ireland's Emerald Isle!
Then swell the song, both loud and long,
Till rocks and forest quiver,
God save our Queen, and Heaven bless
The Maple Leaf for ever!

The Maple Leaf, our emblem dear,
The Maple Leaf for ever!
God Save our Queen and Heaven bless
The Maple Leaf for ever!

"I think I will write about the maple leaf," Alexander Muir (1830–1906) told his wife after returning from a stroll with a friend one October evening in 1867. While Muir was walking under a silver maple tree, a leaf had landed on his coat sleeve, lodged there, and resisted his efforts to brush it off. His friend said, "There, Muir! There's your text! The maple leaf is the emblem of Canada! Build your poem on that!"

That night the Scottish-born schoolteacher composed the patriotic words and stirring tune of "The Maple Leaf for Ever." Before nightfall he mailed the manuscript to a competition for patriotic poetry sponsored by the Caledonia Society of Montreal. His composition placed second and earned Muir the sum of fifty dollars. He allotted twenty dollars to printing the sheet music in 1868. He lived long enough to realize that he had written a song that had become a patriotic favourite in English Canada, rivalling the National Anthem in popularity.

No one now recalls the patriotic composition that placed first! Interestingly, the silver maple tree that produced the leaf that inspired the song is still standing at 62 Laing Street in the East End of Toronto. It is identified with a plaque first erected in 1937.

The lyrics reproduced here were sung by generations of school students. They were sung, as the sheet music advises, "*con spirito,*" at least until the 1960s, when the song passed completely out of favour (and hence out of the school curriculum). Today the lyrics are avoided for a number of reasons. They are felt to be excessively patriotic, too nationalistic, even jingoistic; they are said to be anglophile and hence francophobe. There has never been a French version. The lyrics have been much revised over the years. One version pays tribute to the French heritage. In it, the last two lines of the first verse read: "With Lily, Thistle, Shamrock, Rose, / The Maple Leaf for ever."

THE
True
North

SONG
Uvavnuk

The great sea
Has set me adrift,
It moves me as the weed in a great river,
Earth and the great weather
Move me,
Have carried me away
And move my inward parts with joy.

This song, so brief, so beautiful, captures the spirit of nature, of mankind, and of poetry. It was composed and sung by Uvavnuk, an Inuit *angakok* or shaman. He was a resident of Cape Elizabeth, north of Lyon Inlet, Melville Peninsula, Northwest Territories. The explorer Knud Rasmussen recorded the words in Inuktitut and then translated them into Danish. They were then translated into English by W. Worster for their appearance in Rasmussen's *Intellectual Culture of the Iglulik Eskimos: Report of the Fifth Thule Expedition, 1921–24* (1929). So powerful are the simple words and emotions that they have survived two translations.

THE SONG OF THE STARS
Traditional

We are the stars which sing;
We sing with our light;
We are the birds of fire;
We fly over the sky.
Our light is a voice;
We make a road for spirits,
For the spirits to pass over.
Among us are three hunters
Who chase a bear;
There never was a time
When they were not hunting.
We look down on the mountains.
This is the Song of the Stars.

This lovely lyric expresses the Native people's connection with the sky and the world of the spirits. It was collected by the journalist and linguist Charles G. Leland from the Passamaquoddy on Campobello Island, N.B., in 1882. He preserved this simple but beautiful lyric, translating it from the Algonkian and publishing it in *The Algonquin Legends of New England; or Myths and Folk Lore of the Micmac, Passamaquoddy, and Penobscot Tribes* (1884).

JACQUES CARTIER
Thomas D'Arcy McGee

In the seaport of St. Malo 'twas a smiling morn in May,
When the Commodore Jacques Cartier to the westward sailed
    away;
In the crowded old Cathedral all the town were on their knees
For the safe return of kinsmen from the undiscovered seas;
And every autumn blast that swept o'er pinnacle and pier
Filled manly hearts with sorrow, and gentle hearts with fear.

A year passed o'er St. Malo—again came round the day,
When the Commodore Jacques Cartier to the westward sailed
    away;
But no tidings from the absent had come the way they went,
And tearful were the vigils that many a maiden spent;
And manly hearts were filled with gloom, and gentle hearts
    with fear,
When no tidings came from Cartier at the closing of the year.

But the earth is as the Future, it hath its hidden side,
And the Captain of St. Malo was rejoicing in his pride
In the forests of the North—while his townsmen mourned his
    loss,
He was rearing on Mount-Royal the fleur-de-lis and cross;
And when two months were over and added to the year,
St. Malo hailed him home again, cheer answering to cheer.

He told them of a region, hard, ironbound, and cold,
Where no seas of pearl abounded, nor mines of shining gold,
Where the wind from Thulé freezes the word upon the lip,
And the ice in Spring comes sailing athwart the early ship;
He told them of the frozen scene until they thrill'd with fear,
And piled fresh fuel on the hearth to make them better cheer.

But then he changed the strain—he told how soon are cast
In early Spring the fetters that hold the waters fast;
How the Winter causeway broken is drifted out to sea,
And rills and rivers sing with pride the anthem of the free;
How the magic wand of Summer clad the landscape to his eyes,
Like the dry bones of the just when they wake in Paradise.

He told them of the Algonquin braves—the hunters of the wild;
Of how the Indian mother in the forest rocks her child;
Of how, poor souls, they fancy in every living thing
A spirit good or evil, that claims their worshipping;
Of how they brought their sick and maim'd for him to breathe
    upon,
And of the wonders wrought for them through the Gospel of
    St. John.

He told them of the river, whose mighty current gave
Its freshness for a hundred leagues to ocean's briny wave;
He told them of the glorious scene presented to his sight,
What time he reared the cross and crown on Hochelaga's height,
And of the fortess cliff that keeps of Canada the key,
And they welcomed back Jacques Cartier from his perils o'er
    the sea.

Imbedded in the memory of many readers is the first line of the narrative that begins, "In fourteen hundred ninety-two, Columbus sailed the ocean blue." Few remember its second line ("And found this land, land of the Free, beloved by you, beloved by me"), and nobody recalls its title or the name of its author ("The History of the U.S." by Winifred Sackville Stoner).

A fair number of Canadians recall the words "In the seaport of St. Malo 'twas a smiling morn in May," the first line of the narrative poem "Jacques Cartier" composed by Thomas D'Arcy McGee (1825–1868). Unlike Stoner's verse, which identifies highlights in the history of the United States from Christopher Columbus's landfall in 1492 to the end of the First World War in 1918, McGee's poem focuses on the achievements of the first two voyages made by Jacques Cartier, the navigator and discoverer of the St Lawrence. Born in St Malo, France, Cartier made three trans-Atlantic voyages in all; the poem conflates those of 1534 and 1535, excluding the third voyage, which took place in 1541. McGee focuses on the pride Cartier took in his achievement.

"Jacques Cartier" was included in *Canadian Ballads and Occasional Verses* (1858) and reprinted in *The Poems of Thomas D'Arcy McGee* (1869) edited by Mrs. Mary Anne Sadlier. "'Jacques Cartier' is a favourite poem in Canada," wrote the anthologist William Douw Lighthall in 1898. Its popularity faded in the 1960s.

NORTHWEST PASSAGE
Stan Rogers

Ah, for just one time, I would take the Northwest Passage
To find the hand of Franklin reaching for the Beaufort Sea
Tracing one warm line through a land so wide and savage
And make the Northwest Passage to the sea.

Westward from the Davis Strait, 'tis there 'twas said to lie
The sea-route to the Orient for which so many died
Seeking gold and glory, leaving weathered broken bones
And a long-forgotten cairn of stones.

Three centuries thereafter, I take passage overland
In the footsteps of brave Kelsey, where his "sea of flowers"
     began
Watching cities rise before me, then behind me sink again
This tardiest explorer, driving hard across the plain.

Ah, for just one time, I would take the Northwest Passage
To find the hand of Franklin reaching for the Beaufort Sea
Tracing one warm line through a land so wide and savage
And make the Northwest Passage to the sea.

And through the night, behind the wheel, the mileage clicking
     West
I think upon Mackenzie, David Thompson and the rest
Who cracked the mountain ramparts, and did show a path for
     me
To trace the roaring Fraser to the sea.

Ah, for just one time, I would take the Northwest Passage
To find the hand of Franklin reaching for the Beaufort Sea
Tracing one warm line through a land so wide and savage
And make the Northwest Passage to the sea.

How then am I so different from the first men through this way?
Like them I left a settled life, I threw it all away
To seek a Northwest Passage at the call of many men
To find there but the road back home again.

Ah, for just one time, I would take the Northwest Passage
To find the hand of Franklin reaching for the Beaufort Sea
Tracing one warm line through a land so wide and savage
And make the Northwest Passage to the sea.

These are the lyrics of an extremely powerful song. The words "one warm line," once heard sung, reverberate in memory.

The song memorializes the voyage of Sir John Franklin and his crew, who perished in 1847 in an attempt to prove the existence of the Northwest Passage across the Arctic Sea. The other adventurers are Henry Kelsey, who explored the prairies, and Alexander Mackenzie, David Thompson, and Simon Fraser, who crossed the continent to behold the Pacific Ocean.

With rough gusto, Stan Rogers (1949–1983) sings "Northwest Passage" on his album *Northwest Passage* (Fogarty's Cove Music, 1981).

AN ANTI-CONFEDERATION SONG
Traditional

Hurrah for our own native isle, Newfoundland!
Not a stranger shall hold one inch of its strand!
Her face turns to Britain, her back to the Gulf.
Come near at your peril, Canadian Wolf!

Ye brave Newfoundlanders who plough the salt sea
With hearts like the eagle so bold and so free,
The time is at hand when you'll all have to say
If Confederation will carry the day.

Cheap tea and molasses they say they will give,
All taxes take off that the poor man may live;
Cheap nails and cheap lumber our coffins to make,
And homespun to mend our old clothes when they break.

If they take off the taxes how then will they meet
The heavy expense of the country's upkeep?
Just give them the chance to get us in this scrape
And they'll chain us like slaves with pen, ink, and red tape.

Would you barter the rights that your fathers have won,
Your freedom transmitted from father to son?
For a few thousand dollars of Canadian gold,
Don't let it be said that your birthright was sold.

Then hurrah for our own native isle, Newfoundland!
Not a stranger shall hold one inch of its strand!
Her face turns to Britain, her back to the Gulf.
Come near at your peril, Canadian Wolf!

The Dominion of Canada was created in 1867 with the federal
union of four former British colonies: New Brunswick, Nova Scotia,
Ontario, Quebec. Two years later, Newfoundlanders held a vote to
decide whether or not to accept the invitation to join Confederation.
The men and women opposed to Confederation won the day with
lively campaign lyrics such as "An Anti-Confederation Song." It was

sung throughout the Great Island and it has remained popular to this day. The Newfoundlanders' resolve to remain independent of Canada (but dependent on Great Britain) lasted until 1949 when Newfoundland and Labrador entered into the federal union.

The full text of this song, which appears in *Old-Time Poetry and Songs of Newfoundland* (1940) edited by Gerald S. Doyle, is reprinted from *Canada's Story in Song* (Toronto: W. J. Gage Limited, 1960) edited by Edith Fowke and Alan Mills.

THE RIDERS OF THE PLAINS
Unknown

Oh! let the prairies echo with
   The ever-welcome sound—
Ring out the boots and saddles,
   Its stinging notes resound.
Our horses toss their bridled heads,
   And chafe against the reins—
Ring out—ring out the marching call
   For the Riders of the Plains.

O'er many a league of prairie wide
   Our pathless way must be;
And round it roams the fiercest tribes
   Of Blackfoot and of Cree.
But danger from their savage hands
   Our dauntless hearts disdain—
The hearts that bear the helmet up—
   The Riders of the Plains!

The thunderstorm sweeps o'er our way
   But onward still we go;
We scale the weary mountains' range,
   Descend the valleys low;
We face the broad Saskatchewan,
   Made fierce with heavy rains—
With all its might it cannot check
   The Riders of the Plains.

We track the sprouting cactus land,
   When lost to white men's ken,
We startle there the creatures wild
   And fight them in their den;
For where'er our leaders bid,
   The bugle sounds its strains,
In marching sections forward go
   The Riders of the Plains.

The Fire King stalks the broad prairie,
   And fearful 'tis to see
The rushing wall of flame and smoke
   Girdling round rapidly.
'Tis there we shout defiance
   And mock its fiery chains—
For safe the cleared circle guards
   The Riders of the Plains.

For us no cheerful hostelries
   Their welcome gates unfold—
No generous board, or downy bed,
   Await our troopers bold.
Beneath the starry canopy
   At eve, when daylight wanes,
There lie the hardy slumberers—
   The Riders of the Plains.

But that which tries the courage sore
   Of horseman and of steed,
Is want of blessed water—
   Blessed water is our need.
We'll face, like men, whate'er befalls.
   Of perils, hardships, pains—
Oh! God, deny not water to
   The Riders of the Plains!

We muster but three hundred
   In all this Great Lone Land,
Which stretches from Superior's waves
   To where the Rockies stand;
But not one heart doth balk,
   No coward voice complains,
That far too few in numbers are
   The Riders of the Plains.

In England's mighty Empire
  Each man must take his stand:
Some guard her honoured flag at sea,
  Some bear it well by land.
It's not our part to face her foes—
  Then what to us remains?
What duty does our country give
  The Riders of the Plains?

Our mission is to plant the right
  Of British freedom here—
Restrain the lawless savages,
  And protect the pioneer.
And 'tis a proud and daring trust
  To hold these vast domains
With but three hundred mounted men—
  The Riders of the Plains.

Here is a rousing verse about the Riders of the Plains . . . known today as the Mounted Police, the Horsemen, the Force, the Mounties, and the RCMP!

The Force was established to police the Prairies in 1873 as the North West Mounted Police, then the Royal North West Mounted Police, and finally the Royal Canadian Mounted Police. Within Canada, the RCMP represents the maintenance of law and order. Throughout the world, the Force stands as a symbol of Canada. Its exploits are celebrated in song, musical, story, movie, and verse.

"The Riders of the Plains" appeared anonymously in the columns of the *Saskatchewan Herald* (Battleford, Sask.), September 23, 1878. It is reprinted from the interesting booklet *Wake the Prairie Echoes: The Mounted Police Story in Verse* (Saskatoon:

Western Producer Book Service, 1973), collected by the Saskatchewan History and Folklore Society.

The author of these verses is unknown, though the original publication conveys a clue or two: "*W.S.*, N.W.M.P. / Cobourg, July 1878." Whoever W.S. might have been, it is hard not to celebrate along with him the Force's mission "to plant the right," an echo of the Force's official motto: *Uphold the right.*

A PSALM OF MONTREAL
Samuel Butler

The City of Montreal is one of the most rising and, in many respects, most agreeable on the American continent, but its inhabitants are as yet too busy with commerce to care greatly about the masterpieces of old Greek art. In the Montreal Museum of Natural History I came upon two plaster casts, one of the Antinous and the other of the Discobolus—not the good one, but in my poem, of course, I intend the good one—banished from public view to a room where were all manner of skins, plants, snakes, insects, etc., and, in the middle of these, an old man stuffing an owl.

"Ah," said I, "so you have some antiques here; why don't you put them where people can see them?"

"Well, sir," answered the custodian, "you see they are rather vulgar."

He then talked a great deal and said his brother did all Mr. Spurgeon's printing.

The dialogue—perhaps true, perhaps imaginary, perhaps a little of the one and a little of the other—between the writer and this old man gave rise to the lines that follow:

Stowed away in a Montreal lumber room
The Discobolus standeth and turneth his face to the wall;
Dusty, cobweb-covered, maimed, and set at naught,
Beauty crieth in an attic and no man regardeth:
                              O God! O Montreal!

Beautiful by night and day, beautiful in summer and winter,
Whole or maimed, always and alike beautiful—
He preached gospel of grace to the skins of owls
And to one who seasoneth the skins of Canadian owls:
                              O God! O Montreal!

When I saw him I was wroth and I said, "O Discobolus!
Beautiful Discobolus, a Prince both among gods and men!
What doest thou there, how camest thou hither, Discobolus,
Preaching gospel in vain to the skins of owls?
                              O God! O Montreal!

And I turned to the man of skins and said unto him, "O thou
    man of skins,
Wherefore hast thou done thus to shame the beauty of the
    Discobolus?"
But the Lord had hardened the heart of the man of skins
And he answered, "My brother-in-law is haberdasher to Mr.
    Spurgeon."
                              O God! O Montreal!

"The Discobolus is put here because he is vulgar,
He has neither vest nor pants with which to cover his limbs;
I, Sir, am a person of most respectable connections—
My brother-in-law is haberdasher to Mr. Spurgeon."
                              O God! O Montreal!

Then I said, "O brother-in-law to Mr. Spurgeon's haberdasher,
Who seasonest also the skins of Canadian owls,
Thou callest trousers 'pants,' whereas I call them 'trousers,'
Therefore thou art in hell-fire and may the Lord pity thee!"
                                        O God! O Montreal!

"Preferrest thou the gospel of Montreal to the gospel of Hellas,
The gospel of thy connection with Mr. Spurgeon's haberdashery
    to the gospel of the Discobolus?"
Yet none the less blasphemed the beauty saying, "The
    Discobolus hath no gospel,
But my brother-in-law is haberdasher to Mr. Spurgeon."
                                        O God! O Montreal!

This deftly written satire on our customs and pretentions has a
familiar refrain: "O God! O Montreal!" These four words are
remembered and savoured to this day. Here is how this satiric verse
came to be written.

The English author Samuel Butler (1835–1902) spent some
months in Montreal in 1874–75 to pursue commercial interests in
a tanning company (all of which came to naught). While here he
was struck by the fact that social pretentions and sexual prudery
extended even into the "lumber room" of the Montreal Museum of
Natural History where a poor plaster cast of the Discobolus (the
naked discus-thrower sculpted by Myron in ancient Greece) was
stored, being considered too "vulgar" to display. The original of
this sculpture has been lost but copies reside in the Vatican and the
British Museum. Butler, incredulous, composed "A Psalm of
Montreal" which appeared in *The Spectator,* May 18, 1878. The
text is taken from *The Note-Books of Samuel Butler* (1926) edited
by Henry Festing Jones.

Visiting Montreal almost four decades later, the English poet Rupert Brooke observed, "I made my investigations in Montreal. I have to report that the Discobolus is very well, and, nowadays, looks the whole world in the face, almost quite unabashed." He found it in the gallery of the Art Association of Montreal in Phillips Square.

It would be pleasant to report that visitors to Montreal may visit the Montreal Museum of Fine Art and behold the Discobolus that so intrigued Butler and Brooke. But this pleasure is denied. The statue was part of the Museum's collection until the mid-1960s, when it was loaned, without authorization, for display to a commercial enterprise. Since then it has been untraceable. Perhaps it languishes in some Montreal company's "lumber room" to this day.

Our Lady of the Snows

Rudyard Kipling

(Canadian Preferential Tariff, 1897)

A Nation spoke to a Nation,
    A Queen sent word to a Throne:
"Daughter am I in my mother's house,
    But mistress in my own.
The gates are mine to open,
    As the gates are mine to close,
And I set my house in order,"
    Said our Lady of the Snows.

"Neither with laughter nor weeping,
    Fear or the child's amaze—
Soberly under the White Man's law
    My white men go their ways.
Not for the Gentiles' clamour—
    Insult or threat of blows—
Bow we the knee to Baal,"
    Said our Lady of the Snows.

"My speech is clean and single,
    I talk of common things—
Words of the wharf and the market-place
    And the ware the merchant brings:
Favour to those I favour,
    But a stumbling-block to my foes.
Many there be that hate us,"
    Said our Lady of the Snows.

"I called my chiefs to council
    In the din of a troubled year;
For the sake of a sign ye would not see,
    And a word ye would not hear.
This is our message and answer;
    This is the path we chose:
For we be also a people,"
    Said our Lady of the Snows.

"Carry the word to my sisters—
    To the Queens of the East and the South.
I have proven faith in the Heritage
    By more than the word of the mouth.
They that are wise may follow
    Ere the world's war-trumpet blows,
But I—I am first in the battle,"
    Said our Lady of the Snows.

A Nation spoke to a Nation,
    A Throne sent word to a Throne:
"Daughter am I in my mother's house,
    But mistress in my own.
The gates are mine to open,
    As the gates are mine to close,
And I abide by my Mother's House,"
    Said our Lady of the Snows.

This verse identified our land with snow. We have never been able to shake off the identification. The poem also defined in the eyes of many people a mother-daughter relationship between Great Britain and the Dominion of Canada that persisted until the Second World War, until the Centennial of Confederation in 1967, or until the patriation of the Constitution in 1982—take your choice!

"Our Lady of the Snows" was written with great vigour and little humour, characteristics of the writer Rudyard Kipling (1865–1936), imperialist and public spokesman for the British Empire. It was occasioned by the principle of "British Preference" in matters of trade and tariff that was first incorporated into Prime Minister Sir Wilfrid Laurier's Liberal budget in 1897. The text of the poem first appeared in the London *Times*, April 27, 1897. The text here is reproduced from *Rudyard Kipling's Verse: Definitive Edition* (1940, 1966).

THE ROYAL TOUR

James Reaney

When the King and the Queen came to Stratford
Everyone felt at once
How heavy the Crown must be.
The Mayor shook hands with their Majesties
And everyone presentable was presented
And those who weren't have resented
It, and will
To their dying day.
Everyone had almost a religious experience
When the King and Queen came to visit us
(I wonder what they felt!)
And hydrants flowed water in the gutters
All day.
People put quarters on the railroad tracks
So as to get squashed by the Royal Train
And some people up the line at Shakespeare
Stayed in Shakespeare, just in case—
They did stop too,
While thousands in Stratford
Didn't even see them
Because the Engineer didn't slow down
Enough in time.

And although,
But although we didn't see them in any way
(I didn't even catch the glimpse
The teacher who was taller did
Of a gracious pink figure)
I'll remember it to my dying day.

The first Royal Visit to Canada was made by King George VI and Queen Elizabeth in May and June of 1939. Their Majesties' progress in the "royal blue train" across the country left an indelible impression on monarchists and republicans alike who took this unique opportunity to view the royal couple.

According to Tom MacDonnell's *Daylight upon Magic: The Royal Tour of Canada—1939* (1989), the train passed through the Stratford station on June 6; it was three hours late and the Queen did not appear until it was almost out of sight of the crowd. (The scheduled stop was the neighbouring hamlet of Shakespeare.)

James Reaney did not seem to mind but wrote this delightful poem about the event. "The Royal Tour, 1939" appeared in Reaney's *The Red Heart* (1949). The text is taken from Reaney's *Poems* (Toronto: New Press, 1972) edited by Germaine Warkentin.

Cries
of
Battle

THE GREAT PEACE
Dekanahwideh

I, Dekanahwideh, and the Confederated Chiefs, now uproot the tallest pine tree, and into the cavity thereby made we cast all weapons of war. Into the depth of the earth, deep down into the underwater currents of water flowing to unknown regions, we cast all weapons of strife. We bury them from sight and we plant again the tree. Thus shall the Great Peace be established.

With these memorable words, Dekanahwideh, the Iroquois statesman of mythic stature, founded the Great League of the Iroquois (then the Five and later the Six Nations Confederacy). He did this with the assistance of Hiawatha, the semi-legendary Ojibwa chief, near the present-day site of Kingston, Ont.

This short passage is part of the long text of "The Great Peace," which is traditionally dated to the 1450s. It is found in various sources, including Paul A. W. Wallace's *The White Roots of Peace* (1946). Every few years the entire text of "The Great Peace" is recited in the English language by the elders of the Six Nations Reserve, near Brantford, Ont.

BRAVE WOLFE
Traditional

Come, all you old men all,
Let this delight you,
Come, all you young men all,
Let nought affright you.
Nor let your courage fail
When comes the trial,
Nor do not be dismayed
At the first denial.

I went to see my love.
Thinking to woo her;
I sat down by her side,
Not to undo her;
But when I looked on her
My tongue did quiver;
I could not speak my mind
While I was with her.

"Love, here's a diamond ring,
Long time I've kept it
All for your sake alone,
If you'll accept it.
When you this token view,
Think on the giver;
Madame, remember me,
Or I'm undone forever."

Then forth went this brave youth
And crossed the ocean,
To free America
Of her division.
He landed at Quebec
With all his party,
A city to attack
Both brave and hearty.

Brave Wolfe drew up his men
In a line so pretty,
On the Plains of Abraham
Before the city.
The French came marching down
Arrayed to meet them,
In double numbers 'round
Resolved to beat them.

Montcalm and this brave youth
Together walkèd;
Between two armies they
Like brothers talkèd,
Till each one took his post
And did retire.
'Twas then these numerous hosts
Commenced their fire.

The drums did loudly beat,
With colours flying,
The purple gore did stream,
And men lay dying.
When shot from off his horse
Fell that brave hero.
Long may we lament his loss
That day in sorrow.

Brave Wolfe lay on the ground
Where the guns did rattle,
And to his aide he said,
"How goes the battle?"
"Quebec is all our own,
They can't prevent it."
He said without a groan,
"I die contented."

"Brave Wolfe" is a traditional ballad that recalls the Battle of the Plains of Abraham, which saw Quebec fall to the English troops under the command of Brigadier-General James Wolfe. The battle was fought on September 13, 1759. Both Wolfe and the French commander, the Marquis de Montcalm, died.

The text of the ballad is reproduced from *Ballads and Sea-Songs of Newfoundland* (Cambridge, Mass.: Harvard University Press, 1933), edited by Elizabeth B. Greenleaf and Grace Y. Mansfield.

COME ALL YOU BOLD CANADIANS
Traditional

Come all you bold Canadians, I'd have you lend an ear
Concerning a fine city that would make your courage cheer,
Concerning an engagement—that we had at Sandwich town,
The courage of those Yankee boys so lately we pulled down.

There was a bold commander, brave General Brock by name,
Took shopping at Niagara and down to York he came,
He says, "My gallant heroes, if you'll come along with me,
We'll fight those proud Yankees in the west of Canaday!"

'Twas thus that we replied: "Along with you we'll go.
Our knapsacks we will shoulder without any more ado.
Our knapsacks we will shoulder and forward we will steer;
We'll fight those proud Yankees without either dread or fear."

We travelled all that night and a part of the next day,
With a determination to show them British play.
We travelled all that night and a part of the next day,
With a determination to conquer or to die.

Our commander sent a flag to them and unto them did say:
"Deliver up your garrison or we'll fire on you this day!"
But they would not surrender, and chose to stand their ground,
We opened up our great guns and gave them fire a round.

Their commander sent a flag to us, a quarter he did call.
"Oh, hold your guns, brave British boys, for fear you slay us all.
Our town you have at your command, our garrison likewise."
They brought their guns and ground them right down before
   our eyes.

And now we are all home again, each man is safe and sound.
May the memory of this conquest all through the Province sound.
Success unto our volunteers who did their rights maintain,
And to our bold commander, brave General Brock by name!

This traditional ballad, almost as rousing to read as to sing, cele-
brates the victory of General Sir Isaac Brock over the American
forces at the Battle of Sandwich, Upper Canada, now Ontario,
during the War of 1812. The text, which appears in *Shantymen
and Shantyboys* (New York: The Macmillan Co., 1951) edited by
W. M. Doerflinger, is reprinted from *Singing Our History* (Toronto:
Doubleday, 1984), edited by Edith Fowke.

━

THE *CHESAPEAKE* AND THE *SHANNON*
Traditional

   The *Chesapeake* so bold
   Out of Boston as we're told
Came to take the British frigate neat and handy O,
   And the people in the port
   All came out to see the sport,
While their bands all played up Yankee Doodle Dandy O.

Ere the action had begun
The Yankees made much fun,
Said, "We'll take the British frigate neat and handy O;
And after that we'll dine,
Treat our sweethearts all with wine,
And we'll dance a jig of Yankee Doodle Dandy O."

Our British frigate's name
That for the purpose came
To cool the Yankees' courage neat and handy O
Was the *Shannon*—Captain Broke,
All his crew had hearts of oak,
And in fighting were allowed to be the dandy O."

The fight had scarce begun
When they flinchéd from their guns.
They thought that they had worked us neat and handy O;
But Broke he waved his sword,
Saying, "Come, my boys, we'll board,
And we'll stop them playing Yankee Doodle Dandy O."

When the Britons heard this word
They all quickly sprang on board,
And seized the Yankees' ensign neat and handy O.
Notwithstanding all their brags,
Soon the British raised their flags
On the Yankees' mizzen-peak to be the dandy O.

Here's to Broke and all his crew
Who with courage stout and true
Fought against the Yankee frigate neat and handy O.
Oh, may they ever prove
Both in fighting and in love
That the British tars will always be the dandy O!

So popular was "The *Chesapeake* and the *Shannon*" that there was
even a reference to the boys at Rugby singing it after a game in the
classic English novel *Tom Brown's School Days* (1857).

The spirited sea ballad recalls an important naval engagement in
the War of 1812. It records the stunning victory of the British ship
Shannon, commanded by Captain P. V. Broke, over the American
Chesapeake, under Captain James Lawrence, off the coast of Boston,
Mass., June 1, 1813. Broke had the captive ship towed in triumph to
Halifax. Like the tune, the lyrics are traditional, though they are
modelled on an earlier American victory song called "The
Constitution and the *Guerrière*."

The sea ballad appears in *Ballads and Sea-Songs from Nova
Scotia* (Cambridge, Mass.: Harvard University Press, 1928), edited
by Roy W. Mackenzie, but is reprinted from *Folk Songs of Canada*
(Waterloo: Waterloo Music Company Limited, 1954) edited by
Edith Fowke and Richard Johnston.

THE BATTLE OF QUEENSTON HEIGHTS
Traditional

Upon the Heights of Queenston one dark October day,
Invading foes were marshalled in battle's dread array.
Brave Brock looked up the rugged steep and planned a bold
    attack;
"No foreign flag shall float," he said, "above the Union Jack."

His loyal-hearted soldiers were ready every one,
Their foes were thrice their number, but duty must be done.
They started up the fire-swept hill with loud resounding cheers,
While Brock's inspiring voice rang out: "Push on, York
    Volunteers!"

But soon a fatal bullet pierced through his manly breast,
And loving friends to help him around the hero pressed;
"Push on," he said. "Do not mind me!"—and ere the set of sun
Canadians held the rugged steep, the victory was won.

Each true Canadian soldier laments the death of Brock;
His country told its sorrow in monumental rock;
And if a foe should e'er invade our land in future years,
His undying words will guide us still: "Push on, brave
    Volunteers!"

"Next to the capture of Quebec, the Battle of Queenston Heights is
the most dramatic in Canada's history," wrote Edith Fowke. "The
darkness in which it began, the shifting fortunes on the steep slopes,
and the final precipitous charge have made it a battle long to be
remembered."

This memorable battle in the Niagara Peninsula during the War of 1812 is memorialized in the ballad "The Battle of Queenston Heights." It tells how British commander Sir Isaac Brock led the British regulars and the York volunteers (the Toronto Militia) in an attack that eventually succeeded in driving the Americans from Queenston Heights. Brock was shot to death by an American sniper. His second-in-command, Lieutenant-Colonel John MacDonell, also died in the battle on October 13, 1812.

The lyrics appear in *Canada's Story in Song* (Toronto: W. J. Gage Limited, 1960) edited by Edith Fowke and Alan Mills. Fowke suggests that the lyrics were written to mark the occasion of the unveiling of Brock's Monument in 1824. Alan Mills wrote the folk-style music.

BROCK
Charles Sangster

October 13th, 1859

One voice, one people, one in heart
    And soul, and feeling, and desire!
    Re-light the smouldering martial fire,
    Sound the mute trumpet, strike the lyre,
    The hero deed can not expire.
        The dead still play their part.

Raise high the monumental stone!
    A nation's fealty is theirs,
    And we are the rejoicing heirs,
    The honoured sons of sires whose cares
    We take upon us unawares,
        As freely as our own.

We boast not of the victory,
  But render homage, deep and just,
  To his—to their—immortal dust,
  Who proved so worthy of their trust
  No lofty pile nor sculptured bust
    Can herald their degree.

No tongue need blazon forth their fame—
  The cheers that stir the sacred hill
  Are but mere promptings of the will
  That conquered then, that conquers still;
  And generations yet shall thrill
    At Brock's remembered name.

Some souls are the Hesperides
  Heaven sends to guard the golden age,
  Illuming the historic page
  With records of their pilgrimage;
  True Martyr, Hero, Poet, Sage:
    And he was one of these.

Each in his lofty sphere sublime
  Sits crowned above the common throng,
  Wrestling with some Pythonic wrong,
  In prayer, in thunder, thought, or song;
  Briaereus-limbed, they sweep along,
    The Typhons of the time.

Major-General Sir Isaac Brock led the British forces at the Battle of Queenston Heights on October 13, 1812, but before he could claim victory, he was killed by an American sniper. Brock lies buried beneath the 184-foot monument which bears his name and towers over the hilly countryside and the Niagara River below. The tall, fluted Corinthian column, modelled on Nelson's Monument in Trafalgar Square, was raised in 1824, damaged during the Rebellion of 1837, re-erected in 1854, and rededicated in 1859.

The poet Charles Sangster (1822–1893) was commissioned to mark the occasion, and he did so in high style. "Brock" is one of the few such public poems to be commissioned and composed in this country. It celebrates not so much the person of Brock as the heroic act itself, and particularly the spirit of sacrifice on behalf of generations yet to come.

The poem is reprinted from Sangster's *Hesperus and Other Poems and Lyrics* (1860).

MACDONNELL ON THE HEIGHTS
Stan Rogers

Too thin the line that charged the Heights
And scrambled in the clay.
Too thin the Eastern Township Scot
Who showed them all the way,
And perhaps had you not fallen,
You might be what Brock became
But not one in ten thousand knows your name.

To say the name, MacDonnell,
It would bring no bugle call
But the Redcoats stayed beside you
When they saw the General fall.
'Twas MacDonnell raised the banner then
And set the Heights aflame,
But not one in ten thousand knows your name.

You brought the field all standing with your courage and your
*   luck*
But unknown to most, you're lying there beside old General
*   Brock.*
So you know what it is to scale the Heights and fall just short
*   of fame*
And have not one in ten thousand know your name.

At Queenston now, the General on his tower stands alone
And there's lichen on "MacDonnell" carved upon that weathered
    stone
In a corner of the monument to glory you could claim,
But not one in ten thousand knows your name.

You brought the field all standing with your courage and your
*   luck*
But unknown to most, you're lying there beside old General
*   Brock.*
So you know what it is to scale the Heights and fall just short
*   of fame*
And have not one in ten thousand know your name.

Lieutenant-Colonel John MacDonnell shared the fate of Sir Isaac Brock but not his fame. Both were British officers, both fell at the Battle of Queenston Heights on October 13, 1812. But history is fickle. It recalls Brock and not MacDonnell (or Macdonell—even his name is variously spelled) in accounts of this decisive battle in the War of 1812.

"MacDonnell on the Heights" is a powerful song composed by Stan Rogers (1949–1983) in 1982 and sung by him with great conviction on his album *From Fresh Water* (1982). Writer Chris Gudgeon has noted that in the original version of the lyrics, the key line reads "Not one in ten thousand knows *my* name." The line may seem to be an overstatement, but it is more likely an understament. These days, could three thousand Canadians identify John MacDonnell?

1838
Dennis Lee

The Compact sat in parliament
To legalize their fun.
And now they're hanging Sammy Lount
And Captain Anderson.
And if they catch Mackenzie
They will string him in the rain.
And England will erase us if
Mackenzie comes again.

The Bishop has a paper
That says he owns our land.
The Bishop has a Bible too
That says our souls are damned.
Mackenzie had a printing press.
It's soaking in the Bay.
And who will spike the Bishop till
Mackenzie comes again?

The British want the country
For the Empire and the view.
The Yankees want the country for
A yankee barbecue.
The Compact want the country
For their merrie green domain.
They'll all play finders-keepers till
Mackenzie comes again.

Mackenzie was a crazy man,
He wore his wig askew.
He donned three bulky overcoats
In case the bullets flew.
Mackenzie talked of fighting
While the fight went down the drain.
But who will speak for Canada?
Mackenzie, come again!

This poem for children refers to the aftermath of the failed
Rebellion of 1837–38 in Upper Canada (today's southern
Ontario). The Rebellion was led by the reformer William Lyon

Mackenzie against the forces of the Family Compact headed by Bishop John Strachan. In Mackenzie (grandfather of Prime Minister W. L. Mackenzie King), Lee envisages the embodiment of the spirit of reform, an Upper Canadian version of Bonnie Prince Charlie, Prince Arthur, and other heroes who promise to return to right wrongs. "1838" is reprinted from Dennis Lee's collection *Nicholas Knock and Other People* (Toronto: Macmillan, 1974). It is as lively and as thoughtful as Lee's other rhymes for children of all ages.

—

MEMORIAL CHAMBER INSCRIPTION
Rudyard Kipling

They are too near to be great,
    But our children shall understand
When and how our fate
    Was changed, and by whose hand.

These noble lines were inscribed on the stone tablet that for generations lay in the Memorial Chamber of the Peace Tower of the Central Block of the Parliament Buildings in Ottawa. The tablet was removed from the Memorial Chamber in 1982.

The expressive lines comprise one of six verses of the poem "The Verdicts (Jutland)," which Rudyard Kipling wrote in 1916 to honour the participants in that naval engagement, not only those who died but also those who survived. He refers to all of them as "heroes" and "demi-gods." The final stanza calls them "saviours": "Our children shall measure their worth. / We are content to be blind. . . . / But we know that we walk on a new-born earth / With the saviours of mankind."

The verse is reprinted from *Rudyard Kipling's Verse: Definitive Edition* (1940).

EPITAPHS ON THE WAR: 1914–18
Rudyard Kipling

I

We giving all gained all.
   Neither lament us nor praise.
Only in all things recall,
   It is Fear, not Death that slays.

II

From little towns in a far land we came,
   To save our honour and a world aflame.
By little towns in a far land we sleep;
   And trust that world we won for you to keep!

Rudyard Kipling was commissioned to compose the inscriptions for cenotaphs to honour the War Dead to be erected in the Ontario communities of, respectively, Sudbury and Sault Ste Marie.

Sudbury's inscription (the first one) was never publicly used. The Sault's inscription (the second one) was commissioned by the local newspaper publisher James W. Curran and is publicly displayed.

"Epitaphs on the War: 1914–18" is reprinted from *Rudyard Kipling's Verse: Definitive Edition* (1940).

IN FLANDERS FIELDS
John McCrae

In Flanders fields the poppies blow
Between the crosses, row on row,
   That mark our place; and in the sky
   The larks, still bravely singing, fly
Scarce heard amid the guns below.

We are the Dead. Short days ago
We lived, felt dawn, saw sunset glow,
Loved, and were loved, and now we lie
        In Flanders fields.

Take up our quarrel with the foe:
To you from failing hands we throw
   The torch; be yours to hold it high.
   If ye break faith with us who die
We shall not sleep, though poppies grow
        In Flanders fields.

This poem is the cornerstone of the present collection. It was the unanimous choice of everyone consulted about which poems to include. It is everyone's "favourite."

"In Flanders Fields" is a short poem. It consists of only ninety-seven words (one hundred if you include the three-word title). It is direct and dramatic (the war dead speak to the living), and it challenges the living to keep faith with those who sacrificed their lives on the field of battle. With the possible exception of Rudyard

Kipling's "Recessional," this elegy is the most familiar of all poems occasioned by the Great War.

It was written by Major John McCrae (1872–1918), a medical officer with the First Canadian Contingent. He composed it in twenty minutes on May 3, 1915, during the Second Battle of Ypres, a Flemish town in Belgium. It first appeared anonymously in a column in the popular English magazine *Punch,* December 8, 1915. McCrae died of double pneumonia on January 28, 1918, and his remains were buried at Wimereux Cemetery, Boulogne, France. The poem appears with twenty-eight other poems in McCrae's sole book, *In Flanders Fields and Other Poems* (1919) edited by Sir Andrew Macphail. That text is reproduced here.

It was said that McCrae noted with surprise that his sentiments were shared by so many readers. He would never know just how many readers. After his death a recital of the poem was part of the official Armistice Day program, November 11, 1918. Every year since then, it has been an integral part of the ceremonies surrounding Remembrance Day in Canada and throughout the British Empire and Commonwealth. Poppies have been associated with Remembrance Day since the publication of this poem.

McCrae supplied friends with handwritten copies of the text, no two of which are identical. There is a textual controversy concerning the use of the words "blow" or "grow" in the first and penultimate lines. Both words appear in the poem, but McCrae described the poppies as blowing and not growing in the first line in the published version of the poem. The handwritten copy most often reproduced on postage stamps and bank notes describes the poppies as growing. The fact that this version is recognized by members of the public proves that the poem survives in memory and that its sentiments continue to move immense numbers of people.

HIGH FLIGHT

John Gillespie Magee, Jr.

Oh! I have slipped the surly bonds of Earth
And danced the skies on laughter-silvered wings;
Sunward I've climbed, and joined the tumbling mirth
Of sun-split clouds,—and done a hundred things
You have not dreamed of—wheeled and soared and swung
High in the sunlit silence. Hov'ring there,
I've chased the shouting wind along, and flung
My eager craft through footless halls of air. . . .

Up, up the long, delirious, burning blue
I've topped the wind-swept heights with easy grace
Where never lark, or even eagle, flew—
And, while with silent, lifting mind I've trod
The high untrespassed sanctity of space,
Put out my hand and touched the face of God.

Here is another poem that is close to the beating hearts of Canadians of all ages and walks of life.

John Gillespie Magee, Jr. (1922–1941) was a volunteer with the Royal Canadian Air Force. He was an American citizen, born in Shanghai, who in October 1940 left Yale University to enlist with the RCAF in Montreal. He trained as a pilot in that city and then flew Spitfires with the Royal Air Force in the 412 Squadron in England. While it was reported that he was killed in action, his death was an accident that occurred during a training flight over Lincolnshire, December 11, 1941.

Magee was only nineteen years old when he composed "High Flight." Three months before his death, he wrote it on the back of a letter that he addressed to his mother. "I am enclosing a verse I wrote the other day. It started at 30,000 feet, and was finished soon after I landed. I thought it might interest you." The verse is dated "September 3, 1941." In form it is a well-composed sonnet.

The poem was first published as part of the column "This World of Books" in *The Pittsburgh Post-Gazette,* November 12, 1941, and it subsequently appeared in *Flying* magazine. The original manuscript of the poem is deposited with the Library of Congress, Washington, D.C. Apollo 15 Lunar Module Pilot James Irwin carried a copy of the poem with him when he circled the moon in 1971.

Following Magee's death, it was chosen as the official poem of the Royal Air Force and posted in pilot-training centres throughout the Commonwealth. That ensured RCAF endorsement, so the poem is especially prized by members of the Canadian Armed Forces. It is the anthem of aviators around the world—or wherever the English language is spoken.

There are numerous textual variations. The version reproduced here appears in Linda Granfield's informative biography, *High Flight: A World War II Story* (Montreal: Tundra Books, 1999) illustrated by Michael Martchenko.

THIS WAS MY BROTHER
Mona Gould

For Lt.-Col. Howard McTavish, killed in action at Dieppe

This was my brother
At Dieppe,
Quietly a hero
Who gave his life
Like a gift,
Withholding nothing.

His youth . . . his love . . .
His enjoyment of being alive . . .
His future, like a book
With half the pages still uncut—

This was my brother
At Dieppe—
The one who bult me a doll house
When I was seven,
Complete to the last small picture frame,
Nothing forgotten.

He was awfully good at *fixing* things,
At stepping into the breach when he was needed.

That's what he did at Dieppe;
He was needed.
And even Death must have been a little shamed
At his eagerness!

Howard McTavish of the Royal Canadian Engineers was one member of the Canadian forces who took part in the ill-fated Dieppe Raid, a full-scale attack across the English Channel on the northern French seaport then held securely by German troops. The disastrous raid took place on August 19, 1942.

The tribute was composed by the poet Mona Gould (1908–1999), and it first appeared in her collection *Tasting the Earth* (Toronto: Macmillan, 1943). Since then it has been widely reprinted. It is a simple-seeming poem written with much restraint and care. Its last two lines continue to move readers even after repeated readings.

Seas
and
Ships

A CANADIAN BOAT SONG
Thomas Moore

Written on the River St. Lawrence

Faintly as tolls the evening chime
Our voices keep tune and our oars keep time.
Soon as the woods on shore look dim,
We'll sing at St. Ann's our parting hymn.
Row, brothers, row, the stream runs fast,
The Rapids are near and the daylight's past.

Why should we yet our sail unfurl?
Why is not a breath the brave wave to curl?
But when the wind blows off the shore,
Oh! sweetly we'll rest our weary oar.
Blow, breeze, blow, the stream runs fast,
The Rapids are near and the daylight's past.

Utawas' tide! This trembling moon
Shall see us float over thy surges soon.
Saint of this green isle! hear our prayers,
Oh, grant us cool heaven and favouring airs.
Blow, breezes, blow, the stream runs fast,
The Rapids are near and the daylight's past.

"A Canadian Boat Song" was composed by the Irish poet Thomas
Moore (1779–1852) at Sainte-Anne-de-Bellevue, south of Montreal,
in 1804, while residing with the explorer Simon Fraser in his house
(which is still standing). Moore included the lyric in *Epistles, Odes
and Other Poems* (1806). There he added the following explanation:

"I wrote these words to an air which our boatmen sung to us frequently. The wind was so unfavourable that they were obliged to row all the way, and we were five days in descending the river from Kingston to Montreal, exposed to an intense sun during the day, and at night forced to take shelter from the dews in any miserable hut upon the banks that would receive us. But the magnificent scenery of the St. Lawrence repays all such difficulties."

"A Canadian Boat Song" was once widely recited and even sung. In the nineteenth century, it was the only poem or song about Canada that was familiar to people in England and the United States.

CANADIAN BOAT-SONG
(FROM THE GAELIC)
David Macbeth Moir

Listen to me, as when ye hear our father
   Sing long ago the song of other shores—
Listen to me, and then in chorus gather
   All your deep voices, as ye pull your oars:

   Fair these broad meads—these hoary woods are grand;
   But we are exiles from our fathers' land.

From the lone shieling of the misty island
   Mountains divide us, and the waste of seas—
Yet still the blood is strong, the heart is Highland,
   And we in dreams behold the Hebrides:

Fair these broad meads—these hoary woods are grand;
But we are exiles from our fathers' land.

We ne'er shall tread the fancy-haunted valley,
    Where 'tween the dark hills creeps the small clear stream,
In arms around the patriarch banner rally,
    Nor see the moon on royal tombstones gleam:

Fair these broad meads—these hoary woods are grand;
But we are exiles from our fathers' land.

When the bold kindred, in the time long-vanish'd,
    Conquer'd the soil and fortified the keep,—
No seer foretold the children would be banish'd,
    That a degen'rate Lord might boast his sheep:

Fair these broad meads—these hoary woods are grand;
But we are exiles from our fathers' land.

Come foreign rage—let Discord burst in slaughter!
    O then for clansmen true, and stern claymore—
The hearts that would have given their blood like water,
    Beat heavily beyond the Atlantic roar:

Fair these broad meads—these hoary woods are grand;
But we are exiles from our fathers' land.

These beautiful verses first appeared in print in *Blackwood's Edinburgh Magazine,* September 1829, in an anonymously written article titled "Noctes Ambrosianae." In the article, some imaginary Scots are discussing aspects of their country's history. During the

course of the discussion, the character called North offers the fol-
lowing explanation for the text of the song that follows:

> By the bye, I have a letter this morning from a friend of
> mine now in Upper Canada. He was rowed down the St.
> Lawrence lately, for several days on end, by a set of strapping
> fellows, all born in that country, and yet hardly one of whom
> could speak a word of any tongue but the Gaelic. They sang
> heaps of our old Highland oar-songs, he says, and capitally
> well, in the true Hebridean fashion; and they had others of
> their own, Gaelic too, some of which my friend noted down,
> both words and music. He has sent me a translation of one of
> their ditties—shall I try how it will croon?

North croons it and the character called Shepherd says, "Hech me!
that's really a very affectin' thing, now."

The boat-song *is* deeply affecting. The dark and sombre refrain
is justly famous. Would that "my friend" had written more such
"ditties"!

The scholar G. H. Needler explained in his study of the lyric in
The Lone Shieling (1941), "It is not a translation from a Gaelic
original. Nor is it in any real sense a boat-song, but the lament of
Highlanders from the Hebrides exiled in Upper Canada."

Needler argues that it is the work of David Macbeth Moir
(1798–1851), Scottish physician and versifier, who based the song
on information and insights gained from his correspondence with
John Galt (1799–1839), colonist in Upper Canada and Scottish
novelist. Probably Moir and Galt should be credited as co-authors.
Yet the question of the authorship of this moving lament remains a
matter of interest to this day. Some other possibilities are discussed
by Hubert G. Mayes in "'A Very Affectin' Thing': The Scottish
Origin of the Canadian Boat Song," *The Beaver*, April–May 1991.

THE SONG MY PADDLE SINGS

Pauline Johnson

West wind, blow from your prairie nest,
Blow from the mountains, blow from the west.
The sail is idle, the sailor too;
O! wind of the west, we wait for you.
Blow, blow!
I have wooed you so,
But never a favour you bestow.
You rock your cradle the hills between,
But scorn to notice my white lateen.

I stow the sail, unship the mast:
I wooed you long but my wooing's past;
My paddle will lull you into rest.
O! drowsy wind of the drowsy west,
Sleep, sleep,
By your mountain steep,
Or down where the prairie grasses sweep!
Now fold in slumber your laggard wings,
For soft is the song my paddle sings.

August is laughing across the sky,
Laughing while paddle, canoe and I,
Drift, drift,
Where the hills uplift
On either side of the current swift.

The river rolls in its rocky bed;
My paddle is plying its way ahead;
Dip, dip,
While the waters flip
In foam as over their breast we slip.

And oh, the river runs swifter now;
The eddies circle about my bow.
Swirl, swirl!
How the ripples curl
In many a dangerous pool awhirl!

And forward far the rapids roar,
Fretting their margin for evermore.
Dash, dash,
With a mighty crash,
They seethe, and boil, and bound, and splash.

Be strong, O paddle! be brave, canoe!
The reckless waves you must plunge into.
Reel, reel.
On your trembling keel,
But never a fear my craft will feel.

We've raced the rapid, we're far ahead!
The river slips through its silent bed.
Sway, sway,
As the bubbles spray
And fall in twinkling tunes away.

And up on the hills against the sky,
A fir tree rocking its lullaby,
Swings, swings,
Its emerald wings,
Swelling the song that my paddle sings.

The opening lines of "The Song My Paddle Sings" are known by heart by thousands of Canadians, Americans, and Britishers who have yet to step into a canoe—or have yet to read a line of the poem! Is there another verse that so captures the spirit of canoeing as this one does?

It was composed for the purpose of recitation by the poet and performer Pauline Johnson (1861–1913), the Mohawk Princess known as Tekahionwake. And perform it she did, from coast to coast. It is her most familiar lyric.

"The Song My Paddle Sings" was written in Toronto in 1892, following a canoe trip on Lake Muskoka. It appeared in *The White Wampum* (1895).

The Ships of Yule

Bliss Carman

When I was just a little boy,
Before I went to school,
I had a fleet of forty sail
I called the Ships of Yule;

Of every rig, from rakish brig
And gallant barkentine,
To little Fundy fishing boats
With gunwales painted green.

They used to go on trading trips
Around the world for me,
For though I had to stay on shore
My heart was on the sea.

They stopped at every port of call
From Babylon to Rome,
To load with all the lovely things
We never had at home;

With elephants and ivory
Bought from the King of Tyre,
And shells and silks and sandal-wood
That sailor men admire;

With figs and dates from Samarcand,
And squatty ginger-jars,
And scented silver amulets
From Indian bazaars;

With sugar-cane from Port of Spain,
And monkeys from Ceylon,
And paper lanterns from Pekin
With painted dragons on;

With cocoanuts from Zanzibar,
And pines from Singapore;
And when they had unloaded these
They could go back for more.

And even after I was big
And had to go to school,
My mind was often far away
Aboard the Ships of Yule.

The innocent reveries of childhood are fetchingly captured by Bliss
Carman in the nine stanzas of "The Ships of Yule." This sweet verse
(a favourite of young readers) transports the reader or listener to
distant "ports of call." It was first published in 1909 and is reprint-
ed from *Bliss Carman's Poems* (1929).

THE SHARK

E. J. Pratt

He seemed to know the harbour,
So leisurely he swam;
His fin,
Like a piece of sheet-iron,
Three-cornered,
And with knife-edge,
Stirred not a bubble
As it moved
With its base-line on the water.

His body was tubular
And tapered
And smoke-blue,
And as he passed the wharf
He turned,
And snapped at a flat-fish
That was dead and floating.
And I saw the flash of a white throat,
And a double row of white teeth,
And eyes of metallic grey,
Hard and narrow and slit.

Then out of the harbour,
With that three-cornered fin,
Shearing with a bubble the water
Lithely,
Leisurely,
He swam—
That strange fish,
Tubular, tapered, smoke-blue,
Part vulture, part wolf,
Part neither—for his blood was cold.

E. J. Pratt (1883–1964) was born and raised in Newfoundland so he knew all about the vagaries of the sea, the terrors of the deep, and the cold-blooded creatures of the ocean.

"The Shark" first appeared in Pratt's *Newfoundland Verse* (1923).

Places
Far
and
Near

SOMETHING TO SING ABOUT
Oscar Brand

I have walked 'cross the sand on the Grand Banks of
    Newfoundland,
Lazed on the ridge of the Miramichi.
Seen the waves tear and roar at the stone coast of Labrador,
Watched them roll back to the great northern sea.

From the Vancouver Island to the Alberta Highlands
'Cross the prairie, the Lakes to Ontario's towers.
From the sound of Mount Royal's chimes out to the Maritimes,
Something to sing about, this land of ours.

I have welcomed the dawn from the fields of Saskatchewan,
Followed the sun to the Vancouver shore.
Watched it climb shiny new up the snow peaks of Cariboo,
Up to the clouds where the wild Rockies soar.

From the Vancouver Island to the Alberta Highlands
'Cross the prairie, the Lakes to Ontario's towers.
From the sound of Mount Royal's chimes out to the Maritimes,
Something to sing about, this land of ours.

I have heard the wild wind sing the places that I have been,
Bay Bulls and Red Deer and Strait of Belle Isle.
Names like Grand'Mère and Silverthrone, Moose Jaw and
    Marrowbone,
Trails of the pioneer, named with a smile.

From the Vancouver Island to the Alberta Highlands
'Cross the prairie, the Lakes to Ontario's towers.
From the sound of Mount Royal's chimes out to the Maritimes,
Something to sing about, this land of ours.

I have wandered my way to the wild wood of Hudson Bay,
Treated my toes to Quebec's morning dew.
Where the sweet summer breeze kissed the leaves of the maple
    trees,
Sharing this song that I'm singing to you.

From the Vancouver Island to the Alberta Highlands
'Cross the prairie, the Lakes to Ontario's towers.
From the sound of Mount Royal's chimes out to the Maritimes,
Something to sing about, this land of ours.

Yes, there's something to sing about, tune up a string about
Call out in chorus or quietly hum.
Of a land that's still young and a ballad that's still unsung
Telling the promise of great things to come.

From the Vancouver Island to the Alberta Highlands
'Cross the prairie, the Lakes to Ontario's towers.
From the sound of Mount Royal's chimes out to the Maritimes,
Something to sing about, this land of ours.

Oscar Brand, the Winnipeg-born, New York-based folksinger, com-
posed more than three hundred songs. In the hearts of Canadians,
he is identified with the stirring song "Something to Sing About,"
which he wrote for a 1963 television special. It was chosen as the

theme song for the Canadian pavilion at Expo 67. Versions of the lyrics abound, but there is only one version of the proud and commanding melody!

THE ODE TO NEWFOUNDLAND
Sir Cavendish Boyle

When sunrays crown thy pine-clad hills
   And summer spreads her hand,
When silvern voices tune thy rills,
   We love thee, smiling land.

We love thee, we love thee, we love thee,
   Newfoundland.
We love thee, we love thee, we love thee,
   Newfoundland.

When spreads thy cloak of shimmering white
   At winter's stern command,
Through shortened days and starlit night
   We love thee, frozen land.

We love thee, we love thee, we love thee,
   Newfoundland,
We love thee, we love thee, we love thee,
   Newfoundland.

When blinding storm-gusts fret thy shore,
    And wild waves lash thy strand:
Through spindrift swirl and tempest roar
    We love thee, windswept land.

We love thee, we love thee, we love thee,
    Newfoundland,
We love thee, we love thee, we love thee,
    Newfoundland.

We loved our fathers, so we love,
    Where once they stood we stand:
Their prayer we raise to Heaven above:
    God guard thee, Newfoundland.

We love thee, we love thee, we love thee,
    Newfoundland,
We love thee, we love thee, we love thee,
    Newfoundland.

"Pine-clad hills" are words Newfoundlanders traditionally associate with their Great Island, although pines taking root today in Newfoundland are few and far between.

The memorable words come from "The Ode to Newfoundland" written by Sir Cavendish Boyle (1849–1916) upon his appointment as Governor of Newfoundland (1901–1916). The verses were set to music by C. H. Parry, the noted composer who also arranged William Blake's "Jerusalem." The "Ode" was first performed in public in St John's on January 21, 1902.

The "Ode" has stood the test of time and was adopted by unanimous consent as "the National Ode of our Island Home."

LET ME FISH OFF CAPE ST. MARY'S

Otto P. Kelland

Take me back to my western boat,
Let me fish off Cape St. Mary's,
Where the hagdowns sail and the foghorns wail
With my friends the Browns and the Clearys.
Let me fish off Cape St. Mary's.

Let me feel my dory lift
To the broad Atlantic combers,
Where the tide rips swirl and the wild ducks whirl
Where Old Neptune calls the numbers
'Neath the broad Atlantic combers. . . .

Let me sail up Golden Bay
With my oil skins all a-streamin'. . . .
From the thunder squall—when I hauled me trawl
And my old Cape Ann a-gleamin'
With my oil skins all a-streamin'. . . .

Let me view that rugged shore,
Where the beach is all a-glisten
With the caplin spawn where from dusk to dawn
You bait your trawl and listen
To the undertow a-hissin'.

When I reach that last big shoal
Where the ground swells break asunder,
Where the wild sands roll to the surges toll.
Let me be a man and take it
Where my dory fails to make it.

Take me back to that snug green cove
Where the seas roll up their thunder.
There let me rest in the earth's cool breast
Where the stars shine out their wonder—
And the seas roll up their thunder.

"Let Me Fish off Cape St. Mary's" is marked to be sung "quietly, with free expression." It was written and copyrighted in 1960 by composer-writer Otto P. Kelland (b. 1904), one-time warden of the penitentiary at St John's, Nfld.

This modern folk song celebrates the traditional life of the fisherfolk of Cape St Mary's, the tip of Newfoundland's Avalon Peninsula that separates St Mary's Bay and Placentia Bay.

Northrop Frye has attested to the arresting beauty of the song's final lines. Gordon Pinsent sings the song with a particular sweetness on the LP album *Roots* (1997). These days there is a Cape St. Mary's Ecological Reserve on the peninsula.

FAREWELL TO NOVA SCOTIA
Traditional

The sun was setting in the west,
The birds were singing on ev'ry tree,
All nature seemed inclined for rest,
But still there was no rest for me.

Farewell to Nova Scotia, the sea-bound coast!
Let your mountains dark and dreary be,
For when I am far away on the briny ocean tossed
Will you ever heave a sigh and a wish for me?

I grieve to leave my native land,
I grieve to leave my comrades all,
And my parents whom I hold so dear,
And the bonny, bonny lass that I do adore.

Farewell to Nova Scotia, the sea-bound coast!
Let your mountains dark and dreary be,
For when I am far away on the briny ocean tossed
Will you ever heave a sigh and a wish for me?

The drums they do beat and the wars do alarm.
The captain calls, we must obey,
So farewell, farewell to Nova Scotia's charms,
For it's early in the morning I am far, far away.

Farewell to Nova Scotia, the sea-bound coast!
Let your mountains dark and dreary be,
For when I am far away on the briny ocean tossed
Will you ever heave a sigh and a wish for me?

I have three brothers and they are at rest,
Their arms are folded on their breast,
But a poor simple sailor just like me
Must be tossed and driven on the dark blue sea.

Farewell to Nova Scotia, the sea-bound coast!
Let your mountains dark and dreary be,
For when I am far away on the briny ocean tossed
Will you ever heave a sigh and a wish for me?

"Farewell to Nova Scotia" is the best known of all Nova Scotian songs and surpassingly the most moving of them all. It combines the melancholy of departure with the stirring melody of an old sea chanty. The song is generally called by the first words of the refrain, but other titles are "Nova Scotia Farewell," "Nova Scotia Song," and "Adieu to Nova Scotia." Folklorist Helen Creighton found it widely sung in the 1930s in the Petpeswick and Chezzetcook districts near Halifax. She included it in her collection *Traditional Songs from Nova Scotia* (1950). It was chosen as the theme song of "Singalong Jubilee" (1961–74), the popular CBC-TV program which originated in Halifax. It has been notably sung and recorded by Catherine McKinnon (on the Arc album *Something Old, Something New*).

LOW TIDE ON GRAND PRÉ

Bliss Carman

The sun goes down, and over all
   These barren reaches by the tide
Such unelusive glories fall,
   I almost dream they yet will bide
   Until the coming of the tide.

And yet I know that not for us,
   By any ecstasy of dream,
He lingers to keep luminous
   A little while the grievous stream,
   Which frets, uncomforted of dream—

A grievous stream, that to and fro
   Athrough the fields of Acadie
Goes wandering, as if to know
   Why one beloved face should be
   So long from home and Acadie.

Was it a year or lives ago
   We took the grasses in our hands,
And caught the summer flying low
   Over the waving meadow lands,
   And held it there between our hands?

The while the river at our feet—
    A drowsy inland meadow stream—
At set of sun the after-heat
    Made running gold, and in the gleam
    We freed our birch upon the stream.

There down along the elms at dusk
    We lifted dripping blade to drift,
Through twilight scented fine like musk,
    Where night and gloom awhile uplift,
    Nor sunder soul and soul adrift.

And that we took into our hands
    Spirit of life or subtler thing—
Breathed on us there, and loosed the bands
    Of death, and taught us, whispering,
    The secrets of some wonder-thing.

Then all your face grew light, and seemed
    To hold the shadow of the sun;
The evening faltered, and I deemed
    That time was ripe, and years had done
    Their wheeling underneath the sun.

So all desire and all regret,
    And fear and memory, were naught;
One to remember or forget
    The keen delight our hands had caught;
    Morrow and yesterday were naught.

The night has fallen, and the tide . . .
    Now and again comes drifting home,
Across these aching barrens wide,
    A sigh like driven wind or foam:
    In grief the flood is bursting home.

"Low Tide on Grand Pré" is one of the few Canadian poems that
may be meaningfully read alongside "Dover Beach," Matthew
Arnold's lyrical meditation on mutability. The two poems capture a
human sense of loss and place it in a context that is at once natural
and close to cosmic.

It was written by Bliss Carman (1861–1929) and published in
his first book, *Low Tide on Grand Pré* (1893). It is reprinted from
Bliss Carman's Poems (Toronto: McClelland & Stewart, 1929).
Grand Pré (great meadow) refers to the fertile marshlands on the
shores of Minas Basin, N.S., settled by the Acadians until their fate-
ful expulsion in 1747.

THE SAINT JOHN
George Frederick Clarke

Where have they gone,
De Monts and Champlain,
Gallant adventurers who sailed into the west
To search for a passage to Cathay
And discovered and named you, Saint John?
The Malecites now no more
Make canoes of birchen bark,
Or elm, as in days of yore,
Nor fashion their arrows of flint.

Stockade and wigwam and warriors
Are one with the age-old dust
That nurtures the blood-root and violet,
The Linnaea and anemone;
But you, my river, flow on, flow on to the sea;
Past island, intervale, upland
Where the stately elms stand guard alone.
Oh, my river, you have seen the passing of spruce and pine,
And the hemlock, too, has gone to the housing of man,
Those who gave you your name—
De Monts and Champlain,
Do they know, do they sorrow with me
When they see the elm trees standing alone?
Do they hear the wind in the leaves,
And the bobolinks' joyous and rollicking lay,
The lilt of the river over the bars,
And the leap of the salmon in play?
I hope so:
For I, too, some day, years hence in the centuries unmade,
Should love to lie in the grass under the elm tree's shade,
Listening to the song of the bobolink and the thrush,
Content, with De Monts and Champlain,
With this, for Cathay.

Samuel de Champlain and Pierre du Gua de Monts, while *en route* to China (or Cathay), explored Acadia in 1604 and named the Saint John River in present-day New Brunswick.

A particularly sweet poem, "The Saint John" was written by George Frederick Clarke (1883–1969). It takes pride of place in his chapbook *The Saint John and Other Poems* (1933).

THE ISLAND HYMN

L. M. Montgomery

Fair Island of the sea,
We raise our song to thee,
  The bright and blest;
Loyally now we stand
As brothers, hand in hand,
And sing God save the land
  We love the best.

Upon our princely Isle
May kindest fortune smile
  In coming years;
Peace and prosperity
In all her borders be,
From every evil free,
  And weakling fears.

Prince Edward Isle, to thee
Our hearts shall faithful be
  Where'er we dwell;
Forever may we stand
As brothers, hand in hand,
And sing God save the land
  We love so well.

"The Island Hymn" was recognized as Prince Edward Island's unofficial anthem at the time of the 1973 Centennial celebrations.

It was composed by L.M. Montgomery (1874–1942), the province's most-loved writer, in 1908. A month or so later, she received advance copies from the publisher of her first novel, *Anne of Green Gables*.

Her three verses were set to music by composer Lawrence W. Watson, and the composition was premiered at a concert held in the Opera House, Charlottetown, March 1909. It was an immediate success, though Montgomery herself did not hear it performed until 1929.

The Island
Milton Acorn

Since I'm Island-born home's as precise
as if a mumbly old carpenter,
shoulder-straps crossed wrong,
laid it out,
refigured to the last three-eighths of shingle.

Nowhere that plow-cut worms
heal themselves in red loam;
spruces squat, skirts in sand;
or the stones of a river rattle its dark
tunnel under the elms,
is there a spot not measured by hands;
no direction I couldn't walk
to the wave-lined edge of home.

In the fanged jaws of the Gulf,
a red tongue.
Indians say a musical God
took up his brush and painted it;
named it, in His own language,
"The Island."

Milton Acorn (1923–1986) supported himself for many years as a carpenter. He loved his native province of Prince Edward Island. Both his trade and his love are evident in "The Island," which is reprinted from his collection *I've Tasted My Blood* (1969).

THE COUNTRY NORTH OF BELLEVILLE
Al Purdy

Bush land scrub land—
         Cashel Township and Wollaston
Elzevir McClure and Dungannon
green lands of Weslemkoon Lake
where a man might have some
         opinion of what beauty
is and none deny him
                  for miles—

Yet this is the country of defeat
where Sisyphus rolls a big stone
year after year up the ancient hills
picnicking glaciers have left strewn
with centuries' rubble
                              backbreaking days
                              in the sun and rain
when realization seeps slow in the mind
without grandeur or self deception in
                              noble struggle
of being a fool—

A country of quiescence and still distance
a lean land
        not like the fat south
with inches of black soil on
        earth's round belly—
And where the farms are
        it's as if a man stuck
both thumbs in the stony earth and pulled

                it apart
                to make room
enough between the trees
for a wife
        and maybe some cows and
        room for some
of the more easily kept illusions—
And where the farms have gone back
to forest
        are only soft outlines
        shadowy differences—

Old fences drift vaguely among the trees
      a pile of moss-covered stones
gathered for some ghost purpose
has lost meaning under the meaningless sky
      —they are like cities under water
and the undulating green waves of time
      are laid on them—

This is the country of our defeat
      and yet
during the fall plowing a man
might stop and stand in a brown valley of the furrows
      and shade his eyes to watch for the same
      red patch mixed with gold
      that appears on the same
      spot in the hills
      year after year
      and grow old
plowing and plowing a ten-acre field until
the convolutions run parallel with his own brain—

And this is a country where the young
      leave quickly
unwilling to know what their fathers know
or think the words their mothers do not say—

Herschel Monteagle and Faraday
lakeland rockland and hill country
a little adjacent to where the world is
a little north of where the cities are and
sometime
we may go back there
                              to the country of our defeat
Wollaston Elzevir and Dungannon
and Weslemkoon lake land
where the high townships of Cashel
          McClure and Marmora once were—
But it's been a long time since
and we must enquire the way
          of strangers—

Hardscrabble farming was an indelible part of the Ontario experience, but few poets have cared to celebrate that way of life. Al Purdy (1918–2000) was one poet who did, and his free-verse poem "The Country North of Belleville" is its muted epic. It appeared in Purdy's collection *The Cariboo Horses* (1965). Upon his death, the League of Canadian Poets began to refer to Al Purdy as the Voice of the Country.

SUDBURY SATURDAY NIGHT
Tom Connors

The girls are out to Bingo and the boys are gettin' stinko.
We think no more of I.N.C.O. on a Sudbury Saturday Night.
The glasses they will tinkle when our eyes begin to twinkle
And we think no more of I.N.C.O. on a Sudbury Saturday Night.

With Irish Jim O'Connell there and Scotty Jack MacDonald
There's honky Fred'rick Hurgel gettin' tight, but that's all right.
There's happy German Fitzy there with Frenchy gettin' tipsy
And even Joe the Gypsy knows it's Saturday tonight.

Now when Mary, Ann and Mabel come to join us at the table
And tell us how the Bingo went tonight, we'll look a fright,
But if they won the money we'll be lappin' up the honey, boys,
'Cause everything is funny for it's Saturday night.

The girls are out to Bingo and the boys are gettin' stinko.
We think no more of I.N.C.O. on a Sudbury Saturday Night.
The glasses they will tinkle when our eyes begin to twinkle
And we think no more of I.N.C.O. on a Sudbury Saturday Night.

We'll drink the loot we borrowed and recuperate tomorrow
'Cause everything is wonderful tonight, we had a good fight,
We ate the Dilly Pickle and we forgot about the Nickel
And everybody's tickled for it's Saturday tonight.

The songs that we'll be singin', they might be wrong but they'll
    be ringin'
When all the lights of town are shinin' bright and we're all tight,
We'll get to work on Monday but tomorrow's only Sunday
And we're out to have a fun-day for it's Saturday tonight.

The girls are out to Bingo and the boys are gettin' stinko.
We think no more of I.N.C.O. on a Sudbury Saturday Night.
The glasses they will tinkle when our eyes begin to twinkle
And we think no more of I.N.C.O. on a Sudbury Saturday Night.

Stompin' Tom is how the singer-songwriter Tom Connors is known to the public, and "stompin'" is a great description of his performances. His ballads are so lively and so Canadian!

In "Sudbury Saturday Night," he refers to the International Nickel Company (INCO), for many years the mainstay of the economy of Sudbury, Ont. The text appears in *Listen! Songs and Poems of Canada* (1972), edited by Homer Hogan and Dorothy Hogan.

A Place to Stand

Richard Morris & Dolores Claman

Give us a place to stand
and a place to grow
and call this land
On-ta-ri-o,
On-ta-ri-a-ri-o.

A place to live
for you and me
with hopes as high
as the tallest tree.

Give us a land of lakes
and a land of snow
and we will build
On-ta-ri-o.

From western hills
to northern shore
to Niag'ra Falls
where the waters roar.

Give us a land of peace
where the free winds blow
and we will build
On-ta-ri-o.

A place to stand
a place to grow,
On-ta-ri-ta-ri-o.

A place to stand,
a place to grow,
On-ta-ri-a-ri-a-ri—
O-N-T-A-R-I-O.

"A Place to Stand" was composed by the songwriting team of Richard Morris (words) and Dolores Claman (music) for the short film *A Place to Stand*. The film was produced by David Mackay and directed by Christopher Chapman and commissioned by the Ontario Government for the Ontario Pavilion at Expo 67. The song is to be sung with "a swinging march tempo," for it characterizes a period in Ontario's history that was brash, expansive, and progressive. After composing it, however, the songwriting team settled in British Columbia.

RED RIVER VALLEY
Traditional

From this valley they say you are going,
I shall miss your sweet face and your smile;
Just because you are weary and tired,
You are changing your range for a while.
I've been thinking a long time, my darling,
Of the sweet word you never would say;
Now, alas, must my fond hopes all vanish?
For they say you are going away.

Then come sit here a while e'er you leave us,
Do not hasten to bid us adieu,
Just remember the Red River Valley
And the cowboy who loves you so true.

I have promised you, darling, that never
Will words from my lips cause you pain;
And my life it will be yours forever,
If you only will love me again.
Must the past with its joys all be blighted
By the future of sorrow and pain?
Must the vows that were spoken be slighted?
Don't you think you could love me again?

Then come sit here awhile e'er you leave us,
Do not hasten to bid us adieu,
Just remember the Red River Valley
And the cowboy who loves you so true.

There never could be such a longing
In the heart of a poor cowboy's breast,
As dwells in the heart you are breaking,
As I wait in my home in the West.
Do you think of the valley you're leaving?
Oh, how lonely and dreary it'll be!
Do you think of the kind hearts you're hurting,
And the pain you are causing to me?

Then come sit here awhile e'er you leave us,
Do not hasten to bid us adieu,
Just remember the Red River Valley
And the cowboy who loves you so true.

"Red River Valley" is one of the most moving of all traditional love songs. It is also among the most emotional of cowboy ballads. The sturdy words, which almost match the melody's haunting air of melancholy, display a dignity characteristically their own. No one knows who composed it.

In *Singing Our History* (1984), folklorist Edith Fowke suggests it was composed in Manitoba at the time of the Red River Rebellion of 1870. She reproduces the chorus in this fashion: "Come and sit by my side if you love me, / Do not hasten to bid me adieu, / But remember the Red River Valley / And the girl who has loved you so true." Whatever the version of the lyrics, the meaning remains the same and the tune is appealing and haunting.

For a well-loved parody of "Red River Valley," see Christopher Dafoe's "Forty Below," included in the present treasury.

SASKATCHEWAN
William W. Smith

Saskatchewan, the land of snow,
Where winds are always on the blow,
Where people sit with frozen toes,
And why we stay here no one knows.

Saskatchewan, Saskatchewan,
There's no place like Saskatchewan.
We sit and gaze across the plain,
And wonder why it never rains,
And Gabriel blows his trumpet sound;
He says: "The rain, she's gone around."

Our pigs are dying on their feet
Because they have no feed to eat;
Our horses, though of bronco race,
Starvation stares them in the face.

Saskatchewan, Saskatchewan,
There's no place like Saskatchewan.
We sit and gaze across the plain,
And wonder why it never rains,
And Gabriel blows his trumpet sound;
He says: "The rain, she's gone around."

The milk from cows has ceased to flow,
We've had to ship them east, you know;
Our hens are old and lay no eggs,
Our turkeys eat grasshopper legs.

Saskatchewan, Saskatchewan,
There's no place like Saskatchewan.
We sit and gaze across the plain,
And wonder why it never rains,
And Gabriel blows his trumpet sound;
He says: "The rain, she's gone around."

But still we love Saskatchewan,
We're proud to say we're native ones,
So count your blessings drop by drop,
Next year we'll have a bumper crop!

Saskatchewan, Saskatchewan,
There's no place like Saskatchewan.
We sit and gaze across the plain,
And wonder why it never rains,
And Gabriel blows his trumpet sound;
He says: "The rain, she's gone around."

These verses were written in the 1930s by William W. Smith, a businessman of Swift Current, Sask. He set them to the music of the Christian hymn "Beulah Land."

"Saskatchewan, Saskatchewan" is one member of a family of songs that describes the miseries and hardships of farming the plains. Readers may be familiar with "Dakota Land," "Nebraska Land," "Alberta Land," and "Oh Prairie Land."

The Canadian text appears in Edith Fowke and Alan Mills's *Canada's Story in Song* (1960).

TWILIGHT ON THE PRAIRIE
Wilf Carter

When it's twilight on the prairie,
Where the pale blue violets hide,
I sit and long for you, dear,
Just to have you by my side.

In dreams I see you smiling,
Thro' eyes of heav'nly blue,
When it's twilight on the prairie,
I am thinking, dear, of you.

Twilight on the prairie,
Cattle cease to roam;
I'm swinging in my saddle,
Down the trail to home, sweet home.

As I'm riding in the twilight,
On the rolling prairie wide,
I'm swaying in my saddle,
My guitar hangs by my side.

The air is filled with fragrance
From flowers in full bloom,
When it's twilight on the prairie,
On a golden night in June.

Twilight on the prairie,
Cattle cease to roam;
I'm swinging in my saddle,
Down the trail to home, sweet home.

I am thinking as I linger,
Where once we used to stray,
Of songs we sang together,
Long before our parting day.

My lonely heart is aching
For days that once we knew,
When it's twilight on the prairie,
I am dreaming, dear, of you.

Twilight on the prairie,
Cattle cease to roam;
I'm swinging in my saddle,
Down the trail to home, sweet home.

Wilf Carter (1904–1996), one of the founders of Canadian Country
and Western music, was born at Port Hilford, N.S. In his youth he
moved to Alberta, where he was employed as a cowhand or cow-
boy. He began to perform his own compositions and those of oth-
ers and launched a highly successful career as a performing and
recording artist.

In 1933, he wrote the words and music and performed
"Twilight on the Prairie," a classic of Country and Western music
and also of Canadian song.

FAREWELL TO ALBERTA

Traditional

My name is Dan Gold, an old bach'lor I am,
I'm keeping old batch on an elegant plan.
You'll find me out here on Alberta's bush plain
A-starving to death on a government claim.

So come to Alberta, there's room for you all
Where the wind never ceases and the rain always falls,
Where the sun always sets and there it remains
Till we get frozen out on our government claims.

My house it is built of the natural soil,
My walls are erected according to Hoyle,
My roof has no pitch, it is level and plain,
And I always get wet when it happens to rain.

My clothes are all ragged, my language is rough,
My bread is case-hardened and solid and tough,
My dishes are scattered all over the room,
My floor gets afraid at the sight of a broom.

How happy I feel when I roll into bed,
The rattlesnake rattles a tune at my head.
The little mosquito devoid of all fear
Crawls over my face and into my ear.

The little bed-bug so cheerful and bright,
It keeps me up laughing two-thirds of the night,
And the smart little flea with tacks in his toes
Crawls up through my whiskers and tickles my nose.

You may try to raise wheat, you may try to raise rye,
You may stay there and live, you may stay there and die,
But as for myself, I'll no longer remain
A-starving to death on a government claim.

So farewell to Alberta, farewell to the west,
It's backwards I'll go to the girl I love best.
I'll go back to the east and get me a wife
And never eat cornbread the rest of my life.

This traditional song paints a vivid picture of pioneer life on the Prairies in the 1890s and gives an insight into the character of the people who opened the West.

"Farewell to Alberta" is of unknown authorship. It is often sung to the tune of "The Irish Washerwoman." The text is reprinted from *Canada's Story in Song* (1960) edited by Edith Fowke and Alan Mills. Fowke recorded it from the lips of traditional singer Ivan Brandick in the early 1950s.

THE DOUBLE-HEADED SNAKE

John Newlove

Not to lose the feel of the mountains
while still retaining the prairies
is a difficult thing. What's lovely
is whatever makes the adrenalin run;
therefore I count terror and fear among
the greatest beauty. The greatest
beauty is to be alive, forgetting nothing,
although remembrance hurts
like a foolish act, is a foolish act.

Beauty's whatever
makes the adrenalin run. Fear
in the mountains at night-time's
not tenuous, it is not the cold
that makes me shiver, civilized man,
white, I remember
the stories of the Indians,
Sis-i-utl, the double-headed snake.

Beauty's what makes
the adrenalin run. Fear at night
on the level plains, with no horizon
and the stars too bright, wind bitter
even in June, in winter
the snow harsh and blowing,
is what makes me
shiver, not the cold air alone.

And one beauty cancels another. The plains
seem secure and comfortable
at Crow's Nest Pass; in Saskatchewan
the mountains are comforting
to think of; among
the eastwardly diminishing hills
both the flatland and the ridge
seem easy to endure.

As one beauty
cancels another, remembrance
is a foolish act, a double-headed snake
striking in both directions, but I
remember plains and mountains, places
I come from, places I adhere and live in.

John Newlove was born in Regina and has lived in many cities,
including Toronto, Vancouver, and Ottawa. Yet the experience of
the Prairies informs his lyrical reflections on nature in "The
Double-Headed Snake." The poem is reprinted from *Black Night
Window* (1968).

THE ATHABASCA TRAIL

Sir Arthur Conan Doyle

My life is gliding downwards; it speeds swifter to the day
When it shoots the last dark canon to the Plains of Faraway,
But while its stream is running through the years that are to be,
The mighty voice of Canada will ever call to me.
I shall hear the roar of rivers where the rapids foam and tear,
I shall smell the virgin upland with its balsam-laden air,
And shall dream that I am riding down the winding woody vale,
With the packer and the packhorse on the Athabasca Trail.

I have passed the warden cities at the eastern watergate,
Where the hero and the martyr laid the corner stone of State
The *habitant, coureur-des-bois,* and hardy *voyageur,*
Where lives a breed more strong at need to venture or endure?
I have seen the gorge of Erie where the roaring waters run,
I have crossed the Inland Ocean, lying golden in the sun,
But the last and best and sweetest is the ride by hill and dale,
With the packer and the packhorse on the Athabasca Trail.

I'll dream again of fields of grain that stretch from sky to sky,
And the little prairie hamlets, where the cars go roaring by,
Wooden hamlets as I saw them—noble cities still to be
To girdle stately Canada with gems from sea to sea;
Mother of a mighty manhood, land of glamour and of hope,
From the eastward sea-swept Islands to the sunny western slope,
Ever more my heart is with you, ever more till life shall fail,
I'll be out with pack and packer on the Athabasca Trail.

The awesome beauty of the land and the hardy romance of the settlement of the country were subjects to celebrate, but it took British Imperial travellers to rise to the occasion and sing the praises of the land and its pioneers.

Sir Arthur Conan Doyle (1859–1930) responded to the call to find excitement and romance in the undertaking. He delivered a rousing, nationalistic address to the members of the Canadian Club of Ottawa, July 2, 1914. To prolonged cheers, he delivered his parting shot, a recital of his newly composed verse, "The Athabasca Trail."

> Before I sit down I will read a verse or two in which I was able, perhaps, to compress a little more of that feeling which Canada has awakened, than can be done in prose. Poetry is like the pemmican of literature: It is compressed thought, and one can mingle emotion with it, which one cannot always do in prosaic speech. I will read you, if I may, these few lines before I take my seat. I called it 'The Athabasca Trail,' since Athabasca is the place where we have for some time been living an open-air life.

THE SHOOTING OF DAN McGREW
Robert W. Service

A bunch of the boys were whopping it up in the Malamute
    saloon;
The kid that handles the music-box was hitting a jag-time tune;
Back of the bar, in a solo game, sat Dangerous Dan McGrew,
And watching his luck was his light-o'-love, the lady that's
    known as Lou.

When out of the night, which was fifty below, and into the din
    and the glare,
There stumbled a miner fresh from the creeks, dog-dirty, and
    loaded for bear.
He looked like a man with a foot in the grave and scarcely the
    strength of a louse,
Yet he tilted a poke of dust on the bar, and he called for drinks
    for the house.
There was none could place the stranger's face, though we
    searched ourselves for a clue;
But we drank his health, and the last to drink was Dangerous
    Dan McGrew.

There's men that somehow just grip your eyes, and hold them
    hard like a spell;
And such was he, and he looked to me like a man who had
    lived in hell;
With a face most hair, and the dreary stare of a dog whose day
    is done,
As he watered the green stuff in his glass, and the drops fell
    one by one.
Then I got to figgering who he was, and wondering what he'd do,
And I turned my head—and there watching him was the lady
    that's known as Lou.

His eyes went rubbering round the room, and he seemed in a
   kind of daze,
Till at last that old piano fell in the way of his wandering gaze.
The rag-time kid was having a drink; there was no one else on
   the stool,
So the stranger stumbles across the room, and flops down
   there like a fool.
In a buckskin shirt that was glazed with dirt he sat, and I saw
   him sway;
Then he clutched the keys with his talon hands—my God! but
   that man could play.

Were you ever out in the Great Alone, when the moon was
   awful clear,
And the icy mountains hemmed you in with a silence you most
   could *hear;*
With only the howl of a timber wolf, and you camped there in
   the cold,
A half-dead thing in a stark, dead world, clean mad for the
   muck called gold;
While high overhead, green, yellow and red, the North Lights
   swept in bars?—
Then you've a hunch what the music meant . . . hunger and
   night and the stars.

And hunger not of the belly kind, that's banished with bacon
    and beans,
But the gnawing hunger of lonely men for a home and all that
    it means;
For a fireside far from the cares that are, four walls and a roof
    above;
But oh! so cramful of cosy joy, and crowned with a woman's
    love—
A woman dearer than all the world, and true as Heaven is true—
(God! how ghastly she looks through her rouge,—the lady
    that's known as Lou.)

Then on a sudden the music changed, so soft that you scarce
    could hear;
But you felt that your life had been looted clean of all that it
    once held dear;
That someone had stolen the woman you loved; that her love
    was a devil's lie;
That your guts were gone, and the best for you was to crawl
    away and die.
'Twas the crowning cry of a heart's despair, and it thrilled you
    through and through—
"I guess I'll make it a spread misere," said Dangerous Dan
    McGrew.

The music almost died away . . . then it burst like a pent-up
 flood;
And it seemed to say, "Repay, repay," and my eyes were blind
 with blood.
The thought came back of an ancient wrong, and it stung like
 a frozen lash,
And the lust awoke to kill, to kill . . . then the music stopped
 with a crash,
And the stranger turned, and his eyes they burned in a most
 peculiar way;
In a buckskin shirt that was glazed with dirt he sat, and I saw
 him sway;
Then his lips went in in a kind of grin, and he spoke, and his
 voice was calm,
And "Boys," says he, "you don't know me, and none of you
 care a damn;
But I want to state, and my words are straight, and I'll bet my
 poke they're true,
That one of you is a hound of hell . . . and that one is Dan
 McGrew."

Then I ducked my head, and the lights went out, and two guns
 blazed in the dark,
And a woman screamed, and the lights went up, and two men
 lay stiff and stark.
Pitched on his head, and pumped full of lead, was Dangerous
 Dan McGrew,
While the man from the creeks lay clutched to the breast of the
 lady's that's known as Lou.

These are the simple facts of the case, and I guess I ought to
know.
They say that the stranger was crazed with "hooch," and I'm
not denying it's so.
I'm not so wise as the lawyer guys, but strictly between us
two—
The woman that kissed him—and pinched his poke—was the
lady that's known as Lou.

THE CREMATION OF SAM MCGEE
Robert W. Service

There are strange things done in the midnight sun
By the men who moil for gold;
The Arctic trails have their secret tales
That would make your blood run cold;
The Northern Lights have seen queer sights,
But the queerest they ever did see
Was that night on the marge of Lake Lebarge
I cremated Sam McGee.

Now Sam McGee was from Tennessee, where the cotton
blooms and blows.
Why he left his home in the South to roam 'round the Pole,
God only knows.
He was always cold, but the land of gold seemed to hold him
like a spell;
Though he'd often say in his homely way that "he'd sooner
live in hell."

On a Christmas Day we were mushing our way over the
Dawson trail.

Talk of your cold! through the parka's fold it stabbed like a
driven nail.

If our eyes we'd close, then the lashes froze till sometimes we
couldn't see;

It wasn't much fun, but the only one to whimper was Sam
McGee.

And that very night, as we lay packed tight in our robes
beneath the snow,

And the dogs were fed, and the stars o'erhead were dancing
heel and toe,

He turned to me, and "Cap," says he, "I'll cash in this trip, I
guess;

And if I do, I'm asking that you won't refuse my last request."

Well, he seemed so low that I couldn't say no; then he says
with a sort of moan:

"It's the cursèd cold, and it's got right hold till I'm chilled clean
through to the bone.

Yet 'tain't being dead—it's my awful dread of the icy grave that
pains;

So I want you to swear that, foul or fair, you'll cremate my last
remains."

A pal's last need is a thing to heed, so I swore I would not fail;
And we started on at the streak of dawn; but God! he looked
 ghastly pale.
He crouched on the sleigh, and he raved all day of his home in
 Tennessee;
And before nightfall a corpse was all that was left of Sam
 McGee.

There wasn't a breath in that land of death, and I hurried,
 horror-driven,
With a corpse half hid that I couldn't get rid, because of a
 promise given;
It was lashed to the sleigh, and it seemed to say: "You may tax
 your brawn and brains,
But you promised true, and it's up to you to cremate these last
 remains."

Now a promise made is a debt unpaid, and the trail has its
 own stern code.
In the days to come, though my lips were dumb, in my heart
 how I cursed that load.
In the long, long night, by the lone firelight, while the huskies,
 round in a ring,
Howled out their woes to the homeless snows—Oh God! how
 I loathed the thing.

And every day that quiet clay seemed to heavy and heavier grow;
And on I went, though the dogs were spent and the grub was
    getting low;
The trail was bad, and I felt half mad, but I swore I would not
    give in;
And I'd often sing to the hateful thing, and it hearkened with a
    grin.

Till I came to the marge of Lake Lebarge, and a derelict there
    lay;
It was jammed in the ice, but I saw in a trice it was called the
    "Alice May."
And I looked at it, and I thought a bit, and I looked at my
    frozen chum;
Then "Here," said I, with a sudden cry, "is my cre-ma-tor-eum."

Some planks I tore from the cabin floor and I lit the boiler fire;
Some coal I found that was lying around, and I heaped the fuel
    higher;
The flames just soared, and the furnace roared—such a blaze
    you seldom see;
And I burrowed a hole in the glowing coal, and I stuffed in
    Sam McGee.

Then I made a hike, for I didn't like to hear him sizzle so;
And the heavens scowled, and the huskies howled, and the
    wind began to blow.
It was icy cold, but the hot sweat rolled down my cheeks, and
    I don't know why;
And the greasy smoke in an inky cloak went streaking down
    the sky.

I do not know how long in the snow I wrestled with a grisly fear;
But the stars came out and they danced about ere again I
   ventured near;
I was sick with dread, but I bravely said: "I'll just take a peep
   inside.
I guess he's cooked, and it's time I looked"; . . . then the door I
   opened wide.

And there sat Sam, looking cool and calm, in the heart of the
   furnace roar;
And he wore a smile you could see a mile, and he said: "Please
   close that door.
It's fine in here, but I greatly fear you'll let in the cold and
   storm—
Since I left Plumtree, down in Tennesssee, it's the first time I've
   been warm."

> *There are strange things done in the midnight sun*
> *By the men who moil for gold;*
> *The Arctic trails have their secret tales*
> *That would make your blood run cold;*
> *The Northern Lights have seen queer sights,*
> *But the queerest they ever did see*
> *Was that night on the marge of Lake Lebarge*
> *I cremated Sam McGee.*

For sheer excitement, enjoyment, and entertainment, it is hard to
beat the work of Robert W. Service (1874–1958). He came to be
identified as the Bard of the Yukon, but all his life, modest man that
he was, he disclaimed the title of "poet" in favour of that of "verse-
maker" or "rhymester."

Born in Scotland, he immigrated to Western Canada and was working as a bank clerk in Whitehorse, Yukon Territory, when, in 1904–6, he began to compose his energetic northern ballads about the characters and incidents of the Yukon Gold Rush of the 1890s.

"The Shooting of Dan McGrew" and "The Cremation of Sam McGee," two of his earliest narrative ballads, appeared in his first Canadian collection, *Songs of a Sourdough* (1907), which was published in the United States as *The Spell of the Yukon*. His books brought him immediate popularity and prosperity. Thereafter he lived in Europe as a newspaper correspondent and retired to Monte Carlo on the Riviera.

As long as the years of the Yukon Gold Rush continue to fascinate Canadians, we will read and reread and memorize and recite Service's "rhymes."

LAURENTIAN SHIELD
F. R. Scott

Hidden in wonder and snow, or sudden with summer,
This land stares at the sun in a huge silence
Endlessly repeating something we cannot hear.
Inarticulate, arctic,
Not written on by history, empty as paper,
It leans away from the world with songs in its lakes
Older than love, and lost in the miles.

This waiting is wanting.
It will choose its language
When it has chosen its technic,
A tongue to shape the vowels of its productivity.

A language of flesh and roses.

Now there are pre-words,
Cabin syllables,
Nouns of settlement
Slowly forming, with steel syntax,
The long sentence of its exploitation.

The first cry was the hunter, hungry for fur,
And the digger for gold, nomad, no-man, a particle;
Then the bold commands of monopolies, big with machines,
Carving its kingdoms out of the public wealth;
And now the drone of the plane, scouting the ice,
Fills all the emptiness with neighbourhood
And links our future over the vanished pole.

But a deeper note is sounding, heard in the mines,
The scattered camps and the mills, a language of life,
And what will be written in the full culture of occupation
Will come, presently, tomorrow,
From millions whose hands can turn this rock into children.

"Laurentian Shield" is at once the starkest and yet the most humane evocation of the landscape and the spirit of the North on record. It is a wonderful poem and it was composed in 1945 by F. R. Scott (1899–1985), poet and professor of constitutional law at McGill University. He wrote the poem following a trip across "the top of Canada" in the company of the youthful adventurer Pierre Elliott Trudeau. It is reprinted from *The Collected Poems of F.R. Scott* (1981).

THE LONELY LAND
A. J. M. Smith

Cedar and jagged fir
uplift sharp barbs
against the gray
and cloud-piled sky;
and in the bay
blown spume and windrift
and thin, bitter spray
snap
at the whirling sky;
and the pine trees
lean one way.

A wild duck calls
to her mate,
and the ragged
and passionate tones
stagger and fall,
and recover,
and stagger and fall,
on these stones—
are lost
in the lapping of water
on smooth, flat stones.

This is a beauty
of dissonance,
this resonance
of stony strand,
this smoky cry
curled over a black pine
like a broken
and wind-battered branch
when the wind
bends the tops of the pines
and curdles the sky
from the north.

This is the beauty
of strength
broken by strength
and still strong.

"The Lonely Land" was composed by A. J. M. Smith (1902–1980). It is Smith's most anthologized poem (and the one that he stated he most disliked). The poem's final stanza is justly famous. It seems to characterize the pre-Cambrian immensities of the geology and the spirit of the land.

The poem, first published in the journal *Poetry* (Chicago) in 1926, is reprinted from Smith's *Collected Poems* (1962).

La Belle
Province

A LA CLAIRE FONTAINE

Traditional

A la claire fontaine
 M'en allant promener,
J'ai trouvé l'eau si belle
 Que je m'y suis baigné;
   Lui ya longtemps que je t'aime,
   Jamais je ne t'oublierai.

Sur la plus haute branche
 Le rossignol chantait.
Chante, rossignol, chante,
 Toi qui as le coeur gai.
   Lui ya longtemps que je t'aime,
   Jamais je ne t'oublierai.

Tu as le coeur . . . rire,
 Moi je l'ai-t-à pleurer:
J'ai perdu ma maîtresse
 Sans l'avoir mérité.
   Lui ya longtemps que je t'aime,
   Jamais je ne t'oublierai.

Pour un bouquet de roses
 Que je lui refusai.
Je voudrais que la rose
 Fût encore au rosier.
   Lui ya longtemps que je t'aime,
   Jamais je ne t'oublierai.

Je voudrais que la rose
Fût encore au rosier,
Et moi et ma maîtresse
Dans les mêmes amitiés.
Lui ya longtemps que je t'aime,
Jamais je ne t'oublierai.

"A la Claire Fontaine" caused folksong collector Ernest Gagnon to exclaim, "One is not *Canadien* without it."

It first saw life as a traditional love song of Old France. It was a favourite of Champlain's men, who formed the Order of Good Cheer at Port Royal in 1608 to banish the miseries of winter. It was then lustily sung by both the *coureurs de bois* and the *habitants* in New France. Today it is part of every musical gathering of Quebeckers.

The text, collected by Gagnon, is taken from *Canadian Folk Songs (Old and New)* (1927).

At the Clear Running Fountain
English

At the clear running fountain
Sauntering by one day,
I found it so compelling
I bathed without delay;
Your love long since overcame me,
Ever in my heart you'll stay.

I found it so compelling
   I bathed without delay;
Under an oak tree shady
   I dried the damp away.
      Your love long since overcame me,
      Ever in my heart you'll stay.

There where the highest branch is,
   Sir Nightingale sang hey!
Sing, Nightingale, keep singing,
   You sing with heart so gay.
      Your love long since overcame me,
      Ever in my heart you'll stay.

You have the heart a-ringing;
   My heart—ah! lack-a-day!
I lost my lovely lady
   In such a blameless way.
      Your love long since overcame me,
      Ever in my heart you'll stay.

For one bouquet of roses
   Which I must say her nay—
I wish that now the roses
   Bloomed on their tree to-day.
      Your love long since overcame me,
      Ever in my heart you'll stay.

I wish that now the roses
  Bloomed on their tree to-day,
And I and she, the lady,
  Were friends the same old way!
    Your love long since overcame me,
    Ever in my heart you'll stay.

"At the Clear Running Fountain" is a faithful translation of "A la Claire Fontaine." Edith Fowke noted its odd history: a medieval jongleur song of Old France that became the unofficial anthem of the French in Canada.

This translation was prepared by publicist and poetaster J. Murray Gibbon (1875–1952) and is reprinted from *Canadian Folk Songs (Old and New)* (1927).

Alouette!
Traditional

Alouette, gentille alouette, alouette, je t'y plumerai.
Alouette, gentille alouette, alouette, je t'y plumerai.

Je t'y plumerai la têt', je t'y plumerai la têt',
Je t'y plumerai la têt', je t'y plumerai la têt',
Et la têt',
Et la têt',
Et la têt',
Et la têt',
Alouett',
Alouett', O. . . .

Je t'y plumerai le bec, je t'y plumerai le bec,
Je t'y plumerai le bec, je t'y plumerai le bec,
Et le bec,
Et le bec,
Et le bec,
Et la têt',
Et la têt',
Et la têt',
Et la têt',
Et la têt',
Alouett',
Alouett', O. . . .

"Alouette!" is a nonsense song with long-standing appeal to Canadians young and old of both language groups.

"This is by far the best known of all Canadian songs," explains the folklorist Edith Fowke. "It has long been used by both French and English Canadians for community singing."

In this traditional French-Canadian song, the *alouette,* or skylark, is warned: "Alouette, gentle alouette, alouette, I will pluck your feathers yet." Verse by verse, different parts of the bird's body are mentioned: *la têt'* (head), *le bec* (beak), *le nez* (nose), *les yeux* (eyes), *le cou* (neck), *les aile's* (wings), *le dos* (back), *les patt's* (feet), *la queue* (tail). . . .

The words and music appear in J. Murray Gibbon's *Canadian Folk Songs (Old and New)* (1927).

VIVE LA CANADIENNE!
Traditional

Vive la Canadienne!
  Vole, mon coeur, vole!
Vive la Canadienne!
  Et ses jolies yeux doux,
Et ses jolies yeux doux, doux, doux,
Et ses jolies yeux doux.

This is the first verse of "Vive la Canadienne!"

Sometime during the seventeenth century, a French Canadian, perhaps a *voyageur,* composed a new set of words for an old French melody and created this lively toast to the *Canadienne* girl. It is widely sung in Quebec to this day.

All six stanzas of "Vive la Canadienne!" appear in J. Murray Gibbon's *Canadian Folk Songs (Old and New)* (1927).

—

VIVE LA CANADIENNE!
English

Of my Canadian girl I sing,
  Gaily our voices ring!
Of my Canadian girl I sing
And her sweet eyes so blue,
  And her sweet eyes so blue, blue, blue,
  And her sweet eyes so blue.

Here's to a lovers' meeting!
  Gaily our voices ring!
Here's to a lovers' meeting!
I know that she is true,
  I know that she is true, true, true,
  I know that she is true.

Quickly our hearts are beating!
  Gaily our voices ring!
Quickly our hearts are beating,
As we go on our way,
  As we go on our way, way, way,
  As we go on our way.

So go the hours a-flying,
  Gaily our voices ring!
So go the hours a-flying
Until our wedding day,
  Until our wedding day, day, day,
  Until our wedding day.

Here are the English words of "Vive la Canadienne!" a once-popular, four-stanza version of the traditional Quebec *chanson*.

The translation was prepared by Edith Fowke for *The Penguin Book of Canadian Folk Songs* (1973). When the song is sung, the last two lines of each verse are repeated.

Un Canadien Errant

Antoine Gérin-Lajoie

Un Canadien errant
    Banni de ses foyers,
Parcourait en pleurant
    Des pays étrangers.
    Des pays étrangers.

Un jour, triste et pensif,
    Assis au bord des flots,
Au courant fugitif
    Il adressa ces mots.
    Il adressa ces mots:

"Si tu vois mon pays,
    Mon pays malheureux,
Va, dis à mes amis
    Que je me souviens d'eux.
    Que je me souviens d'eux.

"O jours si pleins d'appas,
    Vous êtes disparus,
Et ma patrie, hélas!
    Je ne la verrai plus.
    Je ne la verrai plus.

"Non, mais en expirant,
  O mon cher Canada,
Mon regard languissant
  Vers toi se portera.
  Vers toi se portera."

This is the most moving of all laments for the French Canadians who were exiled to Australia following the Rebellion of 1837–38. It must be the most doleful of all *Canadien* and Canadian songs.

"Un Canadien Errant" was written in 1847 by Antoine Gérin-Lajoie (1824–1882), then a young student, later a distinguished essayist, novelist, and librarian.

The text is reprinted from J. Murray Gibbon's *Canadian Folk Songs (Old and New)* (1927).

FROM HIS CANADIAN HOME
English

From his Canadian home
  Banished a wand'rer came,
And full of tears would roam,
  Countries that strangers claim,
And full of tears would roam,
  Countries that strangers claim.

Thoughtful and sad one day,
  Down by a river bed,
As the stream slipped away,
  These were the words he said;
As the stream slipped away,
  These were the words he said:

"If you my land should see,
   My so unhappy land,
Say to my friends from me
   They in my memory stand;
Say to my friends from me
   They in my memory stand.

"O so delightful days,
   Vanished you are—adieu!
And my own land, alas!
   Never again I'll view;
And my own land, alas!
   Never again I'll view.

"Plunged in unhappiness,
   From my dear parents torn,
Now through the tears I pass
   In luckless moments born;
Now through the tears I pass
   In luckless moments born.

"For ever set apart
   From friends that were so sweet,
Alas! no more my heart,
   My heart for grief can beat;
Alas! no more my heart,
   My heart for grief can beat.

"No, yet in dying still,
    O my dear Canada!
My drooping eyes I will
    Turn toward thee afar;
My drooping eyes I will
    Turn toward thee afar."

"From His Canadian Home" is marked to be sung "Plaintively—
Plaintivement." It is a translation of the traditional French-
Canadian song of exile "Un Canadien Errant," composed by
Antoine Gérin-Lajoie and translated by J. Murray Gibbon for his
collection *Canadian Folk Songs: Old and New* (1927).

THE WRECK OF THE "JULIE PLANTE"
William Henry Drummond

A Legend of Lac St. Pierre

On wan dark night on Lac St. Pierre,
    De win' she blow, blow, blow,
An' de crew of de wood scow "Julie Plante"
    Got scar't an' run below—
For de win' she blow lak hurricane
    Bimeby she blow some more,
An' de scow bus' up on Lac St. Pierre
    Wan arpent from de shore.

De captinne walk on de fronte deck,
An' walk de hin' deck too—
He call de crew from up de hole
He call de cook also.
De cook she's name was Rosie,
She come from Montreal,
Was chambre maid on lumber barge,
On de Grande Lachine Canal.

De win' she blow from nor'-eas'-wes',—
De sout' win' she blow too,
W'en Rosie cry "Mon cher captinne,
Mon cher, w'at I shall do?"
Den de captinne t'row de big ankerre,
But still de scow she dreef,
De crew he can't pass on de shore,
Becos' he los' hees skeef.

De night was dark lak' wan black cat,
De wave run high an' fas',
W'en de captinne tak' de Rosie girl
An' tie her to de mas'.
Den he also tak' de life preserve,
An' jomp off on de lak',
An' say, "Good-bye, ma Rosie dear,
I go drown for your sak'."

Nex' morning very early
  'Bout ha'f-pas' two—t'ree—four—
De captinne—scow—an' de poor Rosie
  Was corpses on de shore,
For de win' she blow lak' hurricane
  Bimeby she blow some more,
An' de scow bus' up on Lac St. Pierre,
  Wan arpent from de shore.

Moral

Now all good wood scow sailor man
  Tak' warning by dat storm
An' go an' marry some nice French girl
  An' leev on wan beeg farm.
De win' can blow lak' hurricane
  An' s'pose she blow some more,
You can't get drown on Lac St. Pierre
  So long you stay on shore.

The last two lines of "The Wreck of the 'Julie Plante'" have entered into the folkore of French Canada. Their moral is: Don't go near the water.

    Today it is fashionable to despise dialect humour and disdain the writings of William Henry Drummond (1854–1907). Yet in his own time (and since then), Drummond's recitations and verses were wildly popular with English Canadians and affectionately received by French Canadians. "His is truly the work of a poet and an artist," wrote Louis-Honoré Fréchette in the Foreword to *Dr. W. H. Drummond's Complete Poems* (1926). It should be noted, however, that Fréchette praised only the poet's invention, not his language.

William Henry Drummond was an Irish-born immigrant who worked his way through McGill University, practised medicine, and in later years taught in the university's medical faculty. He was proud to be known as "the *habitant* poet." He felt his idiomatic verses, written in the broken English of French-Canadian lumbermen, canoemen, and farmers, preserved a form of speech and recalled a way of life that was fast passing from the scene.

Drummond's poems and ballads found favour with at least three generations of readers—and reciters. Then they fell into disfavour with critics and educators (who had no idea how to recite them, much less to teach them). It is unlikely that the dialect poetry of Drummond or that of other bards will return to public favour in the near future, despite the fact that poems like these are long-lived. They still retain their remarkable gusto, lively spirits, and good humour.

Today Canadian educators are so fearful of giving offence to ethnic and other groups that they censor any vigorous expression that may seem to characterize or categorize. It was not always so. In the past, educators were appreciative of vigorous expression even when it involved racial profiling. Here, for instance, is an appreciation of dialect verse that appeared in a widely used textbook first published in 1932: "W. H. Drummond's poetry is marked by a fine vein of humour and a rich depth of humanity, and it enjoyed, and still enjoys, a very wide popularity." So wrote Adrian Macdonald, M.A., English Master, The Normal School, Peterborough, Ont. Macdonald was the editor of *A Pedlar's Pack*, an anthology of English-language poetry "Authorized for Use in the Province of Alberta (1940)."

LITTLE BATEESE

William Henry Drummond

You bad leetle boy, not moche you care
How busy you're kipin' your gran'père
Tryin' to stop you ev'ry day
Chasin' de hen aroun' de hay—
W'y don't you geev' dem a chance to lay?
                              Leetle Bateese!

Off on de fiel' you foller de plough
Den w'en you're tire you scare de cow
Sickin' de dog till dey jomp de wall
So de milk ain't good for not'ing at all—
An' you're only five an' a half dis fall,
                              Leetle Bateese!

Too sleepy for sayin' de prayer to-night?
Never min' I s'pose it'll be all right
Say dem to-morrow—ah! dere he go!
Fas' asleep in a minute or so—
An' he'll stay lak dat till de rooster crow,
                              Leetle Bateese!

Den wake us up right away toute suite
Lookin' for somet'ing more to eat,
Makin' me t'ink of dem long leg crane
Soon as dey swaller, dey start again,
I wonder your stomach don't get no pain,
                              Leetle Bateese!

But see heem now lyin' dere in bed,
Look at de arm onderneat' hees head;
If he grow like dat till he's twenty year
I bet he'll be stronger dan Louis Cyr,
An' beat all de voyageurs leevin' here,
                                        Leetle Bateese!

Jus' feel de muscle along hees back,
Won't geev' heem moche bodder for carry pack
On de long portage, any size canoe,
Dere's not many t'ing dat boy won't do,
For he's got double-joint on hees body too,
                                        Leetle Bateese!

But leetle Bateese! please don't forget
We rader you're stayin' de small boy yet,
So chase de chicken an' mak' dem scare,
An' do w'at you lak wit' your ole gran'père,
For w'en you're beeg feller he won't be dere—
                                        Leetle Bateese!

The recitals by Irish-born William Henry Drummond (1854–1907) of his dialect poems about the lives of the French Canadian people always included a performance of "Little Bateese."

Behind the *bonhomie* and hilarity of these poems, the contemporary reader (rather than listener) senses that the subject lacks maturity.

"Little Bateese" is reprinted from *Dr. W. H. Drummond's Complete Poems* (1926). Critic and anthologist A. J. M. Smith wrote in *The Book of Canadian Poetry* (Toronto: W. J. Gage and Company, 1943, rev. ed., 1948), "William Henry Drummond's tender and humorous evocations of the olden times in French Canada are a classic instance of the preservative value of humility, humanity, and good sense."

———

BONNE ENTENTE

F. R. Scott

"One man's meat is another man's poisson." A. Lismer

The advantages of living with two cultures
Strike one at every turn,
Especially when one finds a notice in an office building:
"This elevator will not run on Ascension Day";
Or reads in the Montreal *Star:*
"Tomorrow being the Feast of the Immaculate Conception,
There will be no collection of garbage in the city";
Or sees on the restaurant menu the bilingual dish:

DEEP APPLE PIE
TARTE AUX POMMES PROFONDES

This satiric verse is known, at least in part, to thousands, who still chuckle when it is recalled.

"Bonne Entente" was written by the Montreal poet and professor of constitutional law, F. R. Scott (1899–1985) in 1953 and published in *Events and Signals* (1954). It is reprinted from *The Collected Poems of F. R. Scott* (1981). Scott attributes the bilingual pun at the beginning to the painter Arthur Lismer.

———

Mon Pays

Gilles Vigneault

Mon pays ce n'est pas un pays c'est l'hiver
Mon jardin ce n'est pas un jardin c'est la plaine
Mon chemin ce n'est pas un chemin c'est la neige
Mon pays ce n'est pas un pays c'est l'hiver

Dans la blanche cérémonie
Où la neige au vent se marie
Dans ce pays de poudreire
Mon père a fait bâtir maison
Et je m'en vais être fidèle
A sa manière à son modèle
La chambre d'amis sera telle
Qu'on viendra des autres saisons
Pour se bâtir a côté d'elle

Mon pays ce n'est pas un pays c'est l'hiver
Mon jardin ce n'est pas un refrain c'est rafale
Mon chemin ce n'est pas un maison c'est froidure
Mon pays ce n'est pas un pays c'est l'hiver

De mon grand pays solitaire
Je crie avant que de me taire
A tous les hommes de la terre
Ma maison c'est votre maison
Entre mes quatre murs de glace
Je mets mon temps et mon espace
A préparer le feu la place
Pour les humains sont de ma race

Mon pays ce n'est pas un pays c'est l'hiver
Mon jardin ce n'est pas un jardin c'est la plaine
Mon chemin ce n'est pas un chemin c'est la neige
Mon pays ce n'est pas un pays c'est l'hiver

Mon pays ce n'est pas un pays c'est l'envers
D'un pays qui n'était ni pays ni patrie
Ma chanson ce n'est pas ma chanson c'est ma vie
C'est pour toi que je veux posséder mes hivers. . . .

"Mon Pays" was composed by poet and chansonnier Gilles
Vigneault. It was first published in his collection of poems titled
Avec les vieux mots (1965).

Vigneault wrote about his aim: "I'm trying to make a people—
whom I watch disappear with great anger—believe that its fate can
be reversed." He was successful. "Mon Pays" is so identified with
the Quebec sovereignty movement that it has became the province's
unofficial national anthem.

MY COUNTRY
English

My country it's not a country it's winter
My garden it's not a garden it's the plain
My road it's not a road it's the snow
My country it's not a country it's winter

In the whitish ceremony
Where the snow and wind are married
In this country of the snowdrifts
My father here raised up his house
And to this I will be faithful
To his manner to his fashion
The rooms for guests will be such that
Ones will come from other seasons
To raise up their homes beside his

My country it's not a country it's winter
My refrain it's not a refrain it's a rain
My house it's not a house it's a chill
My country it's not a country it's winter

From my great and lonely country
I'll cry out before I'm silent
To all the men upon the earth
My house it's also your house
Within my four walls of ice
My time I put down and my space
To light the fire to prepare the place
For all mankind is of my race

My country it's not a country it's winter
My garden it's not a garden it's the plain
My road it's not a road it's the snow
My country it's not a country it's winter

My country it's not a country it's its opposite
It's neither countryland nor fatherland
My song it's not my song it's my life
It's for you that I want to keep my winters. . . .

The translation of Gilles Vigneault's "Mon Pays" was prepared by Alexandre L. Amprimoz. It first appeared in John Robert Colombo's *The Poets of Canada* (1978).

GENS DU PAYS (CHANT D'ANNIVERSAIRE)
Gilles Vigneault

Gens du pays c'est votre tour
De vous laisser parle d'amour

Le temps que l'on prend pour dire: Je t'aime
C'est le seul qui reste au bout de nos jours
Les voeux que l'on fait, les fleurs que l'on sème
Chacun les récolte en soi-même
Aux beaux jardins du temps qui court

Gens du pays c'est votre tour
De vous laisser parle d'amour

Le temps de s'amier, le jour de le dire
Fond comme la neige aux doigts du printemps
Fêtons de nos joies, Fêtons de nos rires
Ces yeux où nos regards se mirent
C'est demain que j'avais vingt ans

Gens du pays c'est votre tour
De vous laisser parle d'amour

Le ruisseau des jours aujourd'hui s'arrête
Et forme un étang où chacun peut voir
Comme en un miroir l'amour qu'il reflète
Pour ces coeurs à qui je souhaite
Le temps de vivre leurs espoirs

Gens du pays c'est votre tour
De vous laisser parle d'amour

Popular poet and chansonnier Gilles Vigneault composed and per-formed the very moving "Gens du Pays" to express the euphoria that accompanied the victory of the Parti Québécois in the Quebec election of November 15, 1976. The party's victory marked a turn-ing point in federal-provincial relations and in the sovereignty movement in Quebec.

PEOPLE OF THE LAND
(ANNIVERSARY SONG)
English

People of the land your turn has come
To listen to the voice of love

The time we take to say: I love you
Is all that is left at the end of our days
The wishes we make, the flowers we plant
Each gathers them to himself
In the fair gardens of passing time

People of the land your turn has come
To listen to the voice of love

The time to love, the day to declare
Melts like snow in the fingers of spring
Let's feast on our joys, feast on our laughter
These days that reflect our gaze
Tomorrow, I was twenty

People of the land your turn has come
To listen to the voice of love

The stream of days stops today
And forms a pond where each can see
As in a mirror the reflection of love
To these hearts I wish
The time to live their hopes

People of the land your turn has come
To listen to the voice of love

This translation of Gilles Vigneault's "Gens du Pays" was prepared by poet and scholar Alexandre L. Amprimoz. It first appeared in *Colombo's Book of Canada* (1978).

Nature
AND
Weather

How One Winter Came
in the Lake District

William Wilfred Campbell

For weeks and weeks the autumn world stood still,
    Clothed in the shadow of a smoky haze;
The fields were dead, the wind had lost its will,
And all the lands were hushed by wood and hill,
    In those grey, withered days.

Behind a mist the blear sun rose and set,
    At night the moon would nestle in a cloud;
The fisherman, a ghost, did cast his net;
The lake its shores forgot to chafe and fret,
    And hushed its caverns loud.

Far in the smoky woods the birds were mute,
    Save that from blackened tree a jay would scream,
Or far in swamps the lizard's lonesome lute
Would pipe in thirst, or by some gnarled root
    The tree-toad trilled his dream.

From day to day still hushed the season's mood,
    The streams stayed in their runnels shrunk and dry;
Suns rose aghast by wave and shore and wood,
And all the world, with ominous silence, stood
    In weird expectancy.

When one strange night the sun like blood went down,
    Flooding the heavens in a ruddy hue;
Red grew the lake, the sere fields parched and brown,
Red grew the marshes where the creeks stole down,
    But never a wind-breath blew.

That night I felt the winter in my veins,
    A joyous tremor of the icy glow;
And woke to hear the North's wild vibrant strains,
While far and wide, by withered woods and plains,
    Fast fell the driving snow.

This frequently anthologized nature poem was composed early in his career by the poet William Wilfred Campbell (1861–1918). He had in mind the wind-swept region of Georgian Bay, near Wingham, Ont.

"How One Winter Came in the Lake District" offers a superb account of how Indian summer gives way to the cold of winter. It first appeared in Campbell's *Lake Lyrics and Other Poems* (1889).

⌒

Heat

Archibald Lampman

From plains that reel to southward, dim,
    The road runs by me white and bare;
Up the steep hill it seems to swim
    Beyond, and melt into the glare.
Upward half-way, or it may be
    Nearer the summit, slowly steals
A hay-cart, moving dustily
    With idly clacking wheels.

By his cart's side the wagoner
   Is slouching slowly at his ease,
Half-hidden in the windless blur
   Of white dust puffing to his knees.
This wagon on the height above,
   From sky to sky on either hand,
Is the sole thing that seems to move
   In all the heat-held land.

Beyond me in the fields the sun
   Soaks in the grass and hath his will;
I count the marguerites one by one;
   Even the buttercups are still.
On the brook yonder not a breath
   Disturbs the spider or the midge.
The water-bugs draw close beneath
   The cool gloom of the bridge.

Where the far elm-tree shadows flood
   Dark patches in the burning grass,
The cows, each with her peaceful cud,
   Lie waiting for the heat to pass.
From somewhere on the slope near by
   Into the pale depth of the noon
A wandering thrush slides leisurely
   His thin revolving tune.

In intervals of dreams, I hear
  The cricket from the droughty ground;
The grasshoppers spin into mine ear
  A small innumerable sound.
I lift mine eyes sometimes to gaze;
  The burning sky-line blinds my sight;
The woods far off are blue with haze;
  The hills are drenched in light.

And yet to me not this or that
  Is always sharp or always sweet:
In the sloped shadow of my hat
  I lean at rest and drain the heat;
Nay more, I think some blessèd power
  Hath brought me wandering idly here:
In the full furnace of this hour
  My thoughts grow keen and clear.

"Heat" has always been popular with anthologists of Canadian poetry and teachers of literature. The poem was composed by Archibald Lampman (1861–1899), who describes the sight and sense of the countryside where man and nature meet. It dramatizes in close to hallucinatory language an inner state of mind.

The poem first appeared in *Among the Millet and Other Poems* (1888).

INDIAN SUMMER
William Wilfred Campbell

Along the line of smoky hills
   The crimson forest stands,
And all the day the blue-jay calls
   Throughout the autumn lands.

Now by the brook the maple leans
   With all his glory spread,
And all the sumachs on the hills
   Have turned their green to red.

Now by great marshes wrapt in mist,
   Or past some river's mouth,
Throughout the long, still autumn day
   Wild birds are flying south.

Generations of high-school students were assigned "Indian Summer" as "memory work." For this reason it is one of the most remembered if not treasured of Canadian poems.

The poem celebrates the few weeks that extend from late fall to early winter, the interseasonal period known as Indian Summer, when nature is particularly colourful and rich and the atmosphere is decidedly "smoky."

The poem was written in 1881–83 by William Wilfred Campbell (1858–1918) when he was still a student at the University of Toronto. It is reprinted from *Songs of the Great Dominion* (1889), edited by William Douw Lighthall.

The Song of the Ski

Wilson MacDonald

Norse am I when the first snow falls;
Norse am I till the ice departs.
The fare for which my spirit calls
Is blood from a hundred viking-hearts.

The curved wind wraps me like a cloak;
The pines blow out their ghostly smoke.
I'm high on the hill and ready to go—
A wingless bird in a world of snow:
Yet I'll ride the air
With a dauntless dare
That only a child of the north can know.

The bravest ski has a cautious heart
And moves like a tortoise at the start,
But when it tastes the tang of the air
It leaps away like a frightened hare.
The day is gloomy, the curtains half-drawn,
And light is stunted as at the dawn;
But my foot is sure and my arm is brawn.

I poise on the hill and I wave adieu
(My curving skis are firm and true).
The slim wood quickens, the air takes fire
And sings to me like a gypsy's lyre.
Swifter and swifter grows my flight:
The dark pines ease the unending white.
The lean, cold birches, as I go by,
Are like blurred etchings against the sky.

One am I for a moment's joy
With the falling star and the plunging bird.
The world is swift as an Arab boy;
The world is sweet as a woman's word.
Never came such a pure delight
To a bacchanal or a sybarite:
Swifter and swifter grows my flight,
And glad am I, as I near the leap,
That the snow is fresh and the banks are deep.

Swifter and swifter on I fare,
And soon I'll gloat with the birds on air.
The speed is blinding; I'm over the ridge,
Spanning space on a phantom bridge,
The drifts await me; I float, I fall:
The world leaps like a lunging carp.
I land erect and the tired winds drawl
A lazy rune on a broken harp.

A poem may be unforgettable because it offers an unexpected
image, an arresting phrase, or lines that are deeply meaningful.

"The Song of the Ski" is a memorable poem for its title, its opening lines, and its high spirits. In fact, it is the most remembered and appreciated of the many verses composed by Wilson MacDonald (1880–1967). It first appeared in his collection *Out of the Wilderness* (1926).

MacDonald was a versifier of indefatigable versatility and vitality. He was also a tireless reciter of his own work in town halls and school auditoriums across the country. He regarded himself as a neglected genius. Truth to tell, he had the misfortune in his later years to encounter critics and anthologists who were schooled in the principles of Modernism and Postmodernism. They ridiculed his straightforward ideas, his sentimental expressions, and his ringing rhymes. Yet many of his verses reverberate in memory. Some day someone should compile a *Selected Poems of Wilson MacDonald*. It would be a book with genuine appeal.

Song to the Four Seasons

Paul Hiebert

Spring is here, the breezes blowing,
Four inches of top-soil going, going;
Farm ducks rolling across the prairie;
Spring is here—how nice and airy!

Summer has come, the hoppers are back,
The sun shines bright, the fields shine black,
Cloudlets gather, it looks like rain—
Ah, the patter of hail on the window-pane!

Bounteous harvest, we'll sell at cost—
Tomorrow we'll have an early frost:
Glorious autumn, red with rust;
We'll live on the general store on trust.

A long, quiet winter with plenty of snow,
And plenty of barley; it's eighty below,
Barley in the heater, salt pork in the pantry—
How nice that you never feel cold in this country.

This lyric verse is meant to be recited by Sarah Binks, "the Sweet Songstress of Saskatchewan."

The loveable, insufferable Sarah is the star of the book *Sarah Binks* (1947). This embodiment of the prairie poetess—rather like Edna Jaques—is the creation of academic and poetaster Paul Hiebert (1892–1987). There have been innumerable stage, radio, and television adaptations of this work of tongue-in-cheek humour.

"Song to the Four Seasons" was described by poet and critic A. J. M. Smith as "this delightfully atrocious verse."

SNOWBIRD

Gene MacLellan

Beneath this snowy mantle, cold and clean,
The unborn grass lies waiting for its coat to turn to green.
The snowbird sings the song he always sings
And speaks to me of flowers that will bloom again in spring.

When I was young, my heart was young then, too;
Anything that it would tell me, that's the thing that I would do.
But now I feel such emptiness within,
For the thing I want the most in life is the thing that I can't win.

Spread your tiny wings and fly away,
And take the snow back with you where it came from on that
    day.
The one I love forever is untrue,
And if I could, you know that I would fly away with you.

The breeze along the river seems to say
That he'll only break my heart again should I decide to stay.
So, snowbird, take me with you when you go
To that land of gentle breezes where the peaceful waters flow.

Yeah, if I could, you know that I would fly away with you.

Guitarist Gene MacLellan composed the words and music of "Snowbird" in twenty-five minutes after he observed a flock of snow buntings playing on a beach in Prince Edward Island in 1967.

Singer Anne Murray recorded the work and made it her own. In fact, it became her signature song. She made it an international hit, and the Nashville Songwriters Association chose MacLellan as the best composer of the year, 1970.

MacLellan was the composer of numerous hit songs, including the phenomenally successful inspiration number called "Put Your Hand in the Hand."

The text of "Snowbird" is reprinted from Edith Fowke's *Canadian Vibrations Canadiennes* (1972).

FORTY BELOW

Christopher Dafoe

From this valley we hope to be going,
When at last we can travel alone,
For we're sick of the snow and the dust storms,
In Toronto we'll find a new home.

For it's forty below in the winter,
And it's twenty below in the fall.
It just rises to zero in summer,
And we don't have a springtime at all.

Oh my Grandpa came West in the eighties,
To the prairies where grain grew like grass,
But the Wheat Board and freight rates got Grandpa,
And Grandpa went East, second class.

For it's forty below in the winter,
And it's twenty below in the fall.
It just rises to zero in summer,
And we don't have a springtime at all.

It was raining and snowing this morning,
At the corner of Portage and Main,
Now it's noon and the dust storm is blowing,
And my basement is flooded again.

For it's forty below in the winter,
And it's twenty below in the fall.
It just rises to zero in summer,
And we don't have a springtime at all.

Then come pay for my fare if you love me,
And I'll hasten to bid you adieu,
So goodbye to the Red River Valley,
And the farmers all shivering and blue.

For it's forty below in the winter,
And it's twenty below in the fall.
It just rises to zero in summer,
And we don't have a springtime at all.

"Forty Below" is an amusing (though knowing) parody of the well-loved folk song "Red River Valley" (which is also included in the present treasury).

Believed to be the work of "Anon.," it turned out to be the handiwork of the newspaperman Christopher Dafoe, grandson of newspaper publisher John W. Dafoe. The poem was first published in the younger Dafoe's column, "Coffee Break by Wink," in *The Winnipeg Free Press*, May 30, 1959. Thereafter the lyrics took on a life of their own.

As Dafoe later wrote in the article "Part of the Oral Tradition," *The Beaver*, February–March 1993, "It is a sober experience to become a part—even a small part—of the national oral tradition. To become one with 'Anon.,' that prolific writer of songs and poems and doggerel, brings on me a feeling of great solemnity. It happened to me—as it happens to everyone—quite by accident." He added, "I love Manitoba, but there are moments when I would gladly give it back to the buffalo."

CANADIAN LOVE

Marie-Lynn Hammond

Oh I met him at an ice rink in Flin Flon
'twas a mild night, just 20 below
as we skated in circles he reached for my hand
but what it felt like I'm not sure I know
for I had on two pairs of mittens
and he wore a thick sheepskin glove
but if the trembling I felt wasn't due to the cold
then maybe perhaps it was love

Oh Canadian love, Canadian love
it's either 40 below or it's 90 above
and though it's hard to be yearning
when you're freezing or burning
like the dollar we keep falling—in Canadian love

So we ended up going to his place
where I peeled off my mitts at the door (both pairs)
and after 10 minutes of struggle my boots and my socks
lay in a pool on the floor
then he tenderly took my wool tuque off
and he rolled down my leg warmers too
by now it was 10 to 11 and we
still had a lot left to do

Oh Canadian love, Canadian love
it's either 40 below or it's 90 above
and though it's hard to be yearning
when you're freezing or burning
like the dollar we keep falling—in Canadian love

With a sigh he unknotted my muffler
then he stopped for a much needed rest
I could tell he was getting discouraged—with reason!
for he was still fully dressed
but when he finally unzippered my parka
I caught sight of the clock and cried, "Oh!
It's quarter to 12 and I promised my mother
I'd be home an hour ago!"

Well, he looked like a man who'd been broken
but it wasn't emotional pain
it was just that he couldn't stand having to watch me
put all that stuff back on again

Oh Canadian love, Canadian love
it's either 40 below or it's 90 above
and though it's hard to be yearning
when you're freezing or burning
like the dollar we keep falling—in Canadian love

Well, we met the next summer in Wawa,
an only slightly more hospitable clime;
and if it hadn't been for the black flies and the heat wave
we might just have made it that time

Oh Canadian love, Canadian love
it's either 40 below or it's 90 above
and though it's hard to be yearning
when you're freezing or burning
like the dollar we keep falling—in Canadian love

"A humorous look at love in a cold climate, written for a folk festival years ago" is how composer and performer Marie-Lynne Hammond describes the song "Canadian Love," which she composed in 1985.

She received an invitation to lead a workshop at a folk festival. "In those days, guys always seemed to get the sexy workshops like 'Rebel Songs that Changed the World' and 'Really Fast Train Songs with Lots of Instrumental Breaks So the Guys Can All Try to Out-Solo One Another,' while the gals got stuck with 'Lugubrious Lullabies' or 'Interminable Ballads about Masochistic Women who Die on the Scottish Moors of Broken Hearts.'

"When the artistic director asked me what workshops I'd like to be in, I said, 'Anything but "Love Songs."' On arriving at the festival, I found I was to host a workshop called 'Canadian Love.' In mock revenge I dashed off this ditty."

The unnamed artistic director was wiser than he knew, and Marie-Lynn Hammond rose to the occasion, penning and frequently performing her classic "Canadian Love." She sings "Canadian Love" on her CD *Impromptu* (Vignettes Media).

Longing
for
Love

WHEN YOU AND I WERE YOUNG, MAGGIE

George W. Johnson

I wander'd today to the hill, Maggie,
To watch the scene below,
The creek and the creaking old mill, Maggie,
As we used to, long ago.

The green grove is gone from the hill, Maggie,
Where first the daisies sprung,
The creaking old mill is still, Maggie,
Since you and I were young.

And now we are aged and gray, Maggie,
And the trials of life nearly done;
Let us sing of the days that are gone, Maggie,
When you and I were young.

A city so silent and lone, Maggie,
Where the young and the gay and the best
In polished white mansions of stone, Maggie,
Have each found a place of rest.

Is built where the birds used to play, Maggie,
And join in the songs that were sung
For we sang as gay as they, Maggie,
When you and I were young.

And now we are aged and grey, Maggie,
The trials of life are nearly done.
Let us sing of the days that are gone, Maggie,
When you and I were young.

This sentimental love ballad, once widely sung, was for decades a favourite of barbershop quartets. Its note of nostalgia may be nicely contrasted with the upbeat irony of the Beatles's pop song "When I'm Sixty-Four."

The ballad began life as a poem composed by George Washington Johnson (1839–1917). He included it in his collection of poems, *Maple Leaves* (1864). Here is the story behind the poem.

Born in Wentworth County, Ont., Johnson taught school in the district and fell in love with one of his students, Maggie Clark. The couple were married the year after she graduated, and Johnson's only book was published. The "old mill" stood on the bank of Twenty Mile Creek.

Sad to relate, the young bride died two years later, the same year that J. A. Butterfield, an English composer who was then living in Chicago, set the poem to its mournful music.

The text of "When You and I Were Young, Maggie" is reprinted from an undated songsheet. A slightly different version was included by Ralph L. Woods in *A Treasury of the Familiar* (1942).

IN THE SHADE OF THE OLD APPLE TREE
Harry H. Williams

The oriole with joy was sweetly singing,
The little brook was babbling its tune,
The village bells at noon were gaily ringing,
The world seemed brighter than a harvest moon;
For there within my arms I gently pressed you,
And blushing red, you slowly turned away;
I can't forget the way I once caressed you;
I only pray we'll meet another day.

In the shade of the old apple tree,
Where the love in your eyes I could see,
When the voice that I heard,
Like the song of the bird,
Seemed to whisper sweet music to me;
I could hear the dull buzz of the bee,
In the blossoms as you said to me,
With a heart that is true,
I'll be waiting for you,
In the shade of the old apple tree.

I've really come a long way from the city,
And though my heart is breaking, I'll be brave.
I've brought this bunch of flowers, I think they're pretty,
To place upon a fresh moulded grave;
If you will show me, father, where she's lying,
Or, if it's far, just point it out to me.
Said he, "She told us all when she was dying,
To bury her beneath the apple tree."

Harry H. Williams (1874–1922) wrote the lyrics of "In the Shade of the Old Apple Tree" in 1905. The sentiments of the popular love ballad were inspired, it was said, by a tree that once grew on Glen Edith Drive, located south of Casa Loma, in Toronto.

The melody was the inspiration of the American composer Egbert Van Alstyne, who had teamed up with Williams in 1900 to make good on Tin Pan Alley. This song is their best-known collaboration. (Williams is also remembered as the author of the words of "It's a Long Way to Tipperary." With the music of the Britisher Jack Judge, added in 1908, this song was adopted by the British Army as a marching song in 1914. Tipperary is a lovely town in Ireland.)

The words of "In the Shade of the Old Apple Tree" are reproduced from *A Third Treasury of the Familiar* (1970) edited by Ralph L. Woods.

THE POOR LITTLE GIRLS OF ONTARIO
Traditional

I'll sing you a song of that plaguey pest,
It goes by the name of the Great North-West.
I cannot have a beau at all,
They all skip out there in the fall.

One by one they all clear out,
Thinking to better themselves, no doubt,
Caring little how far they go
From the poor little girls of Ontario.

First I got mashed on Charlie Brown,
The nicest fellow in all the town.
He tipped his hat and sailed away,
And now he's settled in Manitobay.

One by one they all clear out,
Thinking to better themselves, no doubt,
Caring little how far they go
From the poor little girls of Ontario.

Then Henry Mayner with his white cravat,
His high stiff collar and his new plug hat,
He said if he stayed he'd have to beg,
And now he's settled in Winnipeg.

One by one they all clear out,
Thinking to better themselves, no doubt,
Caring little how far they go
From the poor little girls of Ontario.

Then my long-legged druggist with his specs on his nose,
I really thought he would propose,
But he's sold his bottle-shop and now he's gone
Clear out to little Saskatchewan.

One by one they all clear out,
Thinking to better themselves, no doubt,
Caring little how far they go
From the poor little girls of Ontario.

I'll pack my clothes in a carpet sack,
I'll go out there and I'll never come back,
I'll find me a husband and a good one, too,
If I have to go through to Cariboo.

One by one we'll all clear out,
Thinking to better ourselves, no doubt,
Caring little how far we go
From the old, old folks of Ontario.

"The Poor Little Girls of Ontario" is a traditional song that dates back to the 1880s, when Ontarians began to move West. The earliest versions of the complaint refer to "the boys" leaving Thunder Bay for Keewatin in northwestern Ontario to the distress of "the poor little girls."

The version reproduced here, which dates from the turn of the century, was first recorded by Edith Fowke from Mrs. Harley Minifie of Peterborough in 1957. Marked to be performed "plaintively," it has been sung to tunes as unalike as "The Little Brown Jug" and "Yankee Doodle."

The text is taken from *Canada's Story in Song* (1960) edited by Edith Fowke and Alan Mills.

O ROSE-MARIE

Otto Harbach and Oscar Hammerstein II

Oh, sweet Rose-Marie,
It's easy to see
Why all who learn to know you love you;
You're gentle and kind,
Divinely designed,
As graceful as the pines above you.
There's an angel's breath beneath your sigh,
There's a little devil in your eye,
Oh, Rose-Marie. I love you!
I'm always dreaming of you.
No matter what I do,
I can't forget you.
Sometimes I wish that I had never met you!
And yet if I should lose you,
'Twould mean my very life to me;
Of all the queens that ever lived I'd choose you
To rule me, my Rose-Marie.

These are the inane but appealing lyrics of the romantic love song
"O Rose-Marie." It serves as the centrepiece of the Broadway
operetta *Rose-Marie* (1924), with words by Otto Harbach and
Oscar Hammerstein II and music by Rudolf Friml. It tells about the
life and love of a Mountie.

Everybody knows about this operetta, but hardly anybody has
ever seen it staged. Instead people have seen one of the three film
versions. The best of the lot is the 1936 classic Hollywood film
Rose Marie, in which the songs are feelingly sung by Jeanette

MacDonald and Nelson Eddy. "O Rose-Marie" and other prairie-related songs (like "Totem Tomtom") remain popular concert favourites, familiar from the soundtrack.

For the record, there was an uninspired 1954 remake, starring Anne Blyth and Howard Keele, and even a silent-film version (with Joan Crawford) in 1928.

FROM THE HAZEL BOUGH
Earle Birney

I met a lady
   on a lazy street
hazel eyes
   and little plush feet

her legs swam by
   like lovely trout
eyes were trees
   where boys leant out

hands in the dark and
   a river side
round breasts rising
   with the fingers' tide

she was plump as a finch
   and live as a salmon
gay as silk and
   proud as a Brahmin

we winked when we met
   and laughed when we parted
never took time
   to be brokenhearted

but no man sees
   where the trout lie now
or what leans out
   from the hazel bough

"From the Hazel Bough" is an enchanting lyric about love that was written by Earle Birney in 1945–47, when he taught at the University of Toronto and lived on Hazelton Avenue in the Yorkville area of the city.

The text is taken from *The Poems of Earle Birney* (1969).

SONG FOR NAOMI

Irving Layton

Who is that in the tall grasses singing
By herself, near the water?
I can not see her
But can it be her,
Than whom the grasses so tall
Are taller,
My daughter,
My lovely daughter?

Who is that in the tall grasses running
Beside her, near the water?
She can not see there
Time that pursued her
In the deep grasses so fast
And faster
And caught her,
My foolish daughter.

What is the wind in the fair grass saying
Like a verse, near the water?
Saviours that over
All things have power
Make Time himself grow kind
And kinder
That sought her,
My little daughter.

Who is that at the close of the summer
Near the deep lake? Who wrought her
Comely and slender?
Time but attends and befriends her
Than whom the grasses though tall
Are not taller,
My daughter,
My gentle daughter.

Irving Layton wrote "Song for Naomi" to express his great love for
his growing daughter. He wrote it with grace and tenderness and
feeling for the cycles of the natural and human worlds.

The poem appeared in *A Red Carpet for the Sun* (1959).

FIRST PERSON DEMONSTRATIVE
Phyllis Gotlieb

I'd rather
heave half a brick than say
I love you, though I do
I'd rather
crawl in a hole than call you
darling, though you are
I'd rather
wrench off an arm than hug you though
it's what I long to do
I'd rather
gather a posy of poison ivy than
ask if you love me

so if my
hair doesn't stand on end it's because
I never tease it
and if my
heart isn't in my mouth it's because
it knows its place
and if I
don't take a bite of your ear it's because
gristle gripes my guts
and if you
miss the message better get new
glasses and read it twice

This is a gritty, gutsy love poem, so unlike "O Rose-Marie" or "When You and I Were Young, Maggie." Certainly less well known than it ought to be!

"First Person Demonstrative" was written by the poet and science-fiction writer Phyllis Gotlieb. It appeared in her collection *Ordinary Moving* (1969).

~

AS THE MIST LEAVES NO SCAR
Leonard Cohen

As the mist leaves no scar
On the dark green hill,
So my body leaves no scar
On you, nor ever will.

When wind and hawk encounter,
What remains to keep?
So you and I encounter,
Then turn, then fall to sleep.

As many nights endure
Without a moon or star,
So will we endure
When one is gone and far.

"As the Mist Leaves No Scar" is a melancholy little poem written by Leonard Cohen that is almost a song. It has been fondly recalled by innumerable readers.

It is reprinted from Cohen's *Selected Poems, 1956–1968* (1968).

~

SUZANNE TAKES YOU DOWN
Leonard Cohen

Suzanne takes you down
to her place near the river,
you can hear the boats go by
you can stay the night beside her.
And you know that she's half crazy
but that's why you want to be there
and she feeds you tea and oranges
that come all the way from China.
Just when you mean to tell her
that you have no gifts to give her,
she gets you on her wave-length
and she lets the river answer
that you've always been her lover.
   And you want to travel with her,
   you want to travel blind
   and you know that she can trust you
   because you've touched her perfect body
   with your mind.

Jesus was a sailor
when he walked upon the water
and he spent a long time watching
from a lonely wooden tower
and when he knew for certain
only drowning men could see him
he said All men will be sailors then
until the sea shall free them,
but he himself was broken
long before the sky would open,
forsaken, almost human,
he sank beneath your wisdom like a stone.
    And you want to travel with him,
    you want to travel blind
    and you think maybe you'll trust him
    because he touched your perfect body
    with his mind.

Suzanne takes your hand
and she leads you to the river,
she is wearing rags and feathers
from Salvation Army counters.
The sun pours down like honey
on our lady of the harbour
as she shows you where to look
among the garbage and the flowers,
there are heroes in the seaweed
there are children in the morning,
they are leaning out for love
they will lean that way forever
while Suzanne she holds the mirror.
 And you want to travel with her
 and you want to travel blind
 and you're sure that she can find you
 because she's touched her perfect body
 with her mind.

"Suzanne" is one of the most moving, most popular, and most familiar songs of Canadian origin of all time. To hear composer-singer Leonard Cohen perform it is to be mesmerized by the poetic power of the words and the haunting, never-to-be forgotten melody. The Montreal poet composed the lyrics in 1966 and performed the song to considerable acclaim the following summer at the Newport and Mariposa folk festivals.

It is the text of the poem that is reproduced here. "Suzanne Takes You Down" is reprinted from *Selected Poems 1956–1968* (1968). The lyrics differ slightly from the text of the poem. "Suzanne" is the title of the lyrical version which Cohen himself sings on his album *Songs of Leonard Cohen* (1980).

Leonard Cohen's Never Gonna Bring My Groceries In

Nancy White

I was listening to music as I swept the kitchen floor,
I was needing a shampoo and I was pushing forty-four.
And I had one of those flashes that hit you now and then
About experience *manqué* and certain sadly missing men,
And I realized in horror as I stroked my double chin,
Leonard Cohen's never gonna bring my groceries in!

I've a husband and a baby, there's another on the way,
And, like Leonard, I am aching in the place I used to play,
But really, I'm enjoying all this domesticity,
Hey, I never have to deal with Warren Beatty's vanity,
But there's one thing I regret, and my regret is genuine,
Leonard Cohen's never gonna bring my groceries in.

Oh, Leonard and me, together we'd be great,
Strumming our guitars and singing songs while it got late!
(Well, not *too* late, these days I kind of fold about eleven,
But for a little while it would be heaven! heaven, heaven.)
Oh, Leonard and me, we'd be so decadent,
We'd look at all those bottles, wonder where the wine all went.
(Well, frankly, I can't drink it anymore, my head can't take it,
But I know me and Leonard, we could make it. Make it.)

I love each line he's written, except for maybe one:
"Nancy wore green stockings and she slept with everyone."
I thought: "What if somebody thinks he's singing about me?"
'Cause after all, I lived in Montreal in 1963,
And perhaps I was his type when I was young and sweet and
    thin,
But now Leonard's never gonna bring my groceries in.

Oh, Leonard and me, we're soul mates, there's no doubt.
I feel it in my heart, we'd have so much to talk about.
We'd hole up in the Tower of Song with coffee strong and bitter.
That is, of course, if I could get a sitter,
A sitter, a sitter.
Hey, I'm just some singer looking for a sitter.

[Spoken babble—Nancy White's words are heard over a Cohen-
    type "la, la, la, la" chorus.]

*Okay, wait! Leonard! Hey maybe Leonard could babysit.
Yeah, oh he'd be wonderful, the girls would love him. He
can read stories. A poet can always use an extra five dol-
lars an hour. He would be perfect. How can I get his num-
ber? Hmm, Marie-Lynn Hammond she'll have his number.
I know she will. I'm going to call her right now. This is
inspiring. I am so happy! So Leonard Cohen can babysit
and Doug and I can go to the mall and pick out the new
towels for the bathroom. [pause] That's what I really want
to do. Of course, [pause and sexy, sotto voce] maybe I can
be the one to drive the babysitter home tonight.*

Leonard Cohen is so familiar a figure and his "Suzanne" is so memorable a song that before long the icon and the song inspired more than one folksinger to compose and perform a "tribute" song.

The most amusing of these tributes is "Leonard Cohen's Never Gonna Bring My Groceries In." I have reproduced it here, in its entirety, as written and performed by Nancy White, Queen of the Topical Song, on her album *Momnipotent: Songs for Weary Parents* (1990).

Included in the transcript are both the sung and spoken sections. (The reference in the spoken section is to fellow-singer Marie-Lynn Hammond. The reference in the song section is to the song "Seems So Long Ago, Nancy" on Leonard Cohen's CD *Songs from a Room*.)

Here is what the liner notes on Nancy White's CD have to say about this effective tribute song:

> Nancy wrote this song while eleven *[sic]* months pregnant with daughter number two. They say that if you have one child, you can have some kind of other life, but that with two, you're a mommy and that's *it*! Nancy was thinking about this and feeling that maybe this was goodbye to romance and adventure for the *rest of her life*!
>
> She put on Leonard Cohen's glorious new album I'm Your Man [Feb. 1988] to cheer herself up. It didn't work. . . .

Devotion
and
Remembrance

HURON CHRISTMAS CAROL

Jean de Brébeuf

'Twas in the moon of winter time when all the birds had fled,
That Mighty Gitchi Manitou sent angel choirs instead.
Before their light the stars grew dim,
And wandering hunters heard the hymn:
    "Jesus, your King, is born;
    Jesus is born; in excelsis gloria!"

Within a lodge of broken bark the tender Babe was found.
A ragged robe of rabbit skin enwrapped His beauty 'round.
And as the hunter braves drew nigh,
The angel song rang loud and high:
    "Jesus, your King, is born;
    Jesus is born; in excelsis gloria!"

The earliest moon of winter time is not so round and fair
As was the ring of glory on the helpless Infant there.
While Chiefs from far before Him knelt,
With gifts of fox and beaver pelt.
    "Jesus, your King, is born;
    Jesus is born; in excelsis gloria!"

O children of the forest free, O sons of Manitou.
The Holy Child of earth and heav'n is born today for you.
Come kneel before the radiant Boy,
Who brings you beauty, peace and joy.
    "Jesus, your King, is born;
    Jesus is born; in excelsis gloria!"

"Huron Christmas Carol" is the English version of a hymn that was composed by Jean de Brébeuf (1593–1649). He was the Jesuit missionary in charge of the palisaded mission post of Sainte-Marie-Among-the-Hurons, which has been reconstructed on the original site near present-day Midland, Ont.

Brébeuf was an accomplished linguist, and about 1641, eight years before his death as a martyr, he composed the hymn in the Huron language for his Christian converts to sing at Christmas. It was translated into French about a century and a half later. In 1927, the French translation was freely adapted into English by the versifier J.E. Middleton (1872–1960) as "Huron Christmas Carol." It is also known as "Jesous Ahatonhia" (which in Huron means "Jesus, he is born").

"This is perhaps the most truly Canadian of our songs," explained folklorist Edith Fowke, "for it is the only one known to have been sung in Indian, French, and English." Middleton's English version may be lumbering but it is also ingratiating. The first verse is widely recognized.

WHAT A FRIEND WE HAVE IN JESUS
Joseph Medlicott Scriven

What a friend we have in Jesus,
   All our sins and griefs to bear;
What a privilege to carry
   Everything to God in prayer.
Oh, what peace we often forfeit,
   Oh, what needless pain we bear—
All because we do not carry
   Everything to God in prayer.

Have we trials and temptations?
  Is there trouble anywhere?
We should never be discouraged,
  Take it to the Lord in prayer.
Can we find a Friend so faithful,
  Who will all our sorrows share?
Jesus knows our every weakness,
  Take it to the Lord in prayer.

Are we weak and heavy laden,
  Cumbered with a load of care?
Precious Saviour, still our refuge,—
  Take it to the Lord in prayer.
Do thy friends despise, foresake thee?
  Take it to the Lord in prayer:
In his arms he'll take and shield thee,
  Thou wilt find a solace there.

Here are the lyrics of a hymn that has been sung throughout the English-speaking world for more than a century and a half.

The words were written about 1857 by Joseph Medlicott Scriven (1819–1886), a resident of the Port Hope area of Ontario. The poem has an alternate title: "Pray without Ceasing." The verses were set to music by Charles C. Converse, a lawyer and musician who lived in Albany, N.Y. The hymn soon became an international evangelical favourite.

The text is taken from *What a Friend We Have in Jesus and Other Hymns* (1895) written by the Rev. Jas. Cleland.

A LITTLE WHILE
Attributed to Crowfoot

A little while and I will be gone from among you, whither
I cannot tell. From nowhere we came, into nowhere
we go. What is life? It is a flash of a firefly in the
night. It is a breath of a buffalo in the winter time. It
is as the little shadow that runs across the grass and
loses itself in the sunset.

These flowing words and feelings have been attributed to Crowfoot,
the Blackfoot chief, the last of the great chiefs, who died at Blackfoot
Crossing, April 25, 1890. His remains lie buried in a plot overlooking
the Bow River at the town of Gleichen, southeast of Calgary.

The lines are the essence of popular poetry, and the sentiments
were attributed to Crowfoot by the historian John Peter Turner in
The North-West Mounted Police, 1873–1893 (1950). Because
Turner cited no source, the attribution of the lines was questioned.
Fellow historian Hugh Dempsey made no reference to the lines in
his detailed biography of the chief.

A prior source was established by historian Robert S. Carslie.
Unfortunately, the source he found was a fictional one: *King
Solomon's Mines* (1885), a once-popular, frequently filmed adven-
ture novel written by the English novelist Sir H. Rider Haggard.
According to Carslie, writing in "Crowfoot's Dying Speech,"
Alberta History (Summer 1990), the African chieftain Umbopa in
the novel speaks these words:

What is life? . . . It is the glow-worm that shines in the
night-time and is black in the morning; it is the white
breath of the oxen in winter, it is the little shadow that
runs across the grass and loses itself in sunset.

Did Turner Canadianize the African references and ascribe the fictitious Umbopa's words to the real-life Crowfoot? It seems he did. The reader would like to believe that the words are appropriate (though most historians and literary critics would be critical of them because they *are* so poetic).

H. Rider Haggard was one of the most popular novelists of his day, and he had readers in the Canadian West. Ayesha Peak, west of Alberta's Bow Lake, bears the name of the immortal Queen Ayesha of Haggard's ever-popular, lost-race novel *She* (1887).

THE LARGEST LIFE

Archibald Lampman

There is a beauty at the goal of life,
A beauty growing since the world began,
Through every age and race, through lapse and strife
Till the great human soul complete her span.
Beneath the waves of storm that lash and burn,
The currents of blind passion that appall,
To listen and keep watch till we discern
The tide of sovereign truth that guides it all;
So to address our spirits to the height,
And so attune them to the valiant whole,
That the great light be clearer for our light,
And the great soul the stronger for our soul:
To have done this is to have lived, though fame
Remember us with no familiar name.

An instance of a type of poem rarely found in Canadian literature, "The Largest Life" is a lyrical meditation on spiritual values and the fate of mankind.

It is the third and last sonnet in the series titled "The Largest Life." It is reprinted from *The Poems of Archibald Lampman* (1900) edited by Duncan Campbell Scott.

In the Wide Awe
and Wisdom of the Night

Charles G.D. Roberts

In the wide awe and wisdom of the night
I saw the round world rolling on its way,
Beyond significance of depth or height,
Beyond the interchange of dark and day.
I marked the march to which is set no pause,
And that stupendous orbit, round whose rim
The great sphere sweeps, obedient unto laws
That utter the eternal thought of Him.

I compassed time, outstripped the starry speed,
And in my still soul apprehended space,
Till, weighing laws which these but blindly heed,
At last I came before Him face to face—
And knew the Universe of no such span
As the august infinitude of Man.

Like the previous poems, "In the Wide Awe and Wisdom of the Night" is a meditation on spiritual values with mystical overtones or undercurrents.

It was written by Charles G.D. Roberts and published in *Songs of the Common Day* (1893).

—

THE TWENTY-FOURTH OF MAY
Traditional

The twenty-fourth of May
  Is the Queen's Birthday;
If you don't give us a holiday,
  We'll all run away.

Chances are that readers of this book will already have committed to memory this traditional ball-bouncing rhyme.

The idea of setting aside one day each year to celebrate the British Empire was introduced into Ontario's schools in 1898 and before long it became a national holiday. It was immediately popular with schoolchildren because it gave them a holiday from school on the Monday closest to "the twenty-fourth of May," the day of Queen Victoria's birth.

The rhyme appears in this form in Sara Jeannette Duncan's novel *The Imperialist* (1904), which describes the social life of the day in Brantford, Ont. Both the rhyme and the holiday have outlived the British Empire.

—

PÈRE LALEMANT

Marjorie Pickthall

I lift the Lord on high,
Under the murmuring hemlock boughs, and see
The small birds of the forest lingering by
And making melody.
These are mine acolytes and these my choir,
And this mine altar in the cool green shade,
Where the wild soft-eyed does draw nigh
Wondering, as in the byre
Of Bethlehem the oxen heard Thy cry
And saw Thee, unafraid.

My boatmen sit apart,
Wolf-eyed, wolf-sinewed, stiller than the trees.
Help me, O Lord, for very slow of heart
And hard of faith are these.
Cruel are they, yet Thy children. Foul are they,
Yet wert Thou born to save them utterly.
Then make me as I pray
Just to their hates, kind to their sorrows, wise
After their speech, and strong before their free
Indomitable eyes.

Do the French lilies reign
Over Mont Royal and Stadacona still?
Up the St. Lawrence comes the spring again,
Crowning each southward hill
And blossoming pool with beauty, while I roam
Far from the perilous folds that are my home,
There where we built St. Igace for our needs,
Shaped the rough roof tree, turned the first sweet sod,
St. Ignace and St. Louis, little beads
On the rosary of God.

Pines shall Thy pillars be,
Fairer than those Sidonian cedars brought
By Hiram out of Tyre, and each birch-tree
Shines like a holy thought.
But come no worshippers; shall I confess,
St. Francis-like, the birds of the wilderness?
O, with Thy love my lonely head uphold.
A wandering shepherd I, who hath no sheep;
A wandering soul, who hath no scrip, nor gold,
Nor anywhere to sleep.

My hour of rest is done;
On the smooth ripple lifts the long canoe;
The hemlocks murmur sadly as the sun
Slants his dim arrows through.
Whither I go I know not, nor the way,
Dark with strange passions, vexed with heathen charms,
Holding I know not what of life or death;
Only be Thou beside me day by day,
Thy rod my guide and comfort, underneath
Thy everlasting arms.

"Père Lalemant" lends a dramatic voice to the perceptions and passions of Gabriel Lalemant, the Jesuit missionary martyred alongside Jean de Brébeuf by the Iroquois at Huronia on March 16, 1649.

It was written with great lyrical skill, unobtrusive rhymes, and quiet drama by Marjorie Pickthall (1883–1922). The poem first appeared in *The Drift of Pinions* (1913).

VESTIGIA

Bliss Carman

I took a day to search for God,
And found Him not. But as I trod
By rocky ledge, through woods untamed,
Just where one scarlet lily flamed,
I saw his footprint in the sod.

Then suddenly, all unaware,
Far off in the deep shadows, where
A solitary hermit thrush
Sang through the holy twilight hush—
I heard His voice upon the air.

And even as I marvelled how
God gives us Heaven here and now,
In a stir of wind that hardly shook
The poplar trees beside the brook—
His hand was light upon my brow.

At last with evening as I turned
Homeward, and thought what I had learned
And all that there was still to probe—
I caught the glory of His robe
Where the last fires of sunset burned.

Back to the world with quickening start
I looked and longed for any part
In making saving Beauty be ...
And from that kindly ecstasy
I knew God dwelt within my heart.

"Vestigia" was quite popular with high-school teachers because it
lent itself to analysis and discussion. Despite this, once read, it
lingers in the memory. The word *vestigia* is Latin for "footsteps."

The argument of the verse is surprisingly modern in that it
seeks to locate God in the world of nature and in the human heart
rather than in religious scriptures or in book learning.

The poem expresses the pantheistic beliefs of the poet Bliss Carman (1861–1929), at least those of 1920, and is reprinted from *Bliss Carman's Poems* (1929).

CHANGE
Raymond Knister

I shall not wonder more, then,
But I shall know.

Leaves change, and birds, flowers,
And after years are still the same.

The sea's breast heaves in sighs to the moon,
But they are moon and sea forever.

As in other times the trees stand tense and lonely,
And spread a hollow moan of other times.

You will be you yourself,
I'll find you more, not else,
For vintage of the woeful years.

The sea breathes, or broods, or loudens,
Is bright or is mist and the end of the world;
And the sea is constant to change.

I shall not wonder more, then,
But I shall know.

This poem is a favourite of many readers. It is a philosophical meditation on change and changelessness.

"Change" was written by the poet Raymond Knister (1899–1932), and it seems to prefigure his tragic death by drowning. Knister's remains were buried in Port Dover Cemetery, north of the Ontario town of Port Dover on Lake Erie. The Knister plot is marked with a flat slab of blue marble on which is inscribed the full text of this moving poem.

The text of the poem is reprinted from Knister's *Collected Poems* (1949) edited by Dorothy Livesay.

On Seeing the Statuettes
of Ezekiel and Jeremiah
in the Church of Notre Dame

Irving Layton

They have given you French names
   and made you captive, my rugged
troublesome compatriots;
   your splendid beards, here, are epicene,
plaster white
      and your angers
unclothed with Palestinian hills quite lost
in this immense and ugly edifice.

You are bored—I see it—sultry prophets
   with priests and nuns
(What coarse jokes must pass between you!)
   and with those morbidly religious
i.e. my prize brother-in-law
                    ex-Lawrencian
pawing his rosary, and his wife
sick with many guilts.

Believe me I would gladly take you
   from this spidery church
its bad melodrama, its musty smell of candle
   and set you both free again
in no make-believe world
              of sin and penitence
but the sunlit square opposite
alive at noon with arrogant men.

Yet cheer up Ezekiel and you Jeremiah
   who were once cast into a pit;
I shall not leave you here incensed, uneasy
   among alien Catholic saints
but shall bring you from time to time
              my hot Hebrew heart
as passionate as your own, and stand
with you here awhile in aching confraternity.

The Romanesque exterior of the Church of Notre-Dame, a basilica
in Montreal modelled on the *façade* of St Peter's in Rome, inspired
Irving Layton to compose "On Seeing the Statuettes of Ezekiel and
Jeremiah in the Church of Notre-Dame."
    The text is taken from Irving Layton's *Collected Poems* (1965).

O GREAT SPIRIT
Chief Dan George

O Great Spirit, whose voice I hear in the minds, and whose breath gives life to the world, hear me. I come to you as one of your many children. I am small and weak. I need your strength and your wisdom. May I walk in beauty. Make my eyes ever behold the red and purple sunset. Make my hands respect the things that you have made and my ears sharp to hear your voice. Make me wise so that I may know the things you have taught your children, the lessons you have hidden in every leaf and rock. Make me strong, not to be superior to my brothers, but to be able to fight my greatest enemy, myself. Make me ever ready to come to you with straight eyes, so that when life fades as the fading sunset, my spirit may come to you without shame.

"O Great Spirit" was composed by Chief Dan George (1899–1981), Native leader, elected chief of the Salish, orator, and actor on radio, television, and cinema.

He delivered this prayer at the close of a television program devoted to him and his ideals for his people and for all people. It was broadcast by CBC-TV on "Telescope," September 7, 1970. Chief Dan George was the author of two books of inspiring prose poems titled *My Heart Soars* (1974) and *My Spirit Soars* (1982).

TEARS ARE NOT ENOUGH

Bryan Adams & Jim Vallance

As every day goes by
How can we close our eyes
Until we open up our hearts?

We can learn to share
And show how much we care
Right from the moment that we start.

Seems like overnight we see
The world in a different light.
Somehow our innocence is lost.
How can we look away,
'Cause every single day,
We've got to help at any cost.

We can bridge the distance
Only we can make the difference
Don't you know that tears are not enough?

If we can pull together,
We can change the world forever.
Heaven knows that tears are not enough.

It's up to me and you
To make the dream come true
It's time to take our message everywhere you know.

C'est l'amour qui nous rassemble
D'ici à l'autre bout du monde.

Let's show them Canada still cares.
Oh, you know that we'll be there.
And if you should try together, you and I,
Maybe we could understand the reasons why.

Fifty-two Canadian recording artists and groups devoted their time
and talent to record "Tears Are Not Enough" in Toronto, February
10–11, 1985.

Revenues from the sales of the Canadian "famine relief song"
were directed to the charity called Northern Lights for Africa
Society. Bryan Adams and Jim Vallance wrote the words; the title
was supplied by Bob Rock and Paul Hyde; the music was composed
by David Foster.

The tune is haunting and there is an affecting simplicity to the
words and the sentiment, especially when compared with the more
direct and less subtle U.S. famine-relief song, "We Are the World."

FOOTPRINTS

Margaret Fishback Powers

One night I had a dream.
I was walking along the beach with my Lord.
Across the dark sky flashed scenes from my life.
For each scene, I noticed two sets
of footprints in the sand,
one belonging to me
and one to my Lord.
When the last scene of my life shot before me
I looked back at the footprints in the sand.
There was only one set of footprints.
I realized that this was at the lowest
and saddest times of my life.
This always bothered me
and I questioned the Lord
about my dilemma.
"Lord, You told me when I decided to follow You,
You would walk and talk with me all the way.
But I'm aware that during the most troublesome
times of my life there is only one set of footprints.
I just don't understand why, when I needed You most,
You leave me."
He whispered, "My precious child,
I love you and will never leave you,
never, ever, during your trials and testings.
When you saw only one set of footprints
it was then that I carried you."

Written by Margaret Fishback—
Thanksgiving, 1964—Echo Lake Youth Camp,
Kingston, Ontario, Canada. Copyright 1964 by
Margaret Fishback Powers.

"Footprints" is one of the most widely read devotional and inspirational poems of our time. Margaret Fishback Powers, an itinerant evangelist, was born Edith Elma Fishback in Tillsonburg, Ont., and later became a resident of Coquitlam, B.C. In her book *Footprints: The Story behind the Poem That Inspired Millions* (New York: Walker & Company, 1998), she explains that she wrote the text at the youth retreat and titled it "I Had a Dream." She lost the manuscript during her move out west in 1980. Thereafter the text, with the title "Footprints," began to appear anonymously on plaques, T-shirts, cards, calendars, posters, etc. She saw it for the first time in 1989 and claimed ownership in *Footprints*, which was an immediate bestseller and widely translated.

There are innumerable versions of the text in print and on the Internet. It should be noted that Powers's claim of authorship has been challenged. Mary Stevenson (1922–1999), who is said to be the granddaughter of Robert Louis Stevenson, maintained that she was inspired to write it in 1936 (at the tender age of fourteen). It was copyrighted in her name as "Footprints in the Sand" in 1984.

The text reproduced here comes from Powers's book *A Heart for Children: Inspirations for Parents & Their Children* (1995).

People
on *the*
Land

I AM A CANADIAN

Duke Redbird

I'm a lobster fisherman in Newfoundland
I'm a clambake in P.E.I.
I'm a picnic, I'm a banquet
I'm mother's homemade pie
I'm a few drafts in a Legion Hall in Fredericton
I'm a kite-flyer in a field in Moncton
I'm a nap on the porch after a hard day's work is done
I'm a snowball fight in Truro, Nova Scotia
I'm small kids playing jacks and skipping rope
I'm a mother who lost a son in the last great war
And I'm a bride with a brand new ring
And a chest of hope
I'm an Easterner
I'm a Westerner
I'm from the North
And I'm from the South
I've swum in two big oceans
And I've loved them both
I'm a clown in Quebec during Carnival
I'm a mass in the Cathedral of St. Paul
I'm a hockey game in the Forum
I'm Rock Richard and Jean Béliveau
I'm a coach for the little league Expos
I'm a baby-sitter for sleep-defying rascals
I'm a canoe trip down the Ottawa
I'm a holiday on the Trent

I'm a mortgage, I'm a loan
I'm last week's unpaid rent
I'm Yorkville after dark
I'm a walk in the park
I'm Winnipeg gold-eye
I'm a hand-made trout fly
I'm a wheat-field and a sunset
Under a prairie sky
I'm Sir John A. Macdonald
I'm Alexander Graham Bell
I'm a pow-wow dancer
And I'm Louis Riel
I'm the Calgary Stampede
I'm a feathered Sarcee
I'm Edmonton at night
I'm a bar-room fight
I'm a rigger, I'm a cat
I'm a ten-gallon hat
And an unnamed mountain in the interior of B.C.
I'm a maple tree and a totem pole
I'm sunshine shows
And fresh-cut flowers
I'm a ferry boat ride to the Island
I'm the Yukon
I'm the Northwest Territories
I'm the Arctic Ocean and the Beaufort Sea
I'm the prairies, I'm the Great Lakes
I'm the Rockies, I'm the Laurentians
I am French
I am English

And I am Métis
But more than this
Above all this
I am a Canadian and proud to be free.

Duke Redbird wrote this personal testament to his feelings and delivered it as part of the multi-media revue based on his writings that was performed in Ottawa on October 17, 1977. The audience included Queen Elizabeth II, who was celebrating her Silver Jubilee on that same date.

Redbird, who will long be associated with the sentiments of "I Am a Canadian," was born of Métis ancestry at the Saugeen Indian Reserve in northern Ontario. The text appears in the booklet *I Am a Canadian* (1977).

The Red Men—A Sonnet
Charles Sangster

My footsteps press where, centuries ago,
    The Red Men fought and conquered; lost and won.
Whole tribes and races, gone like last year's snow,
    Have found the Eternal Hunting-Grounds, and run
The fiery gauntlet of their active days,
    Till few are left to tell the mournful tale!
And these inspire us with such wild amaze
    They seem like spectres passing down a vale
Steeped in uncertain moonlight, on their way
Towards some bourne where darkness blinds the day,
    And night is wrapped in mystery profound.

We cannot lift the mantle of the past:
    We seem to wander over hallowed ground:
We scan the trail of Thought, but all is overcast.

This poem is a thoughtful, touching attempt of a non-Indian to reconnect with the lives of the Native peoples of the past.

    The poem was written by Charles Sangster (1822–1893) but, curiously, he never included it in his volumes of verse. I have reprinted "The Red Men—A Sonnet" from *Selections from Canadian Poets* (1864) edited by Edward Hartley Dewart.

THE WALKER OF THE SNOW

Charles Dawson Shanly

Speed on, speed on, good master!
    The camp lies far away;—
We must cross the haunted valley
    Before the close of day.

How the snow-blight came upon me
    I will tell you as I go,—
The blight of the shadow hunter
    Who walks the midnight snow.

To the cold December heaven
    Came the pale moon and the stars,
As the yellow sun was sinking
    Behind the purple bars.

The snow was deeply drifted
   Upon the ridges drear,
That lay for miles around me
   And the camp for which we steer.

'Twas silent on the hill-side,
   And by the solemn wood
No sound of life or motion
   To break the solitude,

Save the wailing of the moose-bird
   With a plaintive note and low,
And the skating of the red leaf
   Upon the frozen snow.

And said I,—"Though dark is falling,
   And far the camp must be,
Yet my heart it would be lightsome,
   If I had but company."

And then I sang and shouted,
   Keeping measure, as I sped,
To the harp-twang of the snow-shoe
   As it sprang beneath my tread;

Nor far into the valley
   Had I dipped upon my way,
When a dusky figure joined me,
   In a capuchon of gray,

Bending upon the snow-shoes
   With a long and limber stride;
And I hailed the dusky stranger,
   As we travelled side by side.

But no token of communion
   Gave he by word or look,
And the fear-chill fell upon me
   At the crossing of the brook.

For I saw by the sickly moonlight,
   As I followed, bending low,
That the walking of the stranger
   Left no foot-marks on the snow.

Then the fear-chill gathered o'er me,
   Like a shroud around me cast,
As I sank upon the snow-drift
   Where the shadow hunter passed.

And the otter-trappers found me,
   Before the break of day,
With my dark hair blanched and whitened
   As the snow in which I lay.

But they spoke not as they raised me;
   For they knew that in the night
I had seen the shadow hunter,
   And had withered in his blight.

Sancta Maria speed us!
  The sun is falling low,—
Before us lies the Valley
  Of the Walker of the Snow!

"The Walker of the Snow" is the scariest supernatural ballad in the literature of English Canada. It evokes the cold of the winter northlands and the chill in the heart of man.

It was composed by the journalist Charles Dawson Shanly (1811–1875) and first published in *The Atlantic Monthly*, May 1859. The version reprinted here is taken from the pages of that magazine (where it appeared anonymously).

The Hamilton-born artist W. Blair Bruce read the ballad in 1888 and was inspired to paint an eerie canvas titled "The Phantom Hunter," which depicts an exhausted hunter with his ghostly spectre about to collapse in a blizzard of snow. Bruce donated the canvas to the city of Hamilton, and the bequest led to the establishment of the Art Gallery of Hamilton, Ont.

WE LIVE IN A RICKETY HOUSE

Alexander McLachlan

We live in a rickety house,
  In a dirty dismal street,
Where the naked hide from day,
  And thieves and drunkards meet.

And pious folks with their tracts,
    When our dens they enter in,
They point to our shirtless backs,
    As the fruits of beer and gin.

And they quote us texts to prove
    That our hearts are hard as stone,
And they feed us with the fact
    That the fault is all our own.

It will be long ere the poor
    Will learn their grog to shun
While it's raiment, food and fire,
    And religion all in one.

I wonder some pious folks
    Can look us straight in the face,
For our ignorance and crime
    Are the Church's shame and disgrace.

We live in a rickety house,
    In a dirty dismal street,
Where the naked hide from day,
    And thieves and drunkards meet.

Alexander McLachlan (1818–1896) immigrated from Scotland to
Upper Canada and farmed near Guelph, Ont. He brought with him
a sense of sturdy independence, a feeling for the underdog, and a
sense of class divisions. These concerns underscore "We Live in a
Rickety House."

The poem is reprinted from McLachlan's *The Immigrant and Other Poems* (1861).

THE FORSAKEN
Duncan Campbell Scott

I

Once in the winter
Out on a lake
In the heart of the north-land,
Far from the Fort
And far from the hunters,
A Chippewa woman
With her sick baby,
Crouched in the last hours
Of a great storm.
Frozen and hungry,
She fished through the ice
With a line of the twisted
Bark of the cedar,
And a rabbit-bone hook
Polished and barbed;
Fished with the bare hook
All through the wild day,
Fished and caught nothing;
While the young chieftain
Tugged at her breasts,

Or slept in the lacings
Of the warm *tikanagan*.
All the lake-surface
Steamed with the hissing
Of millions of iceflakes
Hurled by the wind;
Behind her the round
Of a lonely island
Roared like a fire
With the voice of the storm
In the deeps of the cedars.
Valiant, unshaken,
She took of her own flesh,
Baited the fish-hook,
Drew in a grey-trout,
Drew in his fellows,
Heaped them beside her,
Dead in the snow.
Valiant, unshaken,
She faced the long distance,
Wolf-haunted and lonely,
Sure of her goal
And the life of her dear one:
Tramped for two days,
On the third in the morning,
Saw the strong bulk
Of the Fort by the river,
Saw the wood-smoke
Hang soft in the spruces,
Heard the keen yelp

Of the ravenous huskies
Fighting for whitefish:
Then she had rest.

II

Years and years after,
When she was old and withered,
When her son was an old man
And his children filled with vigour,
They came in their northern tour on the verge of winter,
To an island in a lonely lake.
There one night they camped, and on the morrow
Gathered their kettles and birch-bark,
Their rabbit-skin robes and their mink-traps,
Launched their canoes and slunk away through the islands,
Left her alone forever,
Without a word of farewell,
Because she was old and useless,
Like a paddle broken and warped,
Or a pole that was splintered.
Then, without a sigh,
Valiant, unshaken,
She smothered her dark locks under her kerchief,
Composed her shawl in state,
Then folded her hands ridged with sinews and corded with veins,
Folded them across her breasts spent with the nourishing of
    children,
Gazed at the sky past the tops of the cedars,
Saw two spangled nights arise out of the twilight,

Saw two days go by filled with the tranquil sunshine,
Saw, without pain, or dread, or even a moment of longing:
Then on the third great night there came thronging and
    thronging
Millions of snowflakes out of a windless cloud;
They covered her close with a beautiful crystal shroud,
Covered her deep and silent.
But in the frost of the dawn,
Up from the life below,
Rose a column of breath
Through a tiny cleft in the snow,
Fragile, delicately drawn,
Wavering with its own weakness,
In the wilderness a sign of the spirit,
Persisting still in the sight of the sun
Till day was done.
Then all light was gathered up by the hand of God and hid in
    His breast,
Then there was born a silence deeper than silence,
Then she had rest.

This heart-wrenching account of the endurance of an Indian mother was related by a Hudson's Bay Company factor to poet and Indian affairs agent Duncan Campbell Scott (1862–1947). The incident itself took place at Nipigon, on the north shore of Lake Superior.

In keeping with the spirit of poetry at the turn of the last century, Scott combined realistic and sentimental elements in his retelling of the incident in "The Forsaken," which first appeared in his volume *New World Lyrics and Ballads* (1905).

These days there is much criticism directed against Scott as an administrator who felt that the best interests of the Indian population were represented by a policy of assimilation, yet no one in his day lamented more the passing of the old days or did more to preserve the cultural expression of the Native peoples.

AT THE CEDARS

Duncan Campbell Scott

You had two girls—Baptiste—
One is Virginie—
Hold hard—Baptiste!
Listen to me.

The whole drive was jammed
In that bend at the Cedars,
The rapids were dammed
With the logs tight rammed
And crammed; you might know
The Devil had clinched them below.

We worked three days—not a budge,
"She's as tight as a wedge, on the ledge,"
Says our foreman;
"Mon Dieu! boys, look here,
We must get this thing clear."
He cursed at the men
And we went for it then;
With our cant-dogs arow,
We just gave he-yo-ho;
When she gave a big shove
From above.

The gang yelled and tore
for the shore,
The logs gave a grind
Like a wolf's jaws behind,
And as quick as a flash,
With a shove and a crush,
They were down in a mash,
But I and ten more,
All but Isaàc Dufour,
Were ashore.

He leaped on a lot in the front of the rush,
And shot out from the bind
While the jam roar'd behind;
As he floated along
He balanced his pole
And tossed us a song.
But just as we cheered,
Up darted a log from the bottom,
Leaped thirty feet square and fair,
And came down on his own.

He went up like a block
With the shock,
And when he was there
In the air,
Kissed his hand
To the land;
When he dropped
My heart stopped,
For the first logs had caught him
And crushed him;
When he rose in his place
There was blood on his face.

There were some girls, Baptiste,
Picking berries on the hillside,
Where the river curls, Baptiste,
You know—on the still side
One was drown by the water,
She saw Isaàc
Fall back.

She did not scream, Baptiste,
She launched her canoe;
It did seem, Baptiste,
That she wanted to die too,
For before you could think
The birch cracked like a shell
In that rush of hell,
And I saw them both sink—

Baptiste!—
He had two girls,
One is Virginie,
What God calls the other
Is not known to me.

"At the Cedars" is a widely reprinted poem that in a dramatic fash-
ion captures one of the tragedies that must have been common in
the life of a French-Canadian logging community.

It was written by Duncan Campbell Scott and it first appeared
in his collection *The Magic House* (1893).

THE ONONDAGA MADONNA
Duncan Campbell Scott

She stands full-throated and with careless pose,
This woman of a weird and waning race,
The tragic savage lurking in her face,
Where all her pagan passion burns and glows;
Her blood is mingled with her ancient foes,
And thrills with war and wildness in her veins;
Her rebel lips are dabbled with the stains
Of feuds and forays and her father's woes.

And closer in the shawl about her breast,
The latest promise of her nation's doom,
Paler than she her baby clings and lies,
The primal warrior gleaming from his eyes;
He sulks, and burdened with his infant gloom,
He draws his heavy brows and will not rest.

This vivid portrait of an Indian mother is not soon forgotten. It was written by Duncan Campbell Scott more than a hundred years ago. No one would write it—or publish it—today.

"The Onondaga Madonna" appeared in *Labour and the Angel* (1893).

ON THE WAY TO THE MISSION
Duncan Campbell Scott

They dogged him all one afternoon,
Through the bright snow,
Two whitemen servants of greed;
He knew that they were there,
But he turned not his head;
He was an Indian trapper;
He planted his snow-shoes firmly,
He dragged the long toboggan
Without rest.

The three figures drifted
Like shadows in the mind of a seer;
The snow-shoes were whisperers
On the threshold of awe;
The toboggan made the sound of wings,
A wood-pigeon sloping to her nest.

The Indian's face was calm.
He strode with the sorrow of fore-knowledge,
But his eyes were jewels of content
Set in circles of peace.

They would have shot him;
But momently in the deep forest,
They saw something flit by his side:
Their hearts stopped with fear.
Then the moon rose.
They would have left him to the spirit,
But they saw the long toboggan
Rounded well with furs,
With many a silver fox-skin,
With the pelts of mink and of otter.
They were the servants of greed;
When the moon grew brighter
And the spruces were dark with sleep,
They shot him.
When he fell on a shield of moonlight
One of his arms clung to his burden;
The snow was not melted:
The spirit passed away.

Then the servants of greed
Tore off the cover to count their gains;
They shuddered away into the shadows,
Hearing each the loud heart of the other.
Silence was born.

There in the tender moonlight,
As sweet as they were in life,
Glimmered the ivory features
Of the Indian's wife.

In the manner of Montagnais women
Her hair was rolled with braid;
Under her waxen fingers
A crucifix was laid.

He was drawing her down to the Mission,
To bury her there in spring,
When the bloodroot comes and the windflower
To silver everything.

But as a gift of plunder
Side by side were they laid,
The moon went on to her setting
And covered them with shade.

Duncan Campbell Scott's "On the Way to the Mission" appeared in
New World Lyrics and Ballads (1905). The poem combines both
action and pictorial images. The poignancy of the poem survives
multiple rereadings.

PAUL BUNYAN

Arthur S. Bourinot

He came,
striding
over the mountain,
the moon slung on his back,
like a pack,
a great pine

stuck on his shoulder
swayed as he walked,
as he talked
to his blue ox
Babe;
a huge, looming shadow
of a man,
clad
in a mackinaw coat,
his logger's shirt
open at the throat
and the great mane of hair
matching,
meeting
the locks of night,
the smoke from his cauldron pipe
a cloud on the moon
and his laugh
rolled through the mountains
like thunder
on a summer night
while the lightning of his smile
split the heavens
asunder.
His blue ox, Babe,
pawed the ground
till the earth
trembled
and shook
and a high cliff

toppled and fell;
and Babe's bellow
was fellow
to the echo
of Bunyan's laughter;
and then
with one step
he was in the next valley
dragging the moon after,
the stars
tangled,
spangled
in the branches of the great pine
And as he left,
he whistled in the dark
like a far off train
blowing for a crossing
and plainly heard
were the plodding grunts
of Babe, the blue ox,
trying
to keep pace
from hill to hill,
and then, the sounds,
fading,
dying,
were lost
in the churn of night,—
and all was still.

Here is a celebration of Paul Bunyan with his blue ox Babe. 1
lumberman is the hero of the folklore of French Canada. The lively
verse has been popular with children since its first publication.

"Paul Bunyan," written in 1949, is one of a number of popular
poems from the pen of Arthur S. Bourinot (1893–1969). It is reprint-
ed from *Ten Narrative Poems* (1955).

—

TOM THOMSON
Arthur S. Bourinot

It was a gray day
with a drizzle of rain,
something of fey
in the air
as though the lake,
the islands,
the sky
were watching,
waiting,
waiting for what?
A sense of doom
in the air
with silence everywhere
as though a god
had spoken,
and then a loon laughed
and the spell was broken,
the spell was broken.

And Tom Thomson laughed
and his friends laughed
as he launched his canoe
from the dock
and paddled away
with his lures and his lines
to befool the old trout
they had lost so often
in the bay in the river
below Joe Lake Dam;
and he turned
with a wave of his hand
and was gone.
And a loon laughed
and the old trout
waited in the bay
and the sky and lake watched
but he never came
was never seen again
till his body floated
on the surface
eight days later.

What happened?
No one knows,
no one will ever know;
no one knows
except perhaps the old trout
below Joe Lake Dam
and the lake
and the islands
the loon and the sky
that watched and waited;
no one knows.

And in far off Shoreham,
A.Y. Jackson, painting again,
after a "blighty" in France
heard of the upturned canoe
on the lake
and his dreams of camping
and fishing and painting
once more with his friend
came to an end,
as all dreams come
to an end,
as all dreams come
to an end.

Legend has it in Algonquin
Tom Thomson
watches and looks
from the headland
above the bay
on Canoe Lake,
his palette and brushes
and panels in hand
painting the symphony
of the seasons
of his beloved land
he never finished;
the unfolding year,
the folding leaf,
the gathered sheaf,
the winter snow,
the bright bateaux,
painting, painting;
and the great trout
waits in the river
below Joe Lake Dam
and the loon laughs
and sky and lake watch
and only his voice is still
on land and lake
but his spirit is awake
throughout the land he loved
kindling youth to slake
their thirst in beauty.
His spirit is awake,
a torch and a token,

as though a god had spoken;
his spirit is awake,
his spirit is awake.

What is known is that Tom Thomson drowned in the waters of
Canoe Lake, Algonquin Park, Ont., July 1917. The tragic death
under mysterious circumstances of this powerful painter and sea-
soned outdoorsman prompted and continues to prompt spirited
speculation in articles and books. The full story of Thomson's life
and death has yet to be told.

Pondering the incident led Arthur S. Bourinot (1893–1969) to
write this poem. "Tom Thomson" (1954) is reprinted from *Ten
Narrative Poems* (1955). Bourinot is right about two points at least.
"No one will ever know" the details that led to the death by drown-
ing. "His spirit is awake" in the sense that his art revealed the
colour and form of the landscape of northern Ontario and Quebec,
leading in 1920 to the formation of the famed Group of Seven.

Erosion
E. J. Pratt

It took the sea a thousand years,
A thousand years to trace
The granite features of this cliff,
In crag and scarp and base.

It took the sea an hour one night,
An hour of storm to place
The sculpture of these granite seams
Upon a woman's face.

"Erosion" is among the most vivid and the most anthologized poems written by E. J. Pratt (1883–1964). It appeared in *The Iron Door* (1927).

———

The Browns

Audrey Alexandra Brown

There was a Brown at Stamford, nine hundred years ago,
When Harold fought Hardrada with the Saxon bill and bow;
A poor rough churl with heavy hand and fingers blunt from
    toil—
But not the least he was of those that fought for English soil.

A hind who could not read or write, in hardened leather clad,
No mail to turn the levelled spear, no shining blade he had;
But dearly did he sell his life, pierced through with many a shaft,
And died beside his battleaxe, his hand upon its haft.

There was a Brown at Crecy, when Edward routed France,
First in the rank that knelt to break the cavalry's advance;
A peasant from the plough he was, a rude unlettered thing,
But he had a heart for England, and an arm for England's King.

One skill he had, and nothing more; one art alone he knew—
To string and draw with dying hands the bow of tautened yew;
All that he had to give—his life—a thousand others gave;
But not the least he was of those that filled a Flemish grave.

There was a Brown of Devon, who sailed from Plymouth Hoe
With Francis Drake his admiral, four hundred years ago;
A yeoman born he was, a man of scanty speech and plain—
But well he loved the English fields he never saw again.

Nombre de Dios' bells rang sweet on incense-laden air,
The hour the Spaniards led him forth with chanted praise and
    prayer;
They touched the fagots with the fire. Unflinching at the stake
He showed them how the man can die that dies for England's
    sake.

There was a Brown with Nelson, when on the day of fame
The Nile ran red with Gallic blood and burned with English
    flame;
No pacer of the quarter-deck—a common sailor he;
They found him stark beside his gun, and buried him at sea.

And there were candles lit at night, and London rang with cheers;
Triumphant pealed a thousand bells, their merriest chime for
    years;
Who was there looked for him in vain among the crowds ashore?
Who missed him, save the Gloucester home to which he came
    no more?

There was a Brown in Flanders, whose blue Canadian eyes
Beheld but once the gallant cliffs, the gates of England, rise;
Once, only once, he heard the lark above the shimmering wheat,
And once he saw the mellow spires adown an Oxford street.

Ah, youth is sweet upon the lips!—the wine of life is good;
He poured that wine with steadfast hands one day in Ypres
   wood.
Let it forget him if it may, the land that gave him birth—
There is a glory where he lies in green though alien earth.

One with the nameless are they all; there never was a Brown
Who rose above the rank and file to gain the world's renown;
One with a common host they are, by dale and copse and fen—
But England's made and moulded by the lives of common men.

And while a loyal heart is left to beat for God and King,
Long as above an English field the English throstles sing—
When the bugles call at morning, and the brave old flag's
   unfurled,
There'll be Browns to die for England till the Judgment of the
   world!

Verses like "The Browns" are not being written any more (or, if
they are, educators are not including them in school readers, and
literary editors are giving them short shrift). The work is
Imperialist to the core, but at that core are such values as valour,
self-sacrifice, and freedom. As well, the work is quite demanding.
"The Browns" was studied by Grade 9 students in Ontario schools
in the early 1950s. Today how many high school students—indeed,
how many teachers—would appreciate its references? "The
Browns" was written by Audrey Alexandra Brown (1904–1998)
and is reprinted from her collection A *Dryad in Nanaimo* (1931).
It inspired many a student named Brown.

   The reference to Flanders is footnoted: "The 'Brown in
Flanders' was my eldest brother, Albert Harris Brown, who enlisted

August the ninth, 1914 and went overseas with the first Canadian
contingent. He was wounded in the second battle of Ypres, taken
prisoner, and died in a hospital at Paardeborn on May the twenty-
second, aged twenty-one.—A.A.B."

—

Political Meeting

A. M. Klein

For Camillien Houde

On the school platform, draping the folding seats,
they wait the chairman's praise and glass of water.
Upon the wall the agonized Y initials their faith.

Here all are laic; the skirted brothers have gone.
Still, their equivocal absence is felt, like a breeze
that gives curtains the sounds of surplices.

The hall is yellow with light, and jocular;
suddenly some one lets loose upon the air
the ritual bird which the crowd in snares of singing

catches and plucks, throat, wings, and little limbs.
Fall the feathers of sound, like *alouette's*.
The chairman, now, is charming, full of asides and wit,

building his orators, and chipping off
the heckling gargoyles popping in the hall.
(Outside, in the dark, the street is body-tall,

flowered with faces intent on the scarecrow thing
that shouts to thousands the echoing
of their own wishes.) The Orator has risen!

Worshipped and loved, their favourite visitor,
a country uncle with sunflower seeds in his pockets,
full of wonderful moods, tricks, imitative talk,

he is their idol: like themselves, not handsome,
not snobbish, not of the *Grande Allée! Un homme!*
Intimate, informal, he makes bear's compliments

to the ladies; is gallant; and grins;
goes for the balloon, his opposition, with pins;
jokes also on himself, speaks of himself

in the third person, slings slang, and winks with folklore;
and knows now that he has them, kith and kin.
Calmly, therefore, he begins to speak of war,

praises the virtue of being *Canadien,*
of being at peace, of faith, of family,
and suddenly his other voice: *Where are your sons?*

He is tearful, choking tears; but not he
would blame the clever English; in their place
he'd do the same; maybe.

Where *are* your sons?
                     The whole street wears one face,
shadowed and grim; and in the darkness rises
the body-odour of race.

Camillien Houde, Montreal's ebullient Mayor, counselled young French-Canadian males to evade the draft during the Second World War. A. M. Klein (1909–1972) immortalized Houde and his populace-pleasing manner in this satire in *The Rocking Chair and Other Poems* (1948).

W.L.M.K.

F. R. Scott

How shall we speak of Canada,
Mackenzie King dead?
The Mother's boy in the lonely room
With his dog, his medium and his ruins?

He blunted us.

We had no shape
Because he never took sides,
And no sides
Because he never allowed them to take shape.

He skilfully avoided what was wrong
Without saying what was right,
And never let his on the one hand
Know what his on the other hand was doing.

The height of his ambition
Was to pile a Parliamentary Committee on a Royal
   Commission,
To have "conscription if necessary
But not necessarily conscription,"
To let Parliament decide—
Later.

Postpone, postpone, abstain.

Only one thread was certain:
After World War I
Business as usual,
After World War II
Orderly decontrol.
Always he led us back to where we were before.

He seemed to be in the centre
Because we had no centre,
No vision
To pierce the smoke-screen of his politics.

Truly he will be remembered
Wherever men honour ingenuity,
Ambiguity, inactivity, and political longevity.

Let us raise up a temple
To the cult of mediocrity,
Do nothing by halves
Which can be done by quarters.

Is there a more caustic portrait of a politician than "W.L.M.K."? If so, it has yet to appear in print.

William Lyon Mackenzie King, who served as Prime Minister of Canada from 1921 to 1930 and from 1935 to 1948, met his wily match in poet and law professor F. R. Scott (1899–1985). King died in 1950, so he never had the chance to read this penetrating account of his character and career.

"W.L.M.K." was written in 1954 and published in *The Eye of the Needle* (1957).

THE POET CONFIDES
H. T. J. Coleman

Sometimes I write with the stub of a pencil
On the back of an old envelope,
Or an odd scrap of paper
That I fish up out of an inside pocket.
And sometimes I write on decent paper
With pen and ink.
But always I write (when I write truly)
With my heart's blood.

And it is not I that write,
At least it is not the man
Who bears a conventional name,
And sometimes wears evening clothes,
And has a street address and a telephone number,
And is mentioned in Who's Who.
The one who writes is a very different person,
He has been warmed by the suns of a million summers,
And chilled by the frosts of a million winters,
And gone naked in the jungle,
And followed dim trails through primeval forests,
And suffered indescribable agonies and experienced unimagin-
    able joys,
Before streets or telephones or the banalities of publicity were
    ever thought of.

No! I am not the person you take me for,
But so different, indeed, that you might not care to shake
    hands with me if you saw me truly,
Yet I hope you could pity me even if you could not love me,
For I am the soul of man.

There are few poems at all like "The Poet Confides" in the annals
of Canadian writing. The poem is at once direct and didactic, simul-
taneously pleasing and off-putting.

It was written by H. T. J. Coleman (1872–1964), Professor of
Philosophy, University of British Columbia. It is reprinted from
Coleman's *The Poet Confides* (1928).

The Canadian Authors Meet

F. R. Scott

Expansive puppets percolate self-unction
Beneath a portrait of the Prince of Wales.
Miss Crotchet's muse has somehow failed to function,
Yet she's a poetess. Beaming, she sails

From group to chattering group, with such a dear
Victorian saintliness, as is her fashion,
Greeting the other unknowns with a cheer—
Virgins of sixty who still write of passion.

The air is heavy with "Canadian" topics,
And Carman, Lampman, Roberts, Campbell, Scott
Are measured for their faith and philanthropics,
Their zeal for God and King, their earnest thought.

The cakes are sweet, but sweeter is the feeling
That one is mixing with the *literati*;
It warms the old and melts the most congealing.
Really, it is a most delightful party.

Shall we go round the mulberry bush, or shall
We gather at the river, or shall we
Appoint a poet laureate this Fall,
Or shall we have another cup of tea?

O Canada, O Canada, Oh can
A day go by without new authors springing
To paint the native maple, and to plan
More ways to set the selfsame welkin ringing?

It is said that members of the Canadian Authors Association never forgave F. R. Scott (1899–1985) for directing their way the barbs of "The Canadian Authors Meet"!

The deft satire, written way back in 1927, appeared in *Overture* (1945). According to friend and poet A. J. M. Smith, it was "written on the occasion when the author attended a meeting of the local poetry group to see his present collaborator awarded a prize for a piece of sentimental verse."

FLIGHT OF THE ROLLER-COASTER
Raymond Souster

Once more around should do it, the man confided . . .

And sure enough, when the roller-coaster reached the peak
Of the giant curve above me—screech of its wheels
Almost drowned by the shriller cries of the riders—

Instead of the dip and plunge with its landslide of screams
It rose in the air like a movieland magic carpet, some wonderful
    bird,

And without fuss or fanfare swooped slowly across the amuse-
    ment park,
Over Spook's Castle, ice-cream booths, shooting-gallery; and
    losing no height

Made the last yard above the beach, where the cucumber-cool
Brakeman in the last seat saluted
A lady about to change from her bathing-suit.

Then, as many witnesses duly reported, headed leisurely over
    the water,
Disappearing mysteriously all too soon behind a low-lying
    flight of clouds.

"Flight of the Roller-Coaster" is a poem of incredible grace and
movement about an event that never happened, at least not with the
giant roller-coaster that was for many years the centrepiece of the
Sunnyside amusement park in Toronto's West End. The poem, a
favourite of many readers, was written in the late 1950s by
Raymond Souster and is reprinted from his selected poems, *The
Colour of the Times* (1964).

—

I, ICARUS
Alden Nowlan

There was a time when I could fly. I swear it.
Perhaps, if I think hard for a moment, I can even tell you the
    year.
My room was on the ground floor at the rear of the house.
My bed faced a window.
Night after night I lay on my bed and willed myself to fly.
It was hard work, I can tell you.
Sometimes I lay perfectly still for an hour before I felt my body
    rising from the bed.

I rose slowly, slowly until I floated three or four feet above the
    floor.
Then, with a kind of swimming motion, I propelled myself
    toward the window.
Outside, I rose higher and higher, above the pasture fence,
    above the clothesline, above the dark, haunted trees beyond
    the pasture.
And, all the time, I heard the music of flutes.
It seemed the wind made this music.
And sometimes there were voices singing.

A delightful sense of humour, a no-nonsense language, coupled
with a feeling for fantasy are characteristics of the poetry of Alden
Nowlan (1933–1984).

   "I, Icarus" is reprinted from *The Mysterious Naked Man* (1969).

GRANDFATHER
George Bowering

Grandfather
            Jabez Harry Bowering
strode across the Canadian prairie
hacking down trees

                        & building churches
delivering personal baptist sermons in them
leading Holy holy holy lord god almighty songs in them
red haired man squared off in the pulpit
reading Saul on the road to Damascus at them

Left home
                    big walled Bristol town
at age eight
                    to make a living
buried his stubby fingers in root snarled earth
for a suit of clothes & seven hundred gruelly meals a year
taking an anabaptist cane across the back every day
for four years till he was whipt out of England

Twelve years old
                         & across the ocean alone
to apocalyptic Canada
                         Ontario of bone bending labor
six years on the road to Damascus till his eyes were blinded
with the blast of Christ & he wandered west
to Brandon among wheat kings & heathen Saturday night
young red haired Bristol boy shoveling coal
in the basement of Brandon college five in the morning

Then built his first wooden church & married
a sick girl who bore two live children & died
leaving several pitiful letters & the Manitoba night

He moved west with another wife & built children & churches
Saskatchewan Alberta British Columbia Holy holy holy
lord god almighty
                         struck his labored bones with pain
& left him a postmaster prodding grandchildren with crutches
another dead wife & a glass bowl of photographs
& holy books unopened save the bible by the bed

Till he died the day before his eighty fifth birthday
in a Catholic hospital of sheets white as his hair

I like to think of "Grandfather" in terms of a gale of wind that rush-
es across the Prairies, that rises over the crests of the Rockies, and
that settles down into the Interior and then the Coast of British
Columbia. It brings, to my mind at least, the Prairie poems of Carl
Sandburg. It was written by George Bowering and appeared in his
collection *Points on the Grid* (1964).

Work
and
Labour

I's the B'y
Traditional

I's the b'y that build the boat,
I's the b'y that sails 'er!
I's the b'y that catches the fish
And brings 'em home to Lizer.

Hip yer partner, Sally Tibbo,
Hip yer partner, Sally Brown,
Fogo, Twillingate, Moreton's Harbour,
All around the circle!

Sods and rinds to cover the flake,
Tea and cakes for supper,
Flatfish in the spring of the year
Fried in maggoty butter.

Hip yer partner, Sally Tibbo,
Hip yer partner, Sally Brown,
Fogo, Twillingate, Moreton's Harbour,
All around the circle!

I don't want your maggoty fish,
That's no good fer winter,
I could buy as good as that
Down in Bonavista.

Hip yer partner, Sally Tibbo,
Hip yer partner, Sally Brown,
Fogo, Twillingate, Moreton's Harbour,
All around the circle!

I took Lizer to a dance,
Faith, but she could travel,
Fer every step that she did take
She was up to 'er knees in gravel!

Hip yer partner, Sally Tibbo,
Hip yer partner, Sally Brown,
Fogo, Twillingate, Moreton's Harbour,
All around the circle!

Susan White she's out of sight
Fixin' 'er petticoat border,
Sammy Oliver in the dark
He kissed 'er in the corner.

Hip yer partner, Sally Tibbo,
Hip yer partner, Sally Brown,
Fogo, Twillingate, Moreton's Harbour,
All around the circle!

"I's the B'y" is a traditional Newfoundland dance ditty that is sung with gusto on the Great Island. Gerald S. Doyle included it in his booklet *Old-Time Songs of Newfoundland* (1955). The Leslie Bell Singers popularized it on the mainland in the late 1950s. Alan Mills performs it on the Folkways LP *Folk Songs of Newfoundland* (1953).

SQUID-JIGGIN' GROUND

A. R. Scammell

Oh! this is the place where the fishermen gather
With oil skins and boots and Cape Anns battened down
All sizes of figures with squid lines and jiggers,
They congregate here on the squid-jiggin' ground.

There's men from the Harbour and men from the Tickle,
In all kinds of motor boats, green, gray and brown;
There's a red-headed Tory out here in a dory,
A runnin' down Squires on the squid-jiggin' ground.

There's men of all ages and boys in the bargain,
There's old Billy Chafe and there's young Raymond Brown;
Right yonder is "Bobby" and with him is "Nobby."
They're a-chawin' hard tack on the squid-jiggin' ground.

Holy smoke! What a bussel; all hands are excited.
It's a wonder to me that nobody is drowned.
There's a bussel, confusion, a wonderful hussel;
They're all jiggin' squid on the squid-jiggin' ground.

"I wrote 'Squid-Jiggin' Ground' at the age of fifteen as a school
assignment," boasted the writer and composer A. R. Scammell.
"The names in the song are actual Change Island names." Change
Island is the name of an island next to Fogo Island in Notre Dame
Bay off the north coast of Newfoundland.

Since 1929, "The Squid-Jiggin' Ground" has become known
and sung by Newfoundlanders and by many other fine people

across Canada. The lyrics attest to the outport way of life that has pretty well vanished from the island's coasts.

Scammell had the pleasure of hearing the melody played on the carillon bells in the Peace Tower during the ceremony that marked Newfoundland's entrance into Confederation, April 1, 1949. There is now an A. R. Scammell Academy at Notre Dame Bay. The lyrics are reprinted from Scammell's collection *My Newfoundland: Stories, Poems, Songs* (1966). The composer himself sings a longer version of the lyrics on an album released in 1973.

———

THE BALLAD OF SPRINGHILL
Peggy Seeger

In the town of Springhill, Nova Scotia,
Down in the dark of the Cumberland Mine,
There's blood on the coal and the miners lie
In the roads that never saw sun nor sky,
Roads that never saw sun nor sky.

In the town of Springhill, you don't sleep easy,
Often the earth will tremble and roll,
When the earth is restless, miners die,
Bone and blood is the price of coal,
Bone and blood is the price of coal.

In the town of Springhill, Nova Scotia,
Late in the year of fifty-eight,
Day still comes and the sun still shines,
But it's dark as the grave in the Cumberland Mine,
Dark as the grave in the Cumberland Mine.

Down at the coal face, miners working,
Rattle of the belt and the cutter's blade,
Rumble of rock and the walls close round
The living and the dead men two miles down,
Living and the dead men two miles down.

Twelve men lay two miles from the pitshaft,
Twelve men lay in the dark and sang,
Long, hot days in the miners' tomb,
It was three feet high and a hundred long,
Three feet high and a hundred long.

Three days passed and the lamps gave out
And Caleb Rushton he up and said:
There's no more water nor light nor bread
So we'll live on song and hope instead,
Live on song and hope instead.

Listen to the shouts of the *bareface miners*,
Listen through the rubble for a rescue team,
Six hundred feet of coal and slag,
Hope imprisoned in a three-foot seam,
Hope imprisoned in a three-foot seam.

Eight days passed and some were rescued,
Leaving the dead to lie alone,
Through all their lives they dug a grave,
Two miles of earth for a marking stone,
Two miles of earth for a marking stone.

In the town of Springhill, Nova Scotia,
Down in the dark of the Cumberland Mine,
There's blood on the coal and the miners lie
In the roads that never saw sun nor sky,
Roads that never saw sun nor sky.

This moving ballad was composed by Peggy Seeger, the American-born singer-songwriter whose career is linked with that of Scottish folksinger Ewan MacColl (1915–1989).

She was moved by the pluck and spunk shown by the miners who were caught in the collapse on October 23, 1958, of the Cumberland Mine at Springhill, N.S. The refrain with its reference to "roads" is particularly haunting.

The lyrics of "The Ballad of Springhill" come from *The Ewan MacColl / Peggy Seeger Song Book* (1970).

ALL THROUGH THE 'THIRTIES
Roy Daniells

All through the 'thirties, south of Saskatoon,
A farmer farmed a farm without a crop.
Dust filled the air, the lamp was lit at noon,
And never blade of wheat that formed a top.
One New Year's to the hired man he said,
"I have no money. You must take the deeds.
And I will be the hired man instead,
To shovel snow and fork the tumbleweeds."
So it was done. And when the next year came,
"Take back your farm," the other had to say.

And year by year, alternate, just the same
Till the War came and took them both away.
With such superb resource and self-possession
Canada made it through the long depression.

Great skill went into the writing of this sonnet, which has the air of folklore.

 "All through the 'Thirties" was written by poet and professor Roy Daniells (1902–1979) and published in The Chequered Shade (1963).

THE *MARY ELLEN CARTER*
Stan Rogers

She went down last October in a pouring driving rain
The Skipper, he'd been drinking and the Mate, he felt no pain.
Too close to Three Mile Rock and she was dealt her mortal
 blow
And the *Mary Ellen Carter* settled low.
There was just us five aboard her when she finally was awash
We worked like hell to save her, all heedless of the cost
And the groan she gave us as she went down, it caused us to
 proclaim
That the *Mary Ellen Carter* would rise again.

Well, the owners wrote her off; not a nickel would they spend.
"She gave twenty years of service, boys, then met her sorry end.
But insurance paid the loss to us, so let her rest below,"
Then they laughed at us and said we had to go.
But we talked of her all winter, some days around the clock,
For she's worth a quarter million, afloat and at the dock.
And with every jar that hit the bar we swore we would remain
And make the *Mary Ellen Carter* rise again.

Rise again, rise again, that her name not be lost
To the knowledge of men
Those who loved her best and were with her till the end
Will make the Mary Ellen Carter *rise again.*

All spring now, we've been with her on a barge lent by a friend.
Three dives a day in a hard hat suit and twice I've had the
    bends.
Thank God it's only sixty feet and the currents here are slow
Or I'd never have the strength to go below.
But we've patched her rents, stopped her vents, dogged hatch
    and porthole down
Put cable to her, 'fore and aft and girded her around
Tomorrow, noon, we hit the air and then take up the strain
And make the *Mary Ellen Carter* rise again.

Rise again, rise again, that her name not be lost
To the knowledge of men
Those who loved her best and were with her till the end
Will make the Mary Ellen Carter *rise again.*

For we couldn't leave her there, you see, to crumble into scale.
She'd saved our lives so many times, living through the gale
And the laughing, drunken rats who left her to a sorry grave
They won't be laughing in another day. . . .
And you, to whom adversity has dealt the final blow
With smiling bastards lying to you everywhere you go
Turn to, and put out all your strength of arm and heart and brain
And, like the *Mary Ellen Carter,* rise again!

Rise again, rise again—though your heart it be broken
And life about to end
No matter what you've lost, be it a home, a love, a friend
Like the Mary Ellen Carter, *rise again.*

"This is Stan's signature song," noted Chris Gudgeon in *An Unfinished Conversation: The Life and Music of Stan Rogers* (1993). "The story was simple: some sailors salvage a sunken boat. The song paid tribute to those who go against the grain and still find success—people just like Stan Rogers."

Composer-songwriter Stan Rogers (1949–1983) sings it with defiant determination on the album *Between the Breaks* (1979).

THE STENOGRAPHERS
P. K. Page

After the brief bivouac of Sunday,
their eyes, in the forced march of Monday to Saturday,
hoist the white flag, flutter in the snow storm of paper,
haul it down and crack in the midsun of temper.

In the pause between the first draft and the carbon
they glimpse the smooth hours when they were children—
the ride in the ice-cart, the ice-man's name,
the end of the route and the long walk home;

remember the sea where floats at high tide
where sea marrows growing on the scatter-green vine
or spools of grey toffee, or wasps' nests on water;
remember the sand and the leaves of the country.

Bell rings and they go and the voice draws their pencil
like a sled across snow; when its runners are frozen
rope snaps and the voice then is pulling no burden
but runs like a dog on the winter of paper.

Their climates are winter and summer—no wind
for the kites of their hearts—no wind for a flight;
a breeze at the most, to tumble them over
and leave them like rubbish—the boy-friends of blood.

In the inch of the noon as they move they are stagnant.
The terrible calm of the noon is their anguish;
the lip of the counter, the shapes of the straws
like icicles breaking their tongues are invaders.

Their beds are their oceans—salt water of weeping
the waves that they know—the tide before sleep;
and fighting to drown they assemble their sheep
in columns and watch them leap desks for their fences
and stare at them with their own mirror-worn faces.

In the felt of the morning the calico minded,
sufficiently starched, insert papers, hit keys,
efficient and sure as their adding machines;
yet they weep in the vault, they are taut as net curtains
stretched upon frames. In their eyes I have seen
the pin men of madness in marathon trim
race round the track of the stadium pupil.

"The Stenographers" is a poem that is surprisingly popular with
readers, given the richness of the imagery and the intricacy of the
language. It was recommended for inclusion in this treasury by
almost all of the people I consulted.

It was written by P. K. Page, who herself worked as a stenog-
rapher in Montreal in the 1930s. It appeared in *As Ten as Twenty*
(1946).

＿

ENVOI

Bliss Carman

Have little care that Life is brief,
And less that art is long.
Success is in the silences,
Though fame is in the song.

"Envoi" is suitably placed as the concluding verse in *Bliss Carman's
Poems* (1929).

These four lines are inscribed on the tombstone of Bliss
Carman (1861–1929), Forest Hill Cemetery, Fredericton, N.B.

＿

Stuff
and
Nonsense

SWEET MAIDEN OF PASSAMAQUODDY

James De Mille

Sweet maiden of Passamaquoddy,
    Shall we seek for communion of souls
Where the deep Mississippi meanders,
    Or the distant Saskatchewan rolls?

Oh no,—for in Maine will I find thee,
    A sweetly sequestrated nook,
Where the winding Skoodoowabskookis
    Conjoins with the Skoodoowabskook.

There wanders two beautiful rivers
    With many a winding and crook;
The one is the Skoodoowabskookis:
    The other—the Skoodoowabskook.

Ah, sweetes of haunts! tho' ummentioned
    In Geography, Atlas, or Book,
How fair is the Skoodoowabskookis
    When joining the Skoodoowabskook!

Our cot shall be close by the waters
    Within that sequestrated nook—
Reflected in Skoodoowabskookis
    And mirrored in Skoodoowabskook!

You shall sleep to the music of leaflets
    By Zephyrs in wantonness shook,
And dream of the Skoodoowabskooksis,
    And, perhaps, of the Skoodoowabskook!

When awakened by the hens and the roosters,
    Each morn, you shall joyously look
On the junction of Skoodoowabskooksis,
    With soft gliding Skoodoowabskook!

Your food shall be fish from the waters,
    Drawn forth on the point of a hook,
From murmuring Skoodoowabskooksis
    Or wandering Skoodoowabskook!

You shall quaff the most sparkling of water,
    Drawn forth from a silvery brook
With flows to the Skoodoowabskooksis
    And then to the Skoodoowabskook!

And *you* shall preside at the banquet,
    And *I* shall wait on thee as cook:
And we'll talk of the Skoodoowabskooksis,
    And sing of the Skoodoowabskook!

Let others sing loudly of Saco
    Of Quoddy, and Tattamagouche,
Of Kennebecasis, and Quaco,
    Of Merigonishe, and Buctouche.

Of Nashwaak, and Magaguadavique,
    Or Memmerimammericook—
There's none like the Skoodoowabskooksis
    Excepting the Skoodoowabskook!

"I seized paper and pen and dashed off the following 'Lines to Florance Huntingdon, Passamaquoddy, Maine,'" explained James De Mille (1838–1880), professor and novelist, in *The New Dominion and True Humourist,* April 16, 1870. "I remember very little about the composition of that delectable effusion. I found it afterwards in the above state, but could only recall a few circumstances connected with writing it."

Thus did the novelist describe the composition of this amusing (if exasperating) verse included in *The Minnehaha Mines,* a novel published serially in that Saint John publication. Some day the novel may be given the book publication it may deserve. In the meantime, readers may enjoy De Mille's celebrated tongue-twister on East Coast place names.

THE INDIAN NAMES OF ACADIE
James De Mille

The memory of the Red Man,
    How can it pass away,
While his names of music linger
    On each mount and stream and bay?
While *Musquodobit's* waters
    Roll sparkling to the main;
While falls the laughing sunbeam
    On *Chegogin's* fields of grain.

While floats our country's banner
   O'er *Chebucto's* glorious wave;
And frowning cliffs of *Scaterie*
   The trembling surges brave;
While breezy *Aspotogon*
   Lifts high its summit blue,
And sparkles on its winding way
   The gentle *Sissibou.*

While *Escasoni's* fountains
   Pour down their crystal tide;
While *Inganish's* mountains
   Lift high their forms of pride;
Or while on *Mabou's* river
   The boatman plies his oar;
Or the billows burst in thunder
   On *Chickaben's* rock-girt shore.

The memory of the Red Man,
   It lingers like a spell
On many a storm-swept headland,
   On many a leafy dell;
Where *Tusket's* thousand islets,
   Like emeralds, stud the deep;
Where *Blomidon,* a sentry grim,
   His endless watch doth keep.

It dwells round *Catalon's* blue lake,
　'Mid leafy forests hid,—
Round fair *Discourse,* and the rushing tides
　Of the turbid *Pisiquid.*
And it lends, *Chebogue,* a touching grace
　To thy softly flowing river,
As we sadly think of the gentle race
　That has passed away for ever.

This verse may be less familiar to readers than James De Mille's "Sweet Maiden of Passamaquoddy," yet "The Indian Names of Acadie" was written in the same vein. It was composed with at least as much craft and with even more emotion.

　　But who wrote it? Some historians attribute it to Richard Huntington, editor and publisher of *The Yarmouth Tribune* in 1855–1883. Yet William Douw Lighthall, in his authoritative volume *Songs of the Great Dominion* (1889), identifies the author as James De Mille. And it *sounds* like it was written by De Mille.

THE KELLIGREWS' SOIREE
John Burke

You may talk of Clara Nolan's Ball
　Or anything you choose,
But it couldn't hold a snuff-box
　To the spree of Kelligrews'.
If you want your eyeballs straightened,
　Just come out next week with me,
And you will have to wear your glasses
　At the Kelligrews' Soiree.

There was birch rhine, tar twine,
Cherry wine and turpentine;
    Jowls and calavances, ginger beer and tea;
Pigs' feet, cats' meat, dumplin's boiled up in a sheet,
Dandelion and crackies teeth
    At the Kelligrews' Soiree.

Oh, I borrowed Clooney's beaver
    As I squared my yards to sail,
And a swallow-tail from Hogan
    That was foxy on the tail;
Billy Cuddahie's old working pants,
    And Patsy Nowlan's shoes,
And an old white vest from Fogarty
    To sport in Kelligrews'.

There was Dan Milley, Joe Lilly,
Tantan and Mrs. Tilley,
Dancing like a little filly,
    'Twould raise your heart to see,
Jim Brine, Din Ryan,
    Flipper Smith and Caroline;
I tell you, boys, we had a time
    At the Kelligrews' Soiree.

Oh, when I arrived at Betsy Snooks'
   That night at half-past eight
The place was blocked with carriages
   Stood waiting at the gate;
With Cluney's funnel on my pate,
   The first word Betsy said,
"Here comes a local preacher
   With the pulpit on his head."

There was Bill Mews, Dan Hughes,
Wilson, Taft, and Teddy Roose,
While Bryant he sat in the blues
   And looking hard at me;
Jim Fling, Tom King
And Johnson champion of the ring,
And all the boxers I could bring
   At the Kelligrews' Soiree.

"The Saratoga Lancers first,"
   Miss Betsy kindly said;
Sure I danced with Nancy Cronan
   And her Grannie on the "Head";
And Hogan danced with Betsy;
   Oh, you should have seen his shoes
As he lashed old muskets from the rack
   That night at Kelligrew's.

There was boiled guineas, cold guineas,
Bullocks' heads and piccaninnies
And everything to catch the pennies,
You'd break your sides to see;
Boiled duff, cold duff,
Apple jam was in a cuff;
I tell you, boys, we had enough
At the Kelligrews' Soiree.

Cooked Flavin struck to the rim;
And a hand I then took in.
You should see George Clooney's beaver
And it flattened to the rim;
And Hogan's coat was like a vest—
The tails were gone, you see;
"Oh," says I, "the devul haul ye
And your Kelligrews' Soiree."

"A classic folklore song known throughout Newfoundland" is how "The Kelligrews' Soiree" was described by J. R. (Joey) Smallwood, long-time premier and some-time folklorist.

It was written by John Burke (1851–1933), "the last of the balladeers," and it captures the colour and excitement of a family's celebration in an outport on the east coast of Conception Bay. It does so in high spirits and in definitive terms!

The text is reproduced from Smallwood's *The Book of Newfoundland* (1937), volume one.

HAIL OUR GREAT QUEEN
James Gay

Hail our great Queen in Her Regalia;
One foot in Canada, the other in Australia.

It has yet to be established that this remarkable couplet, complete
with its unintentional humour, flowed from the wayward pen of
James Gay (1810–1891), the poetaster and resident of Guelph, Ont.
He described himself as "Poet Laureate of Canada and Master of
All Poets" and considered himself the equal of Tennyson and
Longfellow, as noted by William Arthur Deacon in his serio-comic
study, *The Four Jameses* (1927).

ODE ON THE MAMMOTH CHEESE
James McIntyre

Weighing over 7,000 Pounds

We have seen the Queen of cheese,
Laying quietly at your ease,
Gently fanned by evening breeze—
Thy fair form no flies dare seize.

All gaily dressed soon you'll go
To the great Provincial Show,
To be admired by many a beau
In the City of Toronto.

Cows, numerous as a swarm of bees—
Or as leaves upon the trees—
It did require to make thee please,
And stand unrivalled Queen of Cheese.

May you not receive a scar as
We have heard that Mr. Harris
Intends to send you off as far as
The great World's show at Paris.

Of the youth—beware of these—
For some of them might rudely squeeze
And bite your cheek; then songs or glees
We could not sing o' Queen of Cheese.

We'rt thou suspended from balloon
You'd cast a shade, even at noon;
Folks would think it was the moon
About to fall and crush them soon.

"Ode on the Mammoth Cheese" has a special place in the hearts of
fanciers of inadvertently awful verse.

It was written with a straight face by James McIntyre
(1827–1906), Scottish-born casket-maker and poetaster and long-
time resident of Ingersoll, Ont. Over the years McIntyre composed
some eighteen poems on the subject of cheese-making, for, as he
noted, "About 800 Cheese factories are in operation in this
Province of Ontario." For this reason he was dubbed "the Cheese
Poet" by William Arthur Deacon in his tongue-in-cheek satire *The
Four Jameses* (1927, 1974).

The text of the "Ode" follows the one in McIntyre's book *Musings on the Banks of Canadian Thames* (1884). I am willing to bet the "mammoth cheese" was a great round of cheddar, a specialty of the cheese-makers of southern Ontario, then and now.

WHEN THE ICE WORMS NEST AGAIN
Unknown

There's a trusty husky maiden in the Arctic
And she waits for me but it is not in vain
For some day I'll put my mukluks on and ask her
If she'll wed me when the ice worms nest again
In the land of pale blue snow where it's ninety-nine below
And the polar bears are roaming o'er the plain
In the shadow of the Pole I will clasp her to my soul
We'll be married when the ice worms nest again.

For our wedding feast we'll have seal oil and blubber
In our kayak we will roam the bounding main
All the walruses will look at us and rubber
We'll be married when the ice worms nest again
When some night at half-past two I return to my igloo
After sitting with a friend who was in pain.
She'll be waiting for me there with the hambone of a bear
And she'll beat me till the ice worms nest again.

No one knows the name of the author of this amusing song, but the folklorist Edith Fowke called it "the most popular song of the far north" and hazarded a guess that its author was none other than Robert W. Service, the Bard of the Yukon. Certainly Service published a version of the lyrics in his collection *Bath-Tub Ballads* (1938), but the song was being sung in the Yukon at least two decades earlier.

It seems that newcomers to the Yukon were introduced to the "ice worm cocktail," and were fooled by pieces of spaghetti with red ink spots for eyes into believing they were worms that thrived in ice.

The text is taken from C. E. Gillham's *Raw North* (1947) where it is stated that the words and music were composed by Mona Symington, Marion Williamson, and Joyce Kolgan. Its authorship will only be known "when the ice worms nest again."

THERE ONCE WAS A YOUNG MAN OF QUEBEC

Rudyard Kipling

There once was a young man of Quebec
Who was frozen in snow to his neck,
   When asked, "Are your Friz?"
   He replied, "Yes, I is,
But we don't call this cold in Quebec."

Only in Canada is Rudyard Kipling regarded as the author of this limerick. To my knowledge, Kipling wrote no limericks; certainly not this one. Nor did Stephen Leacock (1869–1944) write limericks, except perhaps for this one.

The attribution to Kipling comes from Leacock's essay "Comic Verse: The Lighter Notes," in *Humour and Humanity: An Introduction to the Study of Humour* (1937).

IMERICKS

Traditional

An Eskimo in Athabasca
Let his igloo to friends from Alaska.
    When they asked if his spouse
    Went along with the house,
He replied, "I don't know, but I'll aska."

A tailor, who sailed from Quebec,
In a storm ventured once upon deck;
    But the waves of the sea
    Were as strong as could be,
And he tumbled in up to his neck.

A boy at Sault Ste. Marie
Said, "Spelling is all Greek to me.
    Till they learn to spell 'Soo'
    Without any 'u,'
Or an 'a' or an 'l' or a 't.'"

There was a young girl from Montreal
Who wore a newspaper dress to a ball.
    But her dress caught on fire
    And burnt her entire
Front page—sporting section and all.

These four limericks are traditional ones, collected from various sources, mainly oral. They are reprinted from the Anonymous section of *Colombo's Canadian Quotations* (1974).

RELATIVITY
A. H. Reginald Buller

There was a young lady named Bright
Whose speed was far faster than light;
   She set out one day
   In a relative way
And returned on the previous night.

"Relativity" appeared anonymously in the English humour weekly *Punch*, December 19, 1923. It is often called the most widely known "clean" limerick of all time.

    Following publication, authorship was claimed by A.H. Reginald Buller (1904–1936), Professor of Botany, University of Manitoba, an authority on fungi. Buller's claim of authorship is noted and presumably accepted by W. S. Baring-Gould in *The Lure of the Limerick* (1968).

—

AWAY WITH TUNICS
Sir Raymond Bell

Away with tunics, cocked hats, swords
In proof of stern endeavour
We'll wear (where Adam wore the fig)
The Maple Leaf for Ever.

"Away with Tunics" deserves a far happier fate than languishing unread in the back issue of a diplomatic journal.

It seems that a memo was circulated requiring consular officers to decline politely those foreign honours that might be offered them. This occurred while Lester B. Pearson was Minister of External Affairs (1946–48), and Pearson himself offered a bottle of spirits to the author of the best verse describing the memo.

Lord Garner, British High Commissioner in Ottawa (1956–61), writing in "Mike: An Englishman's View," *International Journal,* Winter 1973–74, identifies the author of the verse published here as Raymond Bell, a member of his staff, now Sir Raymond Bell. Sadly, Lord Garner does not tell us who won the bottle of spirits.

ON THE APPOINTMENT
OF GOVERNOR-GENERAL
VINCENT MASSEY, 1952

B. K. Sandwell

Let the Old World, where rank's yet vital,
Part those who have and have not title.
Toronto has no social classes—
Only the Masseys and the masses.

This undying ditty was drafted and directed by B. K. Sandwell (1876–1954) against the postures and pretensions of members of the Massey family, among whom numbered statesman Vincent Massey and actor Raymond Massey.

"On the Appointment . . ." first appeared in the first edition of *The Blasted Pine* (1957) edited by F. R. Scott and A. J. M. Smith.

A Church Seen in Canada
Theodore Spencer

Oh country doubly split! One way
Tugged eastward; one to U.S.A.:
One way tugged deep toward silver Rome;
One way scotched stubborn here at home;
What panacea for your ills?
(Le Sacré Coeur de Crabtree Mills.)

This squib was written by Theodore Spencer (1902–1949), Boylston Professor of Rhetoric and Oratory at Harvard, who summered in North Hatley in Quebec's Eastern Townships. "A Church Seen in Canada" appeared in Spencer's final collection *An Acre in the Seed* (1949).

"Though both the ephemeral and the lasting are continually brought to our attention," the poet wrote on another occasion, "it is the passing of the ephemeral that remains most vivid to us."

The Layman Turned Critic
Louis Dudek

Seeing an elephant, he sighed with bliss:
"What a wonderful nightingale this is!"

And of a mosquito he observed with a laugh,
"What a curious thing is this giraffe."

Louis Dudek (1918–2001) was a fine poet, critic, teacher, and aphorist.

He is the author of "The Layman Turned Critic" which first appeared in the anthology *The Blasted Pine* (1957) edited by F. R. Scott and A. J. M. Smith and then in his own collection *Laughing Stalks* (1958).

THE PROGRESS OF SATIRE
Louis Dudek

To F.R.S. and A.J.M.S.

Reading a dead poet
Who complained in his time
Against bad laws, bad manners,
And bad weather in bad rhyme,

I thought how glad he'd be
To be living in our time
To damn worse laws, worse manners,
And worse weather in worse rhyme.

F. R. Scott and A. J. M. Smith chose "The Progress of Satire" to be the epigraph to their anthology *The Blasted Pine* (1957; revised edition, 1967). Louis Dudek, who dedicated his poem to these two anthologists, has written one of those verses that never goes stale or out of date.

OH CANADA
John Robert Colombo

Canada could have enjoyed:
   English government,
      French culture,
         and American know-how.

Instead it ended up with:
   English know-how,
      French government,
         and American culture.

"Oh Canada" first appeared in Al Purdy's anthology *The New Romans* (1965). The verse remains ever-popular and ever-true.

ALLIGATOR PIE
Dennis Lee

Alligator pie, alligator pie,
If I don't get some I think I'm gonna die.
Give away the green grass, give away the sky,
But don't give away my alligator pie.

Alligator stew, alligator stew,
If I don't get some I don't what I'll do.
Give away my furry hat, give away my shoe,
But don't give way my alligator stew.

Alligator soup, alligator soup,
If I don't get some I think I'm gonna droop.
Give away my hockey-stick, give away my hoop,
But don't give away my alligator soup.

If there is a youngster in the country who cannot recite from memory with gusto and glee the words of the chant titled "Alligator Pie," that youngster is probably French-speaking.

The verse, rhyme, chant, song, or "versicle" first appeared in *Wiggle to the Laundromat* (1970). It became an instant classic in Dennis Lee's collection *Alligator Pie* (1974). What is interesting is that the "versicle" is composed of three four-line verses. If each verse were re-arranged in five lines, the work would consist of three five-line limericks.

THE WATER TRADER'S DREAM
Robert Priest

All the water traders
who trade in outer space
talk of a distant planet—
a magical, mystical place
that has seas and seas full of water,
sweet water beyond all worth.
They say that planet is green in the sun
and the name of that planet is Earth.

And the people there drink the water,
they dive and swim in it too.
It falls from the sky in water storms
and it comes in the morning as dew.
That sweet, sweet water is everywhere—
Sweet water! Sweet water of Earth!
And traders say that the people there
have no idea what it's worth.

So, the traders have their Earth dreams.
They dream of one silver cup
brought across space from the earthlings
for millions to drink it up.
"Sweet water! Sweet water! Sweet water of Earth!
The people there trade it for gold!
They've no idea what water's worth—
just look how much they've sold!"

They dream the dream of a water storm—
surely it would drive you mad
to have a wind-full of water flung in your face,
to sail in it like Sinbad!
Yes, they say there are whole oceans there
where waves break on the shore,
where winds leave water singing
and sunlight makes it roar!

They say that planet is green in the sun
and the people there call it Earth.

"The Water Trader's Dream" has been widely reprinted and anthologized in Canada and the United States. It was originally broadcast on CBC Radio and it is rebroadcast, it seems, whenever the issue arises of continental water sales (which is quite often).

The poem was written by poet and songwriter Robert Priest in 1981. It appears in his book *A Terrible Case of the Stars* (1994).

Our Home

and

Native Land

THERE IS A LAND
J. A. Ritchie

The wholesome Sea is at her gates,
    Her gates both East and West,
Then is it strange that we should love
    This Land, Our Land, the best?

These oddly affecting lines were composed by the Ottawa barrister and poetaster John Almon Ritchie (1863–1935). They are believed to be derived from his unpublished poem "There Is a Land" (1920).

The verse is notable as the source of the thirteen words that were inscribed in stone and placed over the main entranceway to the Centre Block, Parliament Buildings, Parliament Hill, Ottawa. The words are the following: "THE WHOLESOME SEA IS AT HER GATES . . . HER GATES BOTH EAST AND WEST."

The inscription dates from the reconstruction of the buildings in 1920, following the Great Fire of the previous year. The words and the lines are suggestive of the patriotism of Sir Walter Scott and the prosody of Rudyard Kipling.

TRANS CANADA
F. R. Scott

Pulled from our ruts by the made-to-order gale
We sprang upward into a wider prairie
And dropped Regina below like a pile of bones.

Sky tumbled upon us in waterfalls,
But we were smarter than a Skeena salmon
And shot our silver body over the lip of air
To rest in a pool of space
On the top storey of our adventure.

A solar peace
And a six-way choice.

Clouds, now, are the solid substance,
A floor of wool roughed by the wind
Standing in waves that halt in their fall.
A still of troughs.

The plane, our planet,
Travels on roads that are not seen or laid
But sound in instruments on pilots' ears,
While underneath
The sure wings
Are the everlasting arms of science.

Man, the lofty worm, tunnels his latest clay,
And bores his new career.

This frontier, too, is ours.
This everywhere whose life can only be led
At the pace of a rocket
Is common to man and man,
And every country below is an I land.

The sun sets on its top shelf,
And stars seem farther from our nearer grasp.

I have sat by night beside a cold lake
And touched things smoother than moonlight on still water,
But the moon on this cloud sea is not human,
And here is no shore, no intimacy,
Only the start of space, the road to suns.

F. R. Scott (1899–1985) wrote "Trans Canada" in 1943. The title refers to the national airline, Trans-Canada Air Lines (TCA), the predecessor of today's Air Canada. The poem is reprinted from *The Collected Poems of F. R. Scott* (1981).

CANADA: CASE HISTORY

Earle Birney

This is the case of a high-school land,
deadset in adolescence,
loud treble laughs and sudden fists,
bright cheeks, and gangling presence.
This boy is wonderful at sports
and physically quite healthy;
he's taken to church on Sunday still
and keeps his prurience stealthy.
He doesn't like books except about bears,
collects new coins and model planes
and never refuses a dare.
His Uncle spoils him with candy, of course,

yet shouts him down when he talks at table.
You will note he's got some of his French mother's looks,
though he's not so witty and no more stable.
He's really much more like his father and yet
if you say so he'll pull a great face.
He wants to be different from everyone else
and daydreams of winning the global race.
Parents unmarried and living abroad,
relatives keen to bag the estate,
schizophrenia not excluded,
will he learn to grow up before it's too late?

This satire remains quite popular and never seems to grow stale.
"Canada: Case History" was written by Earle Birney and appeared
in his collection *The Strait of Anian* (1948).

⟶

This Land Is Your Land

Woody Guthrie & The Travellers

This land is your land,
This land is my land,
From Bonavista
To the Vancouver Island,
From the Arctic Circle,
To the Great Lakes waters,
This land was made for you and me.

Le plus cher pays
De toute la terre,
C'est notre pays,
Nous sommes tout frères
D l'Île Vancouver
Jusqu'à Terre-Neuve,
C'est le Canada, c'est notre pays.

When the sun came shining
And I was strolling
And the wheatfields waving
and the dust clouds rolling,
As the thought was living
A voice was chanting, saying,
This land was made for you and me.

This land is your land,
This land is my land,
From Bonavista
To the Vancouver Island,
From the Arctic Circle,
To the Great Lakes waters,
This land was made for you and me.

"This Land Is Your Land" was composed in 1956 by the American singer-songwriter Woody Guthrie (1912–1967). The composer generously encouraged composers and arrangers of other countries to create their own "national" versions.

This invitation was accepted by Martin Bochner, manager of The Travellers, who arranged the Canadian version (complete with one stanza in French). The song became identified with his group, formed in 1954, which consisted of five singers and musicians from Toronto. The Travellers was the first group in English Canada to perform topical and patriotic songs since the Second World War.

FROM COLONY TO NATION

Irving Layton

A dull people,
but the rivers of this country
are wide and beautiful

A dull people
enamoured of childish games,
but food is easily come by
and plentiful

Some with a priest's voice
in their cage of ribs: but
on high mountain-tops and in thunderstorms
the chirping is not heard

Deferring to beadle and censor;
not ashamed for this,
but given over to horseplay,
the making of money

A dull people, without charm
or ideas,
settling into the clean empty look
of a Mountie or dairy farmer
as into a legacy

One can ignore them
(the silences, the vast distances help)
and suppose them at the bottom
of one of the meaner lakes,
their bones not even picked for souvenirs.

Irving Layton exposes and excoriates the meaness and leanness of the Canadian spirit in "From Colony to Nation" which first appeared in his collection *Music on a Kazoo* (1956).

SONG FOR CANADA
Ian Tyson & Peter Gzowski

How come we can't talk to each other any more?
Why can't you see I'm changing too?
We've got by far too long to end it feeling wrong
And I still share too much with you.

Just one great river always flowing to the sea.
One single river flowing in eternity.
Two nations in the land that lies along each shore
But just one river rolling free.

How come you shut me up as if I wasn't there?
What's this new bitterness you've found?
However wronged you were, however strong it hurt,
It wasn't me that hurled you down.

Just one great river always flowing to the sea.
One single river flowing in eternity.
Two nations in the land that lies along each shore
But just one river rolling free.

Why can't you understand? I'm glad you're standing proud;
I know you made it on your own,
But in this pride you earned, I thought you might have learned
That you don't have to stand alone.

Just one great river always flowing to the sea.
One single river flowing in eternity.
Two nations in the land that lies along each shore
But just one river rolling free.

Lonely northern rivers
Come together till you see
One single river rolling in eternity;
Two nations in the land
That lies along each shore
But just one river, you and me.

The mournful words and heartbreaking melody of "Song for Canada" were written by Peter Gzowski (1934–2002) and Ian Tyson in 1965. The song is an English-Canadian lament for the failure of the English and the French in Canada to understand and respect one another.

It was recorded by Ian and Sylvia Tyson for their album *Early Morning Rain* (1965). Once heard, it is not easily forgotten. According to Stephen Cole, writing in "Yo, Canada," *National Post,* April 12, 2001, Bob Dylan recorded a version of the song as part of "The Basement Tapes" in 1966, but it was not included on their official release in 1975.

CA-NA-DA
Bobby Gimby

CA-NA-DA
One little two little three Canadians
We love Thee
Now we are Twenty Million
CA-NA-DA
Four little five little six little Provinces
Proud and Free
Now we are ten and the Territories Sea to Sea
North, South, East, West
There'll be Happy Times
Church Bells will Ring, Ring, Ring
It's the Hundredth Anniversary of Confederation
Ev'rybody Sing, together
CA-NA-DA
Un petit deux petits trois Canadiens
Notre pays
Maintenant nous sommes vingt millions
CA-NA-DA

Quatre petites cinq petites six petites Provinces
Longue vie
Et nous sommes dix plus les Territories longue vie
Hurrah, Vive le Canada!
Three cheers, Hip, Hip, Horray! Le Centenaire!
That's the order of the day
Merrily we roll along
Together, all the way.

The lyrics of "CA-NA-DA" recall the high spirits kindled by the Centennial of Confederation that was celebrated throughout the summer months of the year 1967. Montreal's Expo 67 and Ottawa's July the First anniversary celebrations marked what Pierre Berton has referred to as "Canada's last good year." Since then, it seems, the country has been plagued with problems, togetherness being but one of them.

The words and music of "CA-NA-DA" were composed as the theme for *Preview '67*, a Centennial promotional film released in spring 1966, by trumpeter and bandleader Bobby Gimby (1921–1998). In the guise of Pied Piper, he crossed and recrossed the country performing it, leading choirs of children and adults in an uncharacteristic display of enthusiasm.

Judy LaMarsh, then the federal minister in charge of the anniversary celebrations, wrote in *Bird in a Gilded Cage* (1969): "There had been no original intention of selecting a popular Centennial song, but when 'CA-NA-DA' was put forward, it proved to be so bright and sparkly it was quickly accepted. It was the only thing associated with the Centennial Commission, so far as I am aware, that was not chosen by a committee after a contest."

I AM CANADIAN

Michael Smith & David Swaine

I'm not a lumberjack or a fur trader.
I don't live in an igloo, eat blubber, or own a dogsled.
I don't know Jimmy, Suzie, or Sally from Canada,
although I'm certain they're very nice.
I have a prime minister, not a president.
I speak English and French, not American.
And I pronounce it "about" not "a-boot."
I can proudly sew my country's flag on my backpack.
I believe in peacekeeping not policing; diversity not assimilation.
And that the beaver is a truly proud and noble animal.
A tuque is a hat, a chesterfield is a couch.
And it's pronounced "zed." Okay? not "zee." Zed.
Canada is the second-largest land mass, the first nation of
     hockey,
and the best part of North America!

My name is Joe and I am Canadian!

It might seem strange to offer the readers of a book of poetry the
text of a television commercial (and a beer commercial at that). Yet
the open-minded reader will respond to the power of the words that
express a human need to affirm an identity in the face of ignorance
or indifference. Here is the rhetorical power of declamation. One
thinks of impassioned poems in the same vein written by
Christopher Smart, Ebenezer Elliot, and Vachel Lindsay.
     The text of "I Am Canadian" takes the form of a monologue
delivered by a roughly dressed young man (actor Jeff Douglas),

who carries on about American misconceptions of Canada and Canadians. His patriotic sentiments are expressed with pride tinted with irony.

The press has dubbed the commercial "the sixty-second rant." It is one in a series of "I Am Canadian" commercials prepared to promote Molson's Canadian lager beer. The series was created for Molson Breweries of Canada by the advertising agency Bensimon Byrne D'Arcy and launched on television on March 17, 2000, in movie theatres on March 27, and thereafter through live-with-video auditorium performances before hockey games.

The series was conceived by art director Michael Smith and writer David Swaine and directed by Kevin Donovan.

THE MIGHTY BUCK, THE IMMIGRANT FUCK, AND MELTING POT LUCK
Raymond Filip

Right off the boat, or Boeing,
I admit being tongue-tied.
For I am the language that is lost,
The name that is changed,
The ghost of welcome houses and Saturday schools.
I am men in sheepskin coats from the Old Country;
I am their New Country descendants: women in Persian lamb.
I am Euro-paeans:
Songs you won't sing and dances you won't dance.
I am hard money.
I am the inalienable right to alienation.
The Horatio Alger Algerian, the Haitian electrician,

The Cuban security guard, the cab driver from Calabria,
The Jewish landlord who lives in Florida,
The Vietnamese orphan, the Romany musician.
I am Hutterite, Mennonite, Wahabite, Bahai, Sikh, and
Alcoholic.
I am the Canadian Mosaic: a melting pot on ice.
I am always the next generation,
The child with which good immigrant fiction ends.
I am that child grown up, writing in English,
Mother tongue in mind, adopted tongue in cheek.
You were Commonwealth, I am common loss.
Like a citizen of the world, in exile,
Or an overseas package returned to sender,
I am nothing left to be but Canadian.

Raymond Filip, born in Italy, is a Canadian who lives in Montreal
and writes in English.

I enjoy rereading his poem "The Mighty Buck," etc., because I
feel it expresses what a great many citizens and non-citizens, both
native-born and foreign-born, who live in Canada today, feel about
this country. As well, the language is inventive and the tone is suit-
ably edgy!

The poem is reprinted from Filip's collection *Somebody Told
Me I Look like Everyman* (1978).

CANADIANS
Miriam Waddington

Here are
our signatures:
geese, fish, eskimo
faces, girl-guide
cookies, ink-drawings
tree-plantings, summer
storms and winter
emanations.

We look
like a geography but
just scratch us
and we bleed
history, are full
of modest misery
are sensitive
to double-talk double-take
(and double-cross)
in a country
too wide
to be single in.

Are we real or
did someone invent
us, was it Henry
Hudson Etienne Brûlé
or a carnival
of village girls?
Was it
a flock of nuns
a pity of indians
a gravyboat of
fur-traders, professional
explorers or those
amateur map-makers
our Fathers
of Confederation?

Wherever you are
Charles Tupper Alexander
Galt D'Arcy McGee George
Cartier Ambrose Shea
Henry Crout Father
Ragueneau Lord Selkirk
and John A.—however
far into northness
you have walked—
when we call you
turn around and
don't look so surprised.

This shining poem radiates the spirit and energy of the country. Paragraphs would be required to identify the references, yet the details are incidental to the whole because the poem's power and direction are apparent through the poet's uninhibited and unabashed enthusiasm for the particulars of Canada's history, society, and culture.

"Canadians" was written by Miriam Waddington in 1968, in the aftermath of the celebrations that marked Canada's Centennial. It appeared in her collection *Driving Home: Poems New and Selected* (1972).

Sources

and

Permissions

Herein appear the sources and acknowledgements of the contents of this anthology. Unless otherwise noted, standard source information has been provided. The acknowledgements are as complete as possible. Every reasonable effort has been made to acknowledge the holders of the copyrights of the following literary compositions.

—

With Glowing Hearts

"God Save the King (Queen)": Percy A. Scholes, *The Oxford Companion to Music* (9th edition, 1956). Hansard, Feb. 16, 1968.

"Dieu Protège Notre Reine (Roi)": Hansard, Feb. 16, 1968.

"O Canada" (English): Hansard, June 27, 1980.

"O Canada" (French): Hansard, June 27, 1980.

"O Canada!": R. Stanley Weir, "O Canada!" *After Ypres and Other Verse* (Toronto: The Musson Book Co., Limited, 1917).

"The Maple Leaf for Ever": Alexander Muir's lyrics first appeared in 1867; later, composite version reprinted from *Colombo's Book of Canada* (1978, 1998), edited by John Robert Colombo.

—

The True North

"Song": Words of Uvavnuk recorded in Inuktitut in the Arctic by Knud Rasmussen and translated from his Danish into English by W. Worster; published in Rasmussen's *Intellectual Culture of the Iglulik Eskimos: Report of the Fifth Thule Expedition 1921–24* (1929).

"The Song of the Stars": Traditional song of the Passamaquoddy on Campbello Island, N.B., transcribed and translated from the Algonkian by Charles G. Leland in 1882 and published in Leland's *The Algonquin Legends of New England; or Myths and Folk Lore of the Micmac, Passamaquoddy, and Penobscot Tribes* (1884).

"Jacques Cartier": Thomas D'Arcy McGee, *The Poems of Thomas D'Arcy McGee* (1869) edited by Mrs. Mary Anne Sadlier.

"Northwest Passage": Copyright © 1981. Stan Rogers' lyrics are reprinted from Chris Gudgeon's *An Unfinished Conversation: The Life and Music of Stan Rogers* (Toronto: Viking, 1993, out of print). All songs written by Stan Rogers (SOCAN)—used by permission of Fogarty's Cove Music and Ariel Rogers.

"An Anti-Confederation Song" (Traditional): The full text of this song, which first appeared in *Old-Time Poetry and Songs of Newfoundland* (1940) edited by Gerald S. Doyle, is reprinted from *Canada's Story in Song* (Toronto: W.J. Gage Limited, 1960) edited by Edith Fowke and Alan Mills.

"The Riders of the Plains" (Unknown): "The Riders of the Plains" appeared anonymously in the columns of the *Saskatchewan Herald* (Battleford, Sask.), Sept. 23, 1878, and is reprinted from *Wake the Prairie Echoes: The Mounted Police Story in Verse* (Saskatoon: Western Producer Book Service, 1973) collected by the Saskatchewan History and Folklore Society.

"A Psalm of Montreal": Samuel Butler, "A Psalm of Montreal," *The Spectator,* May 18, 1878; the text is taken from *The Note-Books of Samuel Butler* (1926) edited by Henry Festing Jones.

"Our Lady of the Snows": Rudyard Kipling's verse first appeared in the London Times, April 27, 1897; the text is reprinted from *Rudyard Kipling's Verse: Definitive Edition* (1940, 1966).

"The Royal Tour": James Reaney, *The Red Heart* (1949); the text is taken from Reaney's *Poems* (Toronto: New Press, 1972) edited by Germaine Warkentin. Reprinted by permission of James Reaney and Livingston Cooke/Curtis Brown Canada.

Cries of Battle

"The Great Peace": Traditional attribution to Dekanahwideh; reprinted from Paul A.W. Wallace, *The White Roots of Peace* (1946).

"Brave Wolfe" (Traditional): Reprinted from *Ballads and Sea-Songs of Newfoundland* (Cambridge, Mass.: Harvard University Press, 1933) edited by Elizabeth B. Greenleaf and Grace Y. Mansfield.

"Come All You Bold Canadians" (Traditional): The ballad first appeared in *Shantymen and Shantyboys* (New York: The Macmillan Co., 1951) edited by W.M. Doerflinger; the text is reprinted from *Singing Our History* (Toronto: Doubleday, 1984), edited by Edith Fowke.

"The Chesapeake and the Shannon" (Traditional): The ballad first appeared in *Ballads and Sea-Songs from Nova Scotia* (Cambridge, Mass.: Harvard University Press, 1928) edited by Roy W. Mackenzie; the text is reprinted from *Folk Songs of Canada* (Waterloo: Waterloo Music Company Limited, 1954) edited by Edith Fowke and Richard Johnston.

"The Battle of Queenston Heights" (Traditional): The lyrics appear in *Canada's Story in Song* (Toronto: W.J. Gage Limited, 1960) edited by Edith Fowke and Alan Mills. Fowke suggests that the lyrics were written to mark the occasion of the unveiling of Brock's Monument in 1824. Alan Mills wrote the folk-style music.

"Brock": Charles Sangster, *Hesperus and Other Poems and Lyrics* (1860).

"MacDonnell on the Heights": Stan Rogers, composed in 1984, recorded on his album *From Fresh Water* (1982). The lyrics are reprinted from Chris Gudgeon's *An Unfinished Conversation: The Life and Music of Stan Rogers* (Toronto: Viking, 1993, out of print). All songs written by Stan Rogers (SOCAN)—used by permission of Fogarty's Cove Music and Ariel Rogers.

"1838": Dennis Lee, *Nicholas Knock and Other People* (Toronto: Macmillan, 1974). Reprinted by permission of Westwood Creative Artists.

"Memorial Chamber Inscription": Rudyard Kipling, *Rudyard Kipling's Verse: Definitive Edition* (1940, 1966).

"Epitaphs on the War": 1914–18: Rudyard Kipling, *Rudyard Kipling's Verse: Definitive Edition* (1940).

"In Flanders Fields": John McCrae, *In Flanders Fields and Other Poems* (1919) edited by Sir Andrew Macphail.

"High Flight": There are numerous versions of John Gillespie Magee's poem. The version here appears in Linda Granfield's *High Flight: A World War II Story* (Montreal: Tundra Books, 1999) illustrated by Michael Martchenko.

"This Was My Brother": Mona Gould, *Tasting the Earth* (Toronto: Macmillan, 1943). Reprinted with permission of the Estate and Maria Gould.

—

Seas and Ships

"A Canadian Boat Song": Thomas Moore, *Epistles, Odes and Other Poems* (1806).

"Canadian Boat-Song" (from the Gaelic): David Macbeth Moir is the likely author, according to the scholar G.H. Needler, *The Lone Shieling* (1941). See also Hubert G. Mayes, "A Very Affectin' Thing': The Scottish Origin of the *Canadian Boat Song*," *The Beaver*, April–May 1991.

"The Song My Paddle Sings": Pauline Johnson, *The White Wampum* (1895); reprinted from *Flint and Feather: The Complete Poems of Pauline Johnson (Tekahionwake)* (Toronto: Hodder & Stoughton, 1917).

"The Ships of Yule": Bliss Carman, *Bliss Carman's Poems* (Toronto: McClelland and Stewart, 1929). The poem was written as early as 1909.

"The Shark": E.J. Pratt, *Newfoundland Verse* (1923); reprinted from *The Collected Poems of E.J. Pratt* (Toronto: Macmillan Company of Canada Limited, 2nd ed., 1958), edited by Northrop Frye. Reprinted by permission of the University of Toronto Press, publishers of E.J. Pratt's *Selected Poems* (2000).

Places Far and Near

"Something to Sing About": Oscar Brand, words and music composed in 1963; numerous versions exist. TRO—copyright © 1963. Renewed, 1964. Renewed Hollis Music, Inc., New York, N.Y. Reprinted by permission of Oscar Brand.

"The Ode to Newfoundland": Composed by Sir Cavendish Boyle and first performed in St. John's, Newfoundland, Jan. 21, 1902; the text is reprinted from J.R. Smallwood's *The Book of Newfoundland* (1937).

"Let Me Fish off Cape St. Mary's": Composed by Otto P. Kelland. Text based on the composer's website, January 2002. Permission requested through Creative Book Publishing. Reprinted by permission.

"Farewell to Nova Scotia" (Traditional): Recorded by Helen Creighton in the 1930s in the Petpeswick and Chezzetcook districts near Halifax, Nova Scotia. She included it in her collection *Traditional Songs from Nova Scotia* (1950). The version here is reproduced from *Folk Songs of Canada* (Waterloo: Waterloo Music Company Limited, 1954) edited by Edith Fowke and Richard Johnston.

"Low Tide on Grand Pré": Bliss Carman, *Low Tide on Grand Pré* (1893). It is reprinted from *Bliss Carman's Poems* (Toronto: McClelland & Stewart, 1929).

"The Saint John": George Frederick Clarke, *The Saint John and Other Poems* (Toronto: The Ryerson Press, 1933).

"The Island Hymn": L.M. Montgomery wrote the lyrics in 1908. The text is taken from John Kendall's article "Fair Island of the Sea," *The Island Magazine*, Fall–Winter, 1999. A local choir sings "The Island Hymn" on the multi-media CD of L.M. Montgomery's work titled *The Bend in the Road* (released by the L.M. Montgomery Institute).

"The Island": Milton Acorn, *I've Tasted My Blood* (Toronto: McGraw-Hill Ryerson, 1969). Reprinted by permission.

"The Country North of Belleville": Al Purdy, *The Cariboo Horses* (1965). The text is reprinted from *The Collected Poems of Al Purdy* (Toronto: McClelland and Stewart, 1986) edited by Russell Brown. Reprinted by permission of Howard White of Harbour Publishing.

"Sudbury Saturday Night": Tom Connors's lyrics are reprinted from *Listen! Songs and Poems of Canada* (Toronto: Methuen, 1972) edited by Homer Hogan and Dorothy Hogan. Words and music by Tom Connors © Crown Vetch Music / Used by permission.

"A Place to Stand": Richard Morris (words) and Doloris Claman (music) wrote this song for the short documentary film *A Place to Stand*, produced by David Mackay, directed by Christopher Chapman, commissioned by the Ontario Government for the Ontario Pavilion at Expo 67.

"Red River Valley" (Traditional): There are innumerable versions of the lyrics; this version also appears in Ralph L. Woods's *A Second Treasury of the Familiar* (N.Y.: The Macmillan Company, 1950). Slightly different lyrics appear in *Canada Sings: Community Song Book for Schools, Clubs, Fraternities, Homes, and Community Singing* (Toronto: Gordon V. Thompson Limited, 1983) edited by Hugo Frey, where the attribution is to N.E. Pearson.

"Saskatchewan": Lyrics composed to a popular tune by William W. Smith in the 1930s. The text appears in Edith Fowke and Alan Mills's *Canada's Story in Song* (Toronto: W.J. Gage Limited, 1960).

"Twilight on the Prairie": Wilf Carter. Copyright © Gordon V. Thompson Limited, 1933. Permission requested.

"Farewell to Alberta" (Traditional): "Farewell to Alberta" is often sung to the traditional tune of "The Irish Washerwoman." The text is reprinted from *Canada's Story in Song* (Toronto: W.J. Gage Limited, 1960) edited by Edith Fowke and Alan Mills. Fowke recorded it from the lips of traditional singer Ivan Brandick in the early 1950s.

"The Double-Headed Snake": John Newlove, *Black Night Window* (Toronto: McClelland & Stewart, 1968). *Black Night Window* by John Newlove. Used by permission, McClelland & Stewart Ltd., *The Canadian Publishers*.

"The Athabasca Trail": Sir Arthur Conan Doyle recited this verse at the conclusion of his address to the members of the Canadian Club of Ottawa, July 2, 1914.

"The Shooting of Dan McGrew": Robert W. Service, *Songs of a Sourdough* (1907), published in the United States as *The Spell of the Yukon*. Used by permission Estate of Robert Service c/o M. Wm. Krasilovsky, Agent.

"The Cremation of Sam McGee": Robert W. Service, *Songs of a Sourdough* (1907), published in the United States as *The Spell of the Yukon*. Used by permission of the Estate of Robert Service c/o M. Wm. Krasilovsky, Agent.

"Laurentian Shield": F.R. Scott, *The Collected Poems of F.R. Scott* (Toronto: McClelland and Stewart, 1981). The poem was written in 1945. Reprinted with the permission of William Toye, literary executor for the Estate of F.R. Scott.

"The Lonely Land": A.J.M. Smith, *Collected Poems* (Toronto: Oxford University Press, 1962). The poem was first published in the magazine *Poetry* (Chicago) in 1926. Reprinted with the permission of William Toye, literary executor for the Estate of A.J.M. Smith.

La Belle Province

"A la Claire Fontaine" (Traditional): Collected by folklorist Ernest Gagnon and reprinted from *Canadian Folk Songs (Old and New)* (Toronto: J.M. Dent & Sons, 1927).

"At the Clear Running Fountain" (English): Folksong translated by J. Murray Gibbon and reprinted from *Canadian Folk Songs (Old and New)* (Toronto: J.M. Dent & Sons, 1927).

"Alouette!" (Traditional): The words and music appear in J. Murray Gibbon's *Canadian Folk Songs (Old and New)* (Toronto: J.M. Dent & Sons, 1927).

"Vive la Canadienne!" (Traditional): Words and music appear in J. Murray Gibbon's *Canadian Folk Songs (Old and New)* (1927).

"Vive la Canadienne!" (English): The translation was prepared by Edith Fowke for *The Penguin Book of Canadian Folk Songs* (1973).

"Un Canadien Errant": Words and music of Antoine Gérin-Lajoie's lament appear in J. Murray Gibbon's *Canadian Folk Songs (Old and New)* (Toronto: J.M. Dent & Sons, 1927).

"From His Canadian Home" (English): Translation of Antoine Gérin-Lajoie's lament is taken from J. Murray Gibbon's *Canadian Folk Songs: Old and New* (1927).

"The Wreck of the "Julie Plante": William Henry Drummond, *Dr. W.H. Drummond's Complete Poems* (Toronto: McClelland & Stewart, 1926).

"Little Bateese": William Henry Drummond, *Dr. W.H. Drummond's Complete Poems* (Toronto: McClelland & Stewart, 1926).

"Bonne Entente": F.R. Scott, *Events and Signals* (1954). The text is taken from *The Collected Poems of F.R. Scott* (Toronto: McClelland and Stewart, 1981). Reprinted with the permission of William Toye, literary executor for the Estate of F.R. Scott.

"Mon Pays": Gilles Vigneault, *Avec les vieux mots* (Montréal: Nouvelles Editions de l'ARC, 1965). Reprinted by permission of Les Editions le vent qui vire.

"My Country" (English): Translation of Gilles Vigneault's poem by Alexandre L. Amprimoz, first published in John Robert Colombo's *The Poets of Canada* (Edmonton: Hurtig Publishers, 1978). Les Nouvelles Editions d l'Arc.

"Gens du Pays" (Chant d'anniversaire): Gilles Vigneault, "Gens du Pays" copyright © Nouvelle Editions d l'ARC, Montreal. Reprinted by permission of Les Editions le vent qui vive.

"People of the Land" (Anniversary Song) (English): Translation of Gilles Vigneault's poem by Alexandre L. Amprimoz, first published in John Robert Colombo's *Colombo's Book of Canada* (Edmonton: Hurtig Publishers, 1978).

Nature and Weather

"How One Winter Came in the Lake District": William Wilfred Campbell, *Lake Lyrics and Other Poems* (St. John, N.B.: J. & A. McMillan, 1889).

"Heat": Archibald Lampman, *Among the Millet and Other Poems* (1888); reprinted from *The Poems of Archibald Lampman* (Toronto: The Musson Book Company Limted, 1900) edited by Duncan Campbell Scott.

"Indian Summer": William Wilfred Campbell, written in 1881–83, and reprinted from *Songs of the Great Dominion* (London: Walter Scott, 1889), edited by William Douw Lighthall.

"The Song of the Ski": Wilson MacDonald, *Out of the Wilderness* (Ottawa: Graphic Publishers Ltd., 1926). Permission requested.

"Song to the Four Seasons": Paul Hiebert, *Sarah Binks* (Toronto: Oxford University Press, 1947).

"Song to the Four Seasons" from *Sarah Binks* by Paul Hiebert. Copyright © Oxford University Press, Canada. Reprinted by permission of Oxford University Press Canada.

"Snowbird": Gene MacLellan, composed in 1967, reprinted from Edith Fowke's *Canadian Vibrations Canadiennes* (Toronto: Macmillan of Canada, 1972). Copyright © 1970 by Beechwood Music of Canada. Permission requested.

"Forty Below": Christopher Dafoe, composed and first printed in 1959, as noted by Dafoe, "Part of the Oral Tradition," *The Beaver,* Feb.–March 1993. Reprinted by permission of the author.

"Canadian Love": Marie-Lynn Hammond, composed in 1985, text reproduced from the composer's website, 2000. Lyrics and music copyright © 1982 by Marie-Lynn Hammond. Reprinted by permission of the composer.

Longing for Love

"When You and I Were Young, Maggie": George W. Johnson, *Maple Leaves* (1864). The text of "When You and I Were Young, Maggie" is reprinted from an undated but early songsheet; a slightly different version was included by Ralph L. Woods in *A Treasury of the Familiar* (N.Y.: The Macmillan Company, 1942).

"In the Shade of the Old Apple Tree": Harry H. Williams, composed in 1905, words reproduced from *A Third Treasury of the Familiar* (N.Y.: The Macmillan Company, 1970), edited by Ralph L. Woods.

"The Poor Little Girls of Ontario" (Traditional): Edith Fowke recorded this popular song as sung by Mrs. Harley Minifie, Peterborough, in 1957; the text is taken from *Canada's Story in Song* (Toronto: W.J. Gage Limited, 1960) edited by Edith Fowke and Alan Mills.

"O Rose-Marie": Words by Otto Harbach and Oscar Hammerstein II, music by Rudolf Friml, from the Broadway operetta *Rose-Marie* (1924).

"From the Hazel Bough": Earle Birney, composed 1945–47, text taken from *The Poems of Earle Birney* (Toronto: McClelland & Stewart, 1969). *Selected Poems* by Earle Birney. Used by permission, McClelland & Stewart Ltd. *The Canadian Publishers*.

"Song for Naomi": Irving Layton, *A Red Carpet for the Sun* (1959); text reprinted from *Collected Poems* (Toronto: McClelland and Stewart Limited, 1965). *Collected Poems* by Irving Layton. Used by permission, McClelland & Stewart Ltd. *The Canadian Publishers*.

"First Person Demonstrative": Phyllis Gotlieb, *Ordinary Moving* (1969); text reprinted from *The Works: Collected Poems* (Toronto: Calliope Press, 1978). Reprinted by permission of the author.

"As the Mist Leaves No Scar": Leonard Cohen, *Selected Poems, 1956–1968* (Toronto: McClelland and Stewart Limited, 1968). *Stranger Music* by Leonard Cohen. Used by permission, McClelland & Stewart Ltd. *The Canadian Publishers*.

"Suzanne Takes You Down": Leonard Cohen, *Selected Poems 1956–1968* (Toronto: McClelland and Stewart Limited, 1968). *Stranger Music* by Leonard Cohen. Used by permission, McClelland & Stewart Ltd. *The Canadian Publishers.*

"Leonard Cohen's Never Gonna Bring My Groceries In": Nancy White, *Momnipotent: Songs for Weary Parents* (Multinan, 1990). Nancy White copyright © 1990 Multinan Inc. Reprinted by permission of Nancy White.

—

Devotion and Remembrance

"Huron Christmas Carol": Jean de Brébeuf, composed as "Jesous Ahatonhia" (Huron for "Jesus, he is born") in French about 1641; translated as "Huron Christmas Carol" by J.E. Middleton. A literal English translation of the original Huron text, prepared by the scholar John Steckley, appears in *Colombo's Book of Canada* (1978). An English version via the French translation appears in *The Poets of Canada* (1978), edited by John Robert Colombo. Originally published by the Frederick Harris Music Co. Ltd. Limited.

"What a Friend We Have in Jesus": Joseph Medlicott Scriven, *What a Friend We Have in Jesus and Other Hymns by Joseph Scriven with a Sketch of the Author* (1895) written by the Rev. Jas. Cleland.

"A Little While": Attributed to Crowfoot by John Peter Turner in *The North-West Mounted Police: 1873–1893* (1950). The actual source is a fictional one: Sir H. Rider Haggard's novel *King Solomon's Mines* (1885), once-popular, frequently filmed adventure novel, written by the English novelist Sir H. Rider Haggard. This fact was established by historian Robert S. Carslie, "Crowfoot's Dying Speech," *Alberta History*, Summer 1990.

"The Largest Life": Archibald Lampman, *The Poems of Archibald Lampman* (1900) edited by Duncan Campbell Scott.

"In the Wide Awe and Wisdom of the Night": Charles G.D. Roberts, *Songs of the Common Day* (1893); the text is taken from *Sir Charles G.D. Roberts: Selected Poems* (Toronto: The Ryerson Press, 1955) edited by Desmond Pacey.

"The Twenty-fourth of May" (Traditional): Sara Jeannette Duncan's novel *The Imperialist* (1904). Père Lalemant: Marjorie Pickthall, *The Drift of Pinions* (1913); text reprinted from *The Selected Poems of Marjorie Pickthall* (1957) edited by Lorne Pierce.

"Vestigia": Bliss Carman, composed in 1920, reprinted from *Bliss Carman's Poems* (Toronto: McClelland & Stewart, 1929).

"Change": Raymond Knister, *Collected Poems* (1949) edited by Dorothy Livesay.

"On Seeing the Statuettes of Ezekiel and Jeremiah in the Church of Notre Dame": Irving Layton, *Collected Poems* (Toronto: McClelland and Stewart Limited, 1965). *Collected Poems* by Irving Layton. Used by permission, McClelland & Stewart Ltd. *The Canadian Publishers.*

"O Great Spirit": Chief Dan George, prayer recited on CBC-TV's *Telescope,* Sept. 7, 1970.

"Tears Are Not Enough": Words by Bryan Adams and Jim Vallance; title by Bob Rock and Paul Hyde; music by David Foster. Recorded by Northern Lights for African Society by performing artists on Feb. 10–11, 1985; the lyrics appear in *Who Speaks for Canada?* (Toronto: McClelland & Stewart Inc., 1998), edited by Desmond Morton and Morton Weinfeld. Warner-Chappell and United Way of the Lower Mainland, B.C. Reprinted courtesy United Way of the Lower Mainland, B.C.

"Footprints": Margaret Fishback Powers, composed Thanksgiving Day, Oct. 11, 1964, at Echo Lake Youth Camp, Kingston, Ont.; the text is reproduced from Powers's book *A Heart for Children: Inspirations for Parents & Their Children* (Toronto: HarperCollins Publishers Ltd., 1995). Permission requested.

People on the Land

"I Am a Canadian": Duke Redbird, composed for the celebration of H.R.H. Queen Elizabeth's Silver Jubilee, Ottawa, Oct. 17, 1977; reprinted by permission of Duke Redbird; text taken from *I Am a Canadian* (Toronto: Wacacro Productions Inc., n.d.) by permission of the author.

"The Red Men": Charles Sangster, "The Red Men—A Sonnet," *Selections from Canadian Poets* (1864) edited by Edward Hartley Dewart.

"The Walker of the Snow": Charles Dawson Shanly, *The Atlantic Monthly*, May 1859. The version reprinted here is taken from the pages of that magazine (where it appeared anonymously) and not from its later appearance in the anthology *Songs of the Great Dominion* (London: Walter Scott, 1889), edited by William Douw Lighthall.

"We Live in a Rickety House": Alexander McLachlan, *The Immigrant and Other Poems* (1861).

"The Forsaken": Duncan Campbell Scott, *New World Lyrics and Ballads* (1905); text reprinted from *The Poems of Duncan Campbell Scott* (1926).

"At the Cedars": Duncan Campbell Scott, *The Magic House* (1893); text printed from *Selected Poems of Duncan Campbell Scott* (Toronto: The Ryerson Press, 1954).

"The Onondaga Madonna": Duncan Campbell Scott, *Labour and the Angel* (1893); text reprinted from *Selected Poems of Duncan Campbell Scott* (Toronto: The Ryerson Press, 1954).

"On the Way to the Mission": Duncan Campbell Scott, *New World Lyrics and Ballads* (1905); text reprinted from *Selected Poems of Duncan Campbell Scott* (Toronto: The Ryerson Press, 1954).

"Paul Bunyan": Arthur S. Bourinot, *Ten Narrative Poems* (Ottawa: The Author, 1955). Reprinted by permission of Esme Bourinot Lewis through John G. Aylen.

"Tom Thomson": Arthur S. Bourinot, *Ten Narrative Poems* (Ottawa: The Author, 1955). Reprinted by permission of Esme Bourinot Lewis through John G. Aylen.

"Erosion": E.J. Pratt, *The Iron Door* (1927); text reprinted from *The Collected Poems of E.J. Pratt* (2nd ed., 1958) edited by Northrop Frye. Reprinted by permission of the University of Toronto Press, publishers of E.J. Pratt's *Selected Poems* (2000).

"The Browns": Audrey Alexandra Brown, *A Dryad in Nanaimo* (Toronto: Macmillan Company of Canada Ltd., 1931). Reprinted by permission of Wilma E. Brown.

"Political Meeting": A.M. Klein, *The Rocking Chair and Other Poems* (1948); text reprinted from *The Collected Poems of A.M. Klein* (Toronto: McGraw-Hill Ryerson Limited, 1974), compiled by Miriam Waddington. A.M. Klein, *Selected Poems,* University of Toronto Press (1997). Reprinted with permission of the publisher.

"W.L.M.K.": F.R. Scott, *The Eye of the Needle* (1957); text reprinted from *The Collected Poems of F.R. Scott* (Toronto: McClelland and Stewart, 1981). Reprinted with the permission of William Toye, literary executor for the Estate of F.R. Scott.

"The Poet Confides": H.T.J. Coleman, *The Poet Confides* (Toronto: The Ryerson Press, 1928).

"The Canadian Authors Meet": F.R. Scott, Overture (1945); text reprinted from *The Collected Poems of F.R. Scott* (Toronto: McClelland and Stewart, 1981). Reprinted with the permission of William Toye, literary executor for the Estate of F.R. Scott.

"Flight of the Roller-Coaster": Raymond Souster, *The Colour of the Times* (Toronto: The Ryerson Press, 1964). "Flight of the Roller Coaster" by Raymond Souster is reprinted from *Collected Poems of Raymond Souster* by permission of Oberon Press.

"I, Icarus": Alden Nowlan, *The Mysterious Naked Man* (Toronto: Clarke, Irwin, 1969). Reprinted by permission of Claudine Nowlan, literary executor of the Estate of Alden Nowlan.

"Grandfather": George Bowering, *Points on the Grid* (Toronto: McClelland & Stewart, 1964). *George Bowering Selected* by George Bowering. Used by permission, McClelland & Stewart Ltd. *The Canadian Publishers*.

Work and Labour

"I's the B'y" (Traditional): The text is reproduced from *Volume 1 of Songs of the Newfoundland Outports* (Ottawa: Secretary of State, 1965) collected by Kenneth Peacock, as arranged by Dan Fox.

"Squid-Jiggin' Ground": A.R. Scammell, composed in 1929, *My Newfoundland: Stories, Poems, Songs* (St. John's: Breakwater Books, 1966). Permission requested of Berandol Music Limited.

"The Ballad of Springhill": Peggy Seeger; alternative titles: "Springhill Mine Disaster" and "Springhill Mining Disaster"; words and music composed in 1960 by Petty Seeger; *The Ewan MacColl / Peggy Seeger Song Book* (1970). Copyright © 1960 by Stormking Music Inc. Reprinted by permission of Peggy Seeger.

"All through the 'Thirties": Roy Daniells, *The Chequered Shade* (Toronto: McClelland & Stewart, 1963). Reprinted by permission of Laurenda Daniells on behalf of the Estate of Roy Daniells.

"The *Mary Ellen Carter*": Stan Rogers, written in 1979, sung on his album *Between the Breaks* (1979); text taken from Chris Gudgeon's *An Unfinished Conversation: The Life and Music of Stan Rogers* (Toronto: Viking, 1993, out of print). All songs written by Stan Rogers (SOCAN)—used by permission of Fogarty's Cove Music and Ariel Rogers.

"The Stenographers": P.K. Page, *As Ten as Twenty* (Toronto: The Ryerson Press, 1946). Reprinted by permission of the author and her agent, Kathryn Mulders.

"Envoi": Bliss Carman, *Bliss Carman's Poems* (Toronto: McClelland & Stewart, 1929).

Stuff and Nonsense

"Sweet Maiden of Passamaquoddy": James De Mille, "Lines to Florance Huntingdon, Passamaquoddy, Maine," *The Minnehaha Mines,* published serially in *The New Dominion and True Humourist,* beginning April 16, 1870.

"The Indian Names of Acadie": James De Mille, *Songs of the Great Dominion* (London: Walter Scott, 1889).

"The Kelligrews' Soiree": John Burke, presumably composed in the 1920s, reprinted from J.R. (Joey) Smallwood, *The Book of Newfoundland* (St. John's: Newfoundland Book Publishers, Ltd., 1937), Volume One.

"Hail Our Great Queen": Attributed to James Gay, William Arthur Deacon in his serio-comic study, *The Four Jameses* (1927, 1974).

"Ode on the Mammoth Cheese": James McIntyre, *Musings on the Banks of Canadian Thames* (1884).

"When the Ice Worms Nest Again" (Unknown): Text taken from C.E. Gillham's *Raw North* (1947) where it is stated that the words and music were composed by Mona Symington, Marion Williamson, and Joyce Kolgan.

"There Once Was a Young Man of Quebec": Attributed to Rudyard Kipling by Stephen Leacock in his essay "Comic Verse: The Lighter Notes," *Humour and Humanity: An Introduction to the Study of Humour* (1937).

"Some Limericks" (Traditional): Reprinted from *Colombo's Canadian Quotations* (Edmonton: Hurtig Publishers, 1974). Reprinted by permission of John Robert Colombo.

"Relativity": A.H. Reginald Buller, *Punch,* Dec. 19, 1923.

"Away with Tunics": Sir Raymond Bell, quoted by Lord Garner, "Mike: An Englishman's View," *International Journal* (Canadian Institute of International Affairs), Winter 1973–74.

"On the Appointment of Governor-General Vincent Massey, 1952": B.K. Sandwell, *The Blasted Pine* (Toronto: The Macmillan Company, 1957; revised edition, 1967), edited by F.R. Scott and A.J.M. Smith.

"A Church Seen in Canada': Theodore Spencer, *An Acre in the Seed* (Cambridge: Harvard University Press, 1949).

"The Layman Turned Critic": Louis Dudek, *Laughing Stalks* (1958); reprinted from his *Collected Poetry* (Toronto: Delta Canada, 1971). Reprinted with the permission of Aileen Collins and Michael Gnarowski, Executor of the author's Estate.

"The Progress of Satire": Louis Dudek, epigraph to the anthology *The Blasted Pine* (Toronto: The Macmillan Company, 1957; revised edition, 1967), edited by F.R. Scott and A.J.M. Smith, its dedicatees. Reprinted with the permission of Aileen Collins and Michael Gnarowski, Executor of the author's Estate.

"Oh Canada": John Robert Colombo, printed in 1965, reprinted from *The Sad Truths* (Toronto: Peter Martin Associates, 1976). Reprinted by permission of the author.

"Alligator Pie": Dennis Lee, *Wiggle to the Laundromat* (1970); reprinted from *Alligator Pie* (Toronto: Macmillan, 1974). Reprinted by permission of Westwood Creative Artists.

"The Water Trader's Dream": Robert Priest, *A Terrible Case of the Stars* (Toronto: Puffin Books, 1994). Copyright © 1994 by Robert Priest. Reprinted by permission of the author.

Our Home and Native Land

"There Is a Land": J.A. Ritchie, derived from an unpublished verse titled "There Is a Land" (1920); researchers at the Library of Parliament have yet to determine the original appearance of this four-line composition.

"Trans Canada": F.R. Scott, composed in 1943, *The Collected Poems of F.R. Scott* (Toronto: McClelland and Stewart, 1981). Reprinted with the permission of William Toye, literary executor for the Estate of F.R. Scott.

"Canada: Case History": Earle Birney, *The Strait of Anian* (1948); the text is taken from *The Poems of Earle Birney* (Toronto: McClelland & Stewart, 1969). *Selected Poems* by Earle Birney. Used by permission, McClelland & Stewart Ltd. *The Canadian Publishers*.

"This Land Is Your Land": Woody Guthrie and The Travellers, composed in 1956, arranged by Martin Bochner; innumerable versions and recordings are known, including a different one in *Canada Sings: Community Song Book for Schools, Clubs, Fraternities, Homes, and Community Singing* (Toronto: Gordon V. Thompson Limited, 1983) edited by Hugo Frey. Permission requested of Jerry Gray of The Travellers.

"From Colony to Nation": Irving Layton, *Music on a Kazoo* (1956); reprinted from *Collected Poems* (Toronto: McClelland and Stewart Limited, 1965). *Collected Poems* by Irving Layton. Used by permission, McClelland & Stewart Ltd. *The Canadian Publishers*.

"Song for Canada": Ian Tyson and Peter Gzowski; lyrics, composed in 1965, printed in Marco Adria's *Peter Gzowski: An Electric Life* (Toronto: ECW Press, 1994) and reprinted with the permission of Ian Tyson.

"CA-NA-DA": Bobby Gimby, composed in 1967, © 1967 Centennial Commission. © Assigned 1968 Gordon V. Thompson Ltd. Copyright renewed. All rights reserved. Permission requested of Warner Bros. Publications U.S. Inc., Miami, FL 33014.

"I Am Canadian": Michael Smith and David Swaine, advertising campaign launched March 17, 2000; the text is reprinted from Richard Helm's article "From Eh to Zed: Beer Ad Taps into Canuck Pride," *The Montreal Gazette,* April 15, 2000. Reprinted by permission.

"The Mighty Buck . . .": Raymond Filip, *Somebody Told Me I Look like Everyman* (Vancouver: Pulp Press, 1978). *Backscatter* (Toronto: Guernica, 2001). Reprinted by permission of the author and Antonio D'Alfonso of Guernica Editions.

"Canadians": Miriam Waddington, *Driving Home: Poems New and Selected* (Toronto: Oxford University Press, 1972). "Canadians" from *Collected Poems* by Miriam Waddington. Copyright © Miriam Waddington, 1986. Used by permission of Oxford University Press.

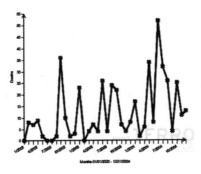

Graph 4. Deaths caused by terrorist attacks in Afghanistan, 2002–4.
Courtesy of MIPT terrorism knowledge database.

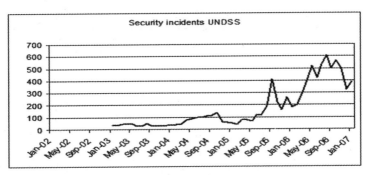

Graph 5: Security incidents 2003–7 according to UNDSS.
Source: UNDSS.

Pakistan, and Islamabad might also have encouraged the Neo-Tali-
ban to strengthen him as a counter-balance to strongly anti-Pakistan
northern factions such as Shura-i Nezar. In the case of the Parlia-
mentary elections of September 2005, the desire not to antagonise
the population seems an even stronger explanation for the Taliban's
mansuetude during election time. Again no significant attacks were
carried out against the polling stations.[27] After the elections US of-
ficers in the field claimed that the Taliban were deliberately lying
low in order to speed up the withdrawal of Coalition forces so that
they could then proceed to overthrow the Karzai regime, but this

115

explanation fails to account for the fact that in the summer of 2005, including up to the elections (18 September), the military activity of the insurgents had been reaching new peaks (see Graph 5).[28] In September UNDSS registered over 400 attacks, by far the highest number recorded thus far. An alternative explanation, also coming from US officers, but accepted by some analysts too, is that the Taliban were hoping to bring a substantial number of sympathisers to the parliament. The Taliban indeed claimed to have their own men among the candidates, but several of the candidates with a Taliban background do not appear to have maintained a good relationship with the Movement and issued statements critical of the insurgency or stated their fear of being assassinated by their former comrades. In any case, the number of candidates with a Taliban past was modest and only four were actually elected. It is unlikely that the Taliban would have determined their attitude towards the elections on the basis of the large number of candidates with a past in Hizb-i Islami,[29] given the rather loose alliance between the two organisations (see 4.9 *Alliances*). The desire to avoid alienating local communities, which wanted to send representatives to the parliament and to the provincial councils, remains the most likely explanation.[30]

Another aspect of the Taliban's effort to secure popular support was their (often clumsy) attempt to manage violence and to target it carefully. Although there are many examples of atrocities carried out by the insurgents, there seems to have been a clear effort to focus the violence on whomever the Taliban considered a collaborator of the government and of the 'occupiers'. There might have been some latitude exercised in the application of the rules issued by the leadership, but in general they appear to have been respected. It is true, for example, that the Taliban did not resort to easy ways of creating havoc such as the large-scale rocketing of cities, which, by contrast, the mujahidin of the 1980s had used widely.[31] 'Collaborationists' were first warned to quit their job and/or stop cooperating with the government and the foreigners. In some cases the Taliban were reported to have walked down the roads of villages with loudspeakers, threatening death to the 'collaborationists', but the recourse to 'night letters' or face-to-face warnings seems to have been more common. After several warnings, the resilient 'collaborationists' would be beaten up or their property damaged. Finally, in case even this tactic failed, the Taliban would proceed to eliminate the 'collaborationist' physically. Of course, in the case of IEDs and suicide bombings unwanted civilian casualties were unavoidable, not least because of the weak technical proficiency of the insurgents (see 4.3 *Demoralisation of the enemy*). However, even in these cases the Taliban sometimes presented their excuses for their mistakes, confirming the existence of a serious concern for their image among the population. According to a DIA document viewed by a journalist, a split occurred within the Taliban leadership concerning the use of suicide bombing, with Mullah Omar and others opposing an increase in its use due to concern with civilian casualties.[32]

Yet another indication of the Taliban's desire to win the 'hearts and minds' of the rural population is the fact that they used to warn rural communities (including small district towns) of planned attacks, giving them the chance to evacuate or at least take shelter. Even if this was presented by NATO as harassment of the population, it was clearly to their benefit. The Taliban paid a price for this, since it often also signalled to the enemy that an ambush was forthcoming. By contrast, attacks in urban areas were never preceded by warnings, leading to high civilian casualties. The Taliban also stayed clear of interfering too much with the life of the inhabitants of the areas under their control. Finally, they would stop depredations and impose law and order, attacking the criminal gangs who had earlier often worked under the protection of the police (see also 2.6 *Recruiting local communities* and 6.3 *Afghan police*). The Taliban's Layeha explicitly forbade practices such as harassing 'innocent people' and searching houses and confiscating weaponry without permission of senior commanders. It also banned recruiting old 1980s jihadis with a bad reputation and fighters sacked by other groups for bad behaviour. If disputes with the population still arose, they had to be resolved by senior commanders or the Council of Ulema or elders, another attempt to prevent arbitrariness in dealing with the villagers (see 3.1 *Cohesiveness of the Taliban*). Reports from the field show that the Taliban were not taxing travellers at the checkpoints, contrary to what the government militias, police and army were doing. They were also not looting farmers' harvests when crossing fields. As a result, many villagers did not perceive the Taliban as a threat, even when they did not directly support them.[33]

4.6 EXPLOITING DIVISIONS AMONG COMMUNITIES

Avoiding ill behaviour towards the villagers could have helped create a generally positive disposition towards the Taliban, but would not have itself sufficed to turn large areas into their strongholds. The next step in the Taliban's strategy was the targeting of rural communities as a source of support in areas where such communities were divided and at odds (see 2.6 *Recruiting local communities*). The Taliban displayed considerable skill in identifying local rivalries and siding with communities opposed to Kabul and its local allies. Where such opposition had not taken root, the Taliban would actively try to create the conditions for this to change. The south-eastern region provides a good example. During 2002–5 the Taliban failed, despite constant attempts, to penetrate Paktia and Khost provinces in the south-east, where the local tribes were on good terms with each other and continued supporting the central government despite numerous grievances.[34] Until the end of 2006 the Taliban had only been able to create a base of support among sectors of the population in Zurmat district, the most tribally mixed districts of Paktia/Khost and one which the tribal élites were unable to control effectively. The assassination of Governor Taniwal in September 2006 was clearly an attempt to destabilise the region. They seemed to have calculated, with some reason, that the need to appoint a new governor would likely lead to competing demands by the various tribes, each claiming the position for itself. Similarly, their attacks on elders and senior clergy were intended to foster social disorder and create cracks which they could then infiltrate. In this case, President Karzai avoided playing the Taliban's game and appointed as a replacement a UN official with extensive experience of the region, but originally from Nangarhar province, presumably in an attempt to avoid upsetting the delicate tribal balance.[35]

By the second half of 2006 the Taliban were experiencing problems with this strategy, as it relied on siding with some communities and against others. The problem is intrinsic to this mode of support-building: while it is relatively easy to pit one community against another and hence build a base of support, to move beyond that and form a wider and more solid alliance is very difficult because many communities have been antagonised in the process. Towards the end of 2006 prominent commanders of the Taliban like Haqqani and Dadullah were reportedly trying to win over the tribes by pledging to share power and resources with them. Exporting the model of mobilisation to areas where the Taliban had weak roots or none at all proved even more problematic. In 2006 Tajik, Hazara and Shi'a commanders were approached to join the jihad, sometimes with success. For example, sources allege that at least two Shi'a commanders from Bamyan and northern Afghanistan agreed to cooperate with the Taliban in the event of a large-scale offensive of the Taliban. However, mobilising such scattered pockets of support among non-Pashtuns was contingent on reaching the critical mass needed to launch a countrywide movement, which proved to be a vicious cycle. In the south, the critical mass had been provided by the madrasa recruits. As of early 2007 no similar groups had yet emerged to play the same role in other regions.[36]

4.7 PROPAGANDA

Gen. David Richards, commander of NATO forces in Afghanistan, reportedly said that he never saw 'a more sophisticated propaganda machine' than the one put together by the Taliban. The propaganda effort was rumoured to be under the responsibility of Qudratullah Jamal (aka Hamid Agha), former Information Minister of the Taliban regime. If he was indeed in charge, he had certainly improved his skills. Compared to the weak, naïve and clumsy public relations displayed by the Taliban of 1996–2001, the Neo-Taliban demonstrated after 2001 a much greater ability to manipulate the press and their interlocutors. Between 2002 and 2005 they already showed an unprecedented readiness to talk with journalists over the satellite phone or sometimes to arrange meetings, although they were still quite reluctant compared to fellow insurgents in other countries. During 2006, however, their availability to the press increased dramatically and Taliban commanders appeared more confident and eager to invite journalists to visit 'liberated' areas. During 2006, for example, they were leaking information to the international press, with the apparent intention of confusing their enemies with regard to where they would strike next and what strategy they would adopt during the coming spring. In one case in November 2006 they announced an impending offensive against Arghandab valley north of Kandahar city, first step towards taking Kandahar city itself. Then they claimed that the plan was to cut off both the Kandahar–Herat road and the Kandahar–Kabul road. They also claimed that a widespread tribal insurrection was in the making and would start in the spring, explaining the relative slow-down in fighting from November with the need to finalise agreements, improve coordination and restock arms dumps inside Afghanistan (see also 4.9 *Alliances*). They also tried to play divide and rule with members of the state administration, hinting that only former communists were cooperating with the government, while former jihadis were helping the Taliban. Similarly, they would leak information to journalists, alleging that a number of non-Islamic countries had offered help to the Taliban, a clear attempt to sow distrust between the US-led coalition on one side and Russia-led front on the other.[37]

There was much more to the Neo-Taliban's propaganda campaign than manipulation of the press. Some aspects of their propaganda and psychological warfare effort were not innovative at all and reproduced practices which had already been used during the 1980s jihad. For example the use of 'night letters', usually handwritten tracts which were widely distributed to villagers or nailed to the doors of houses, mosques and other public buildings. More innovative, though still not a first, was the enlistment of singers to support the cause. Their tape cassettes and CDs (hundreds of titles) were widely and cheaply available for sale in the bazaars of Afghan towns and villages, apparently manufactured by the Taliban and sympathising entrepreneurs. The number and availability of these products increased sharply during 2006. Sales too, despite a government ban, were reportedly increasing during 2006. The Taliban also produced magazines, although their impact must have been more modest given the low levels of literacy, and established both a radio (Voice of Sharia) with mobile transmitters in at least two provinces and a web site (www.alemarah. org) for the delivery of news and propaganda.[38] Where the Taliban were real innovators (together with the Arab jihadis in Iraq) was the introduction of VCDs and DVDs containing explicit propaganda commentary and preaching, featuring topics, ideas and arguments such as:

- heroic and successful episodes of their guerrilla campaign;
- episodes from other 'jihads' elsewhere in the world, primarily Iraq but also Lebanon, Waziristan and Palestine;
- the US invaded Afghanistan like the Soviet Union did and that therefore jihad is justified;
- the conflict is part of a global Christian war against Islam;
- the Kabul government is therefore a mere puppet and the only legitimate authority are the Ulema;
- in the ANA soldiers are not allowed to pray;
- confessions of 'spies' and their execution;
- our low-tech techniques can hold the ground against sophisticated US weaponry;
- success will eventually be achieved and martyrs will win heaven;
- interviews with successful commanders;
- footage showing the effects of US bombings in Afghanistan and Iraq;

- 'Christian' atrocities against Muslims in Poso (Indonesia);
- appeals by prospective suicide bombers for more volunteers;
- US soldiers desecrate bodies of Taliban fighters by burning them;
- the Koran is desecrated in Guantánamo toilets;
- Prophet Muhammad is desecrated in Danish cartoons;
- the convert to Christianity Abdul Rahman is helped by foreigners in getting away with the crime of apostasy.[39]

Like the music tapes, these VCDs and DVDs seem to be commercially manufactured by sympathetic entrepreneurs, probably based in Pakistan, such as:

- Omat productions;
- Manbaul-Jihad;
- Abdullah videos;
- As-sahab.[40]

Initially these products were sold (however cheaply), but were later also distributed for free, which together with their increasing availability in the bazaars suggests that more funding was being channelled into these types of activities. Clearly the Taliban gradually strengthened the role of propaganda in their war effort. Their task was facilitated by the weakness of the psyops effort on the NATO/US side.[41] The importance of propaganda in the Taliban's effort seems to support to some extent Gen. Barno's thesis that the insurgency was an example of 'fourth generation warfare', except that the bulk of the propaganda was not aimed at Western public and governments, but at Afghan and Muslim public opinion. The actual impact of these propaganda efforts on the Afghan population was far from clear at the time of writing, except for the fact that sales of CDs and DVDs seemed to be doing well. The build-up in anti-foreigner sentiment from 2006 onwards (see 2.7 *Changes in recruitment patterns*) might well at one point lead to an enhanced role for pan-Islamic sentiment as a factor of increased recruitment, but there was little evidence of that having been the case up to early 2007.

The reliance on pan-Islamic themes for propaganda purposes might, however, have contributed to mollify the attitude of some sections of the population towards the insurgents, even without leading to much direct recruitment.

4.8 THE THIRD PHASE: 'FINAL OFFENSIVE'?

Until 2006 there was little that could be even remotely described as an attempt of the Taliban to launch a coordinated offensive. The view of US officers is that the Taliban did not mount a coordinated offensive in 2004 because they had been weakened by US counter-insurgency, but it is more likely that they never planned to or were incapable of doing so at that stage. Even if at the beginning of 2004 they had announced their intention to attack and take a major city and to attack US military bases, they were in reality largely busy in-filtrating the territory and establishing infrastructures. By 2006 the situation had changed and they were ready to pursue the ambitious plans stated as early as 2004. Whether the 2006 fighting can effectively be described as an 'offensive' is a matter of debate. It is possible to speculate that the Taliban might have been under pressure from their Arab, Pakistani and other 'donors' to deliver a steady pace of advancement and some high profile victories. It is also possible that the leadership of the Taliban might in any case have planned to escalate its military operations well in advance as a move towards a new stage of the insurgency, taking on US and allied military forces in larger scale engagements. A fourth hypothesis is that the replace-ment of US troops with Canadian troops in Kandahar in the spring of 2006 might have been seen by the insurgents as an indication of the intention of the US to withdraw from the country and as a golden opportunity to score easy victories, boosting the morale of the insurgents and possibly forcing a hasty retreat of the Canadians from Kandahar.[42] Whatever the immediate reason for this decision to escalate and whatever term is used to describe the escalation, there is no question that the Taliban for the first time—at least since what the US military calls Operation Anaconda in March 2002—openly challenged the foreign contingents in a large battle.[43]

In part, the escalation of 2006 was due to special circumstances, beyond the will of the Taliban leadership. In particular, the clashes with the British in Helmand province were likely motivated by the attempt of the British to penetrate the northern strongholds of the Taliban. In fact, the fighting subsided once the British adopted a less aggressive posture at the beginning of the autumn and the Taliban never tried to approach Lashkargah, the provincial capital of Helmand. By contrast, in Kandahar throughout the spring and summer of 2006 the Taliban had moved the focus of their operations very close to the city and the highway, possibly in an attempt to drag the Canadians out of Kandahar and hurt them. The Taliban attempted a single attack on fortified positions at the end of March and then relied on ambushes, roadside bombs and suicide attacks to wear the Canadians out.[44] Although attacks on outposts manned by foreign troops were rare even in 2006, they might have been sufficient for the Taliban to conclude that concentrations of 300–400 Taliban were short of the critical mass needed to overwhelm even company- or platoon-size detachments. Moreover, such attacks were particularly costly in terms of casualties, as the fighters had to expose themselves and face airstrikes both during the attack and when withdrawing. The Taliban leadership and its advisors seem to have concluded that it needed to mobilise larger concentrations in order to achieve the critical mass necessary to inflict serious casualties. This would of course have greatly compounded the problem of manoeuvring and coordinating in the field, a problem of difficult solution given the near absence of educated cadres within the ranks of the Taliban. Together with the desire to limit casualties in its own ranks, this consideration probably reinforced the necessity of drawing the enemy out to fight on the Taliban's ground of choice.

Based on the experience of anti-Soviet jihadis and on their own interpretations of the strategy and tactics of the Soviet army, the leaders of the Taliban seem to have identified the solution to their dilemmas in the vineyards of the area of Pashmul, between the districts of Panjwai and Zhare, a mere 20 km from Kandahar city. The local mujahidin were convinced that the Soviet army could never take Panjwai because its grapevines, drainage ditches, high walled compounds and 'scores of escape tunnels and trenches' built during the 1980s offered good protection from air bombardment as well as shelter from air reconnaissance. Why should the ruse not work against the US Air Force? Moreover, the deployment of Taliban among the villagers of Panjwai and Zhare was probably seen as a deterrent against large-scale air bombardment. During March–July Pashmul had been the staging area of most attacks against Canadian troops, but in August the Taliban tried to make their presence as obvious and as provocative as possible, turning up in large numbers in full daylight, establishing training centres and giving out every signal that they intended to turn the area into a stronghold that could be used to scale up activities in central Kandahar province, including Kandahar city itself. They moved into Pashmul from Maywand district, where they already enjoyed a 'free rein'. Some sources even alleged that the Taliban were planning to infiltrate Arghandab district north of Kandahar, which is contiguous with Panjwai. NATO estimated in the end that as many as 1,500–2,000 Taliban might have been concentrated in the area, although many of them appear to have been local tribesmen allied to the insurgents. In any case, this was certainly by far the largest concentration of insurgents of the whole conflict to date. The build-up lasted several weeks and caused considerable edginess in both Kandahar and Kabul. Eventually the trap set by the Taliban worked, with NATO becoming convinced that a major threat to Kandahar was imminent, the more so since Pashmul is well positioned to threaten the highway connecting Kandahar to Herat. Some signs of infiltration of Taliban fighters into Kandahar were already reported during the summer. However, the offensive mounted by NATO forces was probably bigger and more sophisticated than the Taliban had expected, with US Special Forces trying to cut off the retreat to the insurgents while the Canadians were staging a frontal attack. The Taliban moreover miscalculated NATO's and specifically the Canadians' reluctance to approve the large-scale bombing of populated areas, particularly when accurate targeting was difficult because of the vineyards. NATO instead invited the villagers to leave the area and then launched massive air attacks, which included 2,000lb bombs, despite the fact that substantial numbers of civilians had opted to stay.[45]

The other miscalculation committed by the Taliban leadership concerned the strength of the Soviet Army's determination to take Pashmul, on which assumption the theory of the impregnability of Pashmul was based. It is indeed much more likely that the Soviets were not excessively interested in the area and therefore never invested large resources in taking it. They could certainly have bombed it heavily, had they wished to do so, as the Americans did in September 2006. The final result of the Taliban's miscalculations was hundreds of casualties on their side, although NATO had to pay a political price for the significant civilian losses.[46] Moreover, forced to withdraw by their inability to fight effectively under constant bombardment, the Taliban were subjected to raids by US Special Forces, which inflicted more casualties. The final toll of 1,100 killed, as estimated by NATO, might be an exaggeration or not, but undoubtedly the battle of Pashmul was a serious tactical defeat for the Taliban.[47]

In the immediate aftermath of Pashmul the Taliban did not mount any other major operations and went back to their usual tactic of avoiding direct confrontations with superior NATO forces, as highlighted by operation Baaz Tsuka in the area around Pashmul in December 2006, when the Taliban withdrew without fighting despite having sizeable forces there. However, once the stakes had been raised, it was no simple task for the leadership of the Taliban to fall back on low-scale insurgency tactics. The fact that the Taliban claimed that the withdrawal was contingent on pro-Taliban elders being handed local control by NATO forces might be a sign of how having raised the stakes in the conflict possibly created a problem of image for the Taliban, who had now to live up to its claims of being about to launch a 'final offensive' or 'national uprising'. At the beginning of the autumn of 2006 the Taliban leadership even announced the continuation of large-scale operations throughout the forthcoming winter, in what was seen at the time as an act of defiance. However, as the end of November approached, Mullah Dadullah, military commander of the southern region, announced that the offensive would be postponed to the following spring due to cold weather. Was Dadullah's excuse conceived to mask the weakening of the insurgency after having suffered very heavy losses? Insurgent attacks in November 2006 were 28 per cent fewer than in October, as reported by NATO, then picked up again in December and January. The winter of 2006–7 was not a particularly cold one, but heavy rains in March might have made travel more difficult. It is true that Afghanistan appeared set for a cold winter as November was colder than expected, but the Taliban are also likely to have been buying time while trying to come up with new strategies to upgrade their activities, as well as redeploying fighters. Reports that Mullah Omar was intensifying his efforts to communicate with field commanders and to encourage them also suggest that a further strengthening of military activities was being planned. In particular, the Taliban were reportedly planning to move the focus of their military activities closer to Kabul. Their build-up in Tagab and the infiltration of Kabul's southern surroundings, including an old Hizb-i Islami stronghold like Sarobi valley, the control of which would have allowed cutting the road to Jalalabad, suggest that their intentions were serious (see 2.6 *Recruiting local communities*). By the end of the autumn the situation in a couple of districts in the southern part of Kabul province was showing signs of deterioration and Afghan security forces were not patrolling any more at night. NATO sources were worried that these districts could be used as a 'gateway' to Kabul city. It is possible that in the minds of the Taliban's leaders, combining an offensive in the south with scaled-up operations around Kabul would stretch NATO thin and hamper its ability to fight effectively. The discovery of logistical bases and a field hospital capable of catering for as many as 900 men near Lashkargah, as well as news of a large-scale movement of fighters across the border, suggest serious Taliban planning towards a major effort to cut off the provincial capital of Helmand as well. However, their objectives were confounded by the fact that the adversaries were now aware of the importance of the mountain strongholds and during the winter NATO forces and in particular the British increased the pace of their activities against these areas, in order to disrupt the Talibans' capability to organise a spring offensive. Having enjoyed years of relatively undisturbed control over the logistical redoubts of Helmand, the Taliban were for the first time put under serious pressure, even if most British military activity was concentrated in Garmser and Gereshk, trying to prevent supplies from reaching the Taliban from the shorter route, that is the Pakistani border of Helmand. The Taliban had to start developing alternative routes, for example they tried to pressure the Hazara population of Kijran district (Daikundi) towards allowing the movement of Taliban's caravans between Zabul and Helmand. Indeed, the penetration of Taliban in the southern districts of Daikundi was reported by local Afghan authorities in April 2007. However, even if successfully developing alternative routes, the Taliban's plans for future offensives might have been seriously disrupted in the short term by the British raids.[48]

The fighting around Kandahar in 2006 could be seen as a confirmation that some Maoist concepts of guerrilla warfare seem to have made it in to the mindset of Taliban commanders. Until then their commitment to the 'third phase' had been mostly rhetorical. Some of them had openly talked of 'closing in' on Kandahar, Khost, Jalalabad, Asadabad and Gardez as early as 2003. Bringing the war to the cities of Afghanistan, after having surrounded them, was allegedly part of the Taliban's planning in early 2004, when they claimed to be about to start the 'war of the cities' by the summer. In December of that year the Taliban actually circulated information that the insurgents were infiltrating the cities in the hundreds and indeed a small-scale terrorist campaign started later in Kabul, Mazar-i Sharif, Kandahar and Herat,[49] but this soon petered out. In any case, if the fighting around Kandahar in 2006 was meant to be the beginning of the Taliban's 'third phase', it was clearly a premature move. As of March 2007 they were somewhat toning down their claims to be about to launch a countrywide offensive, shifting the focus once again towards the southern part of the country.

4.9 ALLIANCES

Until 2006 the Taliban did not achieve much success in the formation of alliances with other groups that shared grievances against the central government. The agreement with Hizb-i Islami in 2002 appears to have been more a matter of Gulbuddin Hekmatyar's willingness to emerge from obscurity than the result of a genuine interest on the part of the Taliban leadership. Hizb-i Islami never effectively integrated its forces with the Taliban's, or even successfully coordinated the military effort, although some coordination occurred at the local level. There were also persistent rumours that Hekmatyar might have different strategic aims too, due to his having declared jihad against the foreign forces but not against the government. This was construed by some observers to imply that he might be trying to manoeuvre for a deal with the government, after having infiltrated the state administration with 'former' members of his party, although he explained in one interview that his failure to mention the Afghan government was due to the fact that it was not even worth mentioning. Later again a misquoted interview in March 2007 was interpreted as Hekmatyar offering negotiations without conditions to Kabul, whereas he was just repeating his usual line (and the Taliban's) that foreign troops had to be withdrawn before any negotiations could take place. In any case, towards the end of 2006 Hizb-i Islami seemed intent on strengthening its identity of an insurgent group as separate from the Taliban, appointing for the first time a spokesman (Haroon Zargoun) and beginning to claim military operations for themselves. Hekmatyar admitted to the press the existence of problems in co-ordinating and integrating his forces with the Taliban's, but attributed the failure to the lack of willingness among the ranks of his allies. The fact that he mentioned the lack of resources as an explanation for the low level of Hizb-i Islami's military activities suggests that the lack of cooperation might imply an unwillingness to share resources on the Taliban's side.[50]

Paradoxically, the potential value of Hizb-i Islami to the Taliban might have increased exactly as Hekmatyar was trying to distance himself. As during 2006 the Taliban were rapidly reaching the limits of the area where their activists could reasonably hope to infiltrate (that is their old strongholds in the south and south-east), Hizb-i Islami's old constituencies in the east, north-east, around Kabul and maybe even in the west must have looked attractive to them. Hekmatyar's residual resources were modest but not insignificant. After 2001 his party had been mainly active in eastern Afghanistan (Kunar, Nuristan, Laghman, Nangarhar). Another significant pocket was active in Kapisa (Tagab district) and parts of Kabul province, while some residual capability appeared to exist also in Wardak, Logar, Parwan, Kabul, Paktia, Paktika, Khost, Kandahar, Baghlan, Balkh and Badakhshan, where military activities were, however, very small in scale or non-existent. NATO sources put the strength of Hizb-i Islami very low, at 300–400 fighters in 2006, which looks like an underestimate given the geographical spread of the party's activity. Again, this should be interpreted as an average for active fighters. A total figure of around 1,500 appears more realistic. Hekmatyar's efforts to re-establish contact with his former commanders added to his value to the Taliban. His emissaries were already reported in Kunduz during 2004 and police sources suggested in May 2006 that such networks were being re-activated in Takhar too. In his efforts Hekmatyar scored at least a few successes, particularly in Kapisa province, where his men were reported to have spread their activities beyond Tagab, in Nejab, Kohistan and Kohband districts. Propaganda activities were reported at least in Herat city too. In November 2006 official sources reported the distribution of weapons to local commanders in Kunduz, apparently by pro-Taliban elements. On

December 23 suspected insurgents were arrested in that province and said to be part of a network extending to Baghlan province too. The network included 250 activists of the Taliban, according to security officials, but many of them are likely to have been former Hizbis.[51]

A number of other groups ideologically close to the Taliban are known to operate in Afghanistan (see Table 6), but they are all small and largely insignificant, although a few (like Jamaat-ud-Da'awa Al-Salafia Wal Qitaab, the Bara Bin Malek Front of Mullah Ismail in Kunar and the Nuristani Dawlat-e Enqelabi-ye Islami) might have some influence at the local level, wherever Salafi groups have long had strong roots. It should also be considered that despite ideological contiguities the Salafis do not maintain good relations with the Taliban due to the mistreatment of their leadership by the Taliban regime. The largest insurgent group after the Taliban and Hizb-i Islami, Jaish ul-Muslimeen, was a Taliban offshoot and was reabsorbed in 2005. The Jaish ul-Mahdi was also formed by a former Talib in 2002 and actively cooperates with international jihadi volunteers inside Afghanistan.[52]

As for the international volunteers, 'Al Qaida' or whatever they might be called, their impact on the military capabilities of the insurgency was much greater (see 2.1 *How strong are the Taliban?*), but the relationship with the Taliban appears to have been often uneasy. In early 2007 some press sources reported a disagreement between the two concerning relations with the Pakistani government, to which 'Al Qaida' was reportedly very hostile. In the east at least, the foreign jihadis had their own network of support, separate from that of Hizb-i Islami and the Taliban. In some cases, for example parts of Paktia, local commanders had to ask the foreign volunteers, particularly Arabs, to leave in order not to alienate the population. In Kunar too the Arabs were reported not to be on good terms with Afghan insurgents, who considered them undisciplined and extreme in their behaviour. As a result, the contribution of the volunteers to the advancement of the cause of the insurgency was at best a mixed one.[53]

In order to have some impact on the dynamic of the conflict, the Taliban would have to make alliances with some influential organisation. In fact, from 2005 the leadership showed a new interest for talking to its old northern enemies, possibly a result of their growing self-confidence and of the belief that the Movement had developed into a valuable partner for a countrywide revolt. Taliban sources claimed to have established contacts with personalities of the old Jami'at-i Islami as early as the spring of 2005, confirming rumours circulating in Kabul at that time. According to these sources, the Jami'atis stated their shared hatred for the presence of foreign troops in the country

	2002	2003	2004	2005	2006
Taliban	4,000	7,000	9,500	12,500	17,000
Of which Jaish al Muslimeen			*1000*	*750*	*Re-absorbed into Taliban?*
Hizb-i Islami	800	1,000	1,000	1,250	1,500
Al Qaida			700	1,000	2,000
Jamaat-ud-Da'awa Al-Salafia Wal Qitaab					90 joins Hizb-i Islami in summer 2006
Council of the Secret Army				very small	
Islamic Revolutionary State of Afghanistan	150	150	150	150	100
Jaish al-Mahdi					low hundreds

Table 6. Insurgent groups operating in Afghanistan, strength estimates.
Sources: press reports, interviews with locals and with former members of Hizb-i Islami, UN sources.

and promised to join the fight at a later stage. Taliban sources even claimed that Professor Rabbani, leader of Jami'at, admitted to the Afghan press that his associates were talking to the Taliban. The contacts were reportedly continuing in 2006. UN sources reported that in Badakhshan the rise of Karzai's appointee and former head of the NSD unit in charge of protecting the President (10th Directorate), Zalmay Mojaddedi, contributed to local commanders such as Nazir Mohammed and Sardar Khan, once at odds, forming an opposition alliance. Zalmay Mojaddedi, a minor commander until his appointment to the NSD, won a parliamentary seat in Badakhshan in part at least due to massive support from the security and administrative machinery of the state. Nazir and Sardar had already been alienated by the failure of the central government to reward their loyalty with appointments to positions of power after the demobilisation of the militias they had been commanding. According to some UN sources, approaches between Taliban, conservative mullahs and former jihadi commanders were taking place between the end of 2006 and the beginning of 2007.[54]

These claims of course could just be an attempt to sow discord within the anti-Taliban front. However, sources close to the government and old Jami'atis agreed that northern militias, strongmen and warlords were turning increasingly hostile to the Kabul government during 2006, which they felt had been increasingly marginalising them. NATO sources believed that local conflicts in the north could allow the Taliban to infiltrate the region. The Taliban maintained some influence in Baghdis province after 2001 (see 2.6 *Recruiting local communities*) and from there, in 2006, they were believed to be infiltrating the southern districts of Faryab province, where conflicts among Uzbek warlords, between factions like Junbesh and Jami'at and between Uzbek warlords and Pashtun tribal strongmen created a favourable environment. In December 2006 a rocket attack was reported against Maimana, the provincial capital of Faryab. Between 2005 and 2006 the clear demonstration of government weakness and of the inability of the foreign contingents to control the territory, as well as their obvious overstretching, contributed to lower the threshold beyond which various groups holding grievances against the central government would find it convenient to join the armed opposition. The May 2006 riots in Kabul were widely seen as a demonstration of the government's inability to control even a modest crowd of rioters.[55]

4.10 NEGOTIATIONS

If elements derived from Mao's classical theory were present in the Taliban's strategy, the question remains open of whether this genuinely reflected the determination to conquer political power or whether it was used as a tool of political pressure on the Karzai administration to force it to the negotiating table. For all their image of an extremist movement, there are some indications that the Taliban might have always been aiming for a negotiated settlement. Talks with Karzai had been going on at least since 2003, although it is not clear how far up the Taliban leadership Karzai's contacts were. It appears that the Taliban contacted Kabul through UNAMA and that Kabul agreed to negotiate one month later, after receiving the green light from the US embassy. US military authorities officially endorsed the possibility of talks with 'moderate members' of the Taliban in December of that year. The actual content of the negotiations, however, is not known, nor is it clear whether the 'moderate Taliban' were testing the ground for the leadership of the Movement or were acting on their own initiative and autonomously. After a period of apparent suspension, negotiations were resumed, as admitted by President Karzai himself in 2007.[56]

One possibility is that there might have been different attitudes towards negotiations with Kabul among the Taliban. Even as late as December 2006, after President Karzai launched the idea of parallel 'Peace Jirgas' to be held in both Afghanistan and Pakistan at the beginning of 2007, with the aim of improving the cooperation of the Pakistani side in containing the insurgency, Qari Mohammed Yousuf, who claimed to be a representative of the Taliban in Pakistan but is sometimes dismissed as something short of a genuine spokesman of the Movement, stated that the Taliban might attend the jirgas if they were invited, with some conditions. However, a few days later another Taliban spokesman, Sayed Tayeb Agha, said that the rebels would never participate in such exercises as long as foreign troops were still in Afghanistan. The Taliban might of course have also been indulging in a tactical attempt to sow divisions within the Kabul ruling coalition, between elements favourable to negotiations and others opposing them. However, some facts seem to show that negotiations might indeed have been on the agenda of the leadership of the Taliban. The unofficial truce during the Presidential electoral campaign of 2004 would have made sense particularly if the Taliban were trying to build up Karzai as a legitimate negotiating partner (see 4.5 *Seeking popular support*). Furthermore, the fact that the Taliban until Sping 2007 had never targeted the UN in their terrorist attacks and ambushes is likely to have been due to the fact that they needed this organisation as a broker in negotiations with the government. Otherwise it would have been easy for them to throw the government and its international sponsors into a deep crisis by forcing the departure of the UN mission. This could easily be achieved by assassinating a few international members of staff. Despite many limitations, the UN mission played a key role in shoring up an often incompetent government and in some cases helped in preventing the explosion of local civil wars, for example in the northern half of Afghanistan. If a political deal was ever an organic part of the strategy of the Taliban, it is obvious they would not want to divulge it. Most diplomats would agree that successful negotiations in conflict resolution must always be conducted in secret. In the case of the Taliban, moreover, it would have been difficult to ask the rank-and-file to risk their lives on the battlefield if the leadership had admitted that it was negotiating with Kabul. Given the initial weakness of the Movement, mustering together a credible military threat must have been a priority in order to achieve a strong negotiating position.[57]

Given their rigid ideological background, why would the Taliban have wanted to negotiate? Given available evidence, a definite answer is impossible to give. One might speculate that until 2005 or 2006 the Taliban were not so confident of their ultimate victory and thought that their only chance was to find an accommodation with Kabul. It is also possible that they were forced to include negotiations in their agenda by the Pakistani authorities. These might have sponsored the insurgency as a last resort after attempts to create a legal political party based on the old Taliban (Jami'at-i Khudam-ul Koran, see 3.1 *Cohesiveness of the Taliban*) failed to achieve the aim of guaranteeing Pakistan's influence in Kabul. The Pakistanis might also have feared that a prolonged conflict would have led to the convergence of the two Taliban movements (Pakistani and Afghan) into a single entity (see 1.3 *The role of Pakistan*). Taliban sources repeatedly stated that the departure of foreign troops from Afghanistan was a *conditio sine qua non* for any agreement, which could be interpreted both as a sign of availability to negotiations and as an attempt to avoid negotiations by imposing an unacceptable condition. The former Taliban ambassador to Pakistan, Zaif, seemed to believe that some flexibility in this regard might have been possible and negotiations could have started before a withdrawal of the foreign troops, although such withdrawal would still need to be part of any agreement. The introduction of 'Islamic elements' in the legislation and in the system of government would also be required.[58]

It has also to be considered that there seems to be widespread support for negotiations leading to peace among the Afghan population, a fact which gives a strong incentive to both sides in the conflict to voice support for negotiations even when unwilling to offer reasonable conditions to the adversary. The propaganda purpose of some statements of the Taliban and of the Kabul government appears obvious. For example, while the Taliban made the withdrawal of foreign troops a key demand, in December 2006 President Karzai threw the ball back in their field when he announced that he was prepared to negotiate even with Mullah Omar, as long as he freed himself from 'foreign slavery' (i.e. Pakistan). Another example is that of the Peace Jirgas launched by Karzai in September 2006. Both Karzai and Musharraf tried to create the conditions for better manipulating the jirgas. For example, Karzai appointed three of his close supporters and collaborators among the four members the Afghan Peace Jirga Commission.[59]

4.11 MAO'S EPIGONES, 'FLEAS', 'FOURTH GENERATION' WARRIORS OR INTERNATIONAL JIHADISTS?

As shown in the previous paragraphs, there are valid elements in all three interpretations of the Neo-Taliban's strategy outlined at the beginning of the chapter. Up to 2005 the 'war of the flea' theory seemed to apply well to the Taliban, but the fighting around Kandahar in 2006 represents a departure from that model. At first sight at least, the developments of 2006 strengthen the interpretation of the Taliban insurgency as inspired by Maoist concepts. The idea that some second- or third-hand inspiration was taken from aspects of Mao's theories, purged of their People's War content, received some confirmation already in the form of the phases of infiltration and of stronghold build-up, but until 2005 the third phase had only existed in the shape of some claimed intention of surrounding and taking cities. The 2006 fighting around Kandahar seemed intended to be a first attempt at implementing this third phase and as such lends new credibility to this interpretation. Elements of Mao's theories could have made it to the leadership of the Taliban through some external advisor, or through some old Islamist mujahidin of Hizb-i Islami, some of whom were familiar with these concepts having read Mao.

Mao, however, was not fighting a power much superior in terms of both resources and technology (Japan was not that superior technologically, although it did have superior doctrine, training, resources and organisation). In the context of Afghanistan in 2002–6, like in that of Vietnam, taking a major city was not a realistic enterprise. Compared to Giap, the leadership of the Taliban (or their advisors) could have had the hindsight that militarily a Tet-like offensive was bound to fail. There is no evidence that this was the case and that the Kandahar offensive was not meant to succeed militarily, but on the other hand no military commander could ask his men to sacrifice their lives in a battle without hope. Hence even if the aim was just to create a psychological effect, the leaders of the Taliban would not want to divulge the notion. If this was the case, the theory of 'fourth generation warfare' would seem to fit well with the case of the Taliban, although whether this is really something new in historical terms is open to debate. The Taliban's improving skills in manipulating the press also point in this direction.

Nonetheless, some elements of the strategy of the Taliban do not fit well with any of these theories. Although the Neo-Taliban paid some attention to the manipulation of Western government and public opinion, the bulk of their effort was directed at winning over the Afghan public, as well as a wider Islamic one. It is also not clear whether they really tried to target public opinion and those governments perceived as not fully committed to intervention in Afghanistan. The offensive against Kandahar could be read as an attempt to throw the Canadians off-balance, given that Canadian public opinion was rather cool towards the Afghan mission and that the Conservative government did not have a majority in parliament. However, the Dutch in Uruzgan would have been an easier target, given that their government had already fallen and that elections were forthcoming. According to opinion polls, the Dutch public was even more sceptical of the mission than the Canadian one and the ground in Uruzgan was more favourable to insurgency operations than in central Kandahar province. Still, the summer was relatively quiet in Uruzgan.

This author supports an alternative interpretation, according to which the Neo-Taliban had become much more integrated in a supra-national jihadist movement than the 'old Taliban' ever were and that they increasingly believed that the decisive factor in winning the war would not be Western public opinion, but the support of their Muslim brethren. Hence their priority increasingly became the mobilisation of Muslim opinion worldwide as a source of funding and moral support, as well as of volunteers.[60] Other aspects of their strategy were becoming either subordinated to this, or confined to a secondary role. Ultimately, the belief was that victory would come with the overstretching of the enemy through the creation of 'one, ten, a hundred Iraqs', rather than with country-specific strategies. Since there is little evidence that the leadership of the Neo-Taliban already held this view when they started the insurgency in 2002, it is likely that this strategic view emerged gradually, under the influence of external advisors, financial contributors and allies. The jihadist perspective, moreover, was not necessarily incompatible with most of the characteristics of the 'war of the flea', of Maoist warfare or of 'fourth generation warfare' and the transition from any of them could take place almost seamlessly. Tactics and strategies could be pragmatically picked from the market of ideas and concepts as long as they fit in with the jihadist grand strategy. Given the current status of knowledge, it is impossible to say whether the conversion to a global jihadist strategy is permanent or not. It might have been dictated by the need to secure more funding from particular sources, rather than by a genuine belief in its intrinsic value.

NOTES

1   See Sami Yousafzai and Ron Moreau, 'The mysterious Mullah Omar', *Newsweek*, 5 March 2007.
2   See Jandora (2005). See also Cassidy (2003).
3   Gerges (2006), p. 174.
4   Belasco (2006).
5   'A double spring offensive', *The Economist*, 22 February 2007.
6   For a summary of Hammes' argument see Hammes (2005).
7   Hammes (2006), p. 2, also quoted in Barno; Barno (2006), pp. 16–17.
8   Naylor (2006).
9   The term is borrowed from Taber (1965). See also Johnson and Mason (2007), p. 87.
10 'NATO in Afghanistan', *RFE/RL Afghanistan Report*, vol. 5, no. 20 (1 August 2006); Tim McGirk, 'The Taliban on the run', *Time*, 28 March 2005; personal communication with Niamatullah Ibrahimi, Crisis States Research Centre, Kabul, 24 January 2007; Carlotta Gall, 'Despite years of U.S. pressure, Taliban fight on in jagged hills', *New York Times*, 4 June 2005; Claudio Franco, 'In remote Afghan camp, Taliban explain how and why they fight', *San Francisco Chronicle*, 21 January 2007; 'Socaust media briefing post Op Slipper', 27 September 2006, <http://www.defence.gov.au/media/SpeechTpl.cfm?CurrentId=6034>; Bill Graveland, 'Les talibans: un ennemi difficilement saisissable', *Associated Press*, 27 December 2006; ANA sources, January 2007.
11 Wright (2006a); Borhan Younus, 'Taliban call the shots in Ghazni', *Afghanistan Recovery Report*, no. 213 (25 April 2006); Andrew Maykuth, 'Taliban rampage in Ghazni', *Philadelphia Inquirer*, 10 September 2006; David Rohde, 'Afghan symbol for change becomes a symbol of failure', *New York Times*, 5 September 2006; Brian Hutchinson, 'Taliban execute 26

male Afghans', *CanWest News Service*, 19 December 2006; Claudio Franco, 'Islamic militant insurgency in Afghanistan experiencing "Iraqization"', *Eurasianet*, 8 November 2005; April Witt, 'Afghan political violence on the rise', *Washington Post*, 3 August 2003; Rahmani (2006b); Senlis Council (2006e), pp. 18–19; Declan Walsh, 'Better paid, better armed, better connected – Taliban rise again', *Guardian*, 16 September 2006; Syed Saleem Shahzad, 'Taliban line up the heavy artillery', *Asia Times Online*, 21 December 2006; Kim Sengupta, 'Helmand governor escapes blast as he battles for job', *Independent*, 13 December 2006; 'Man who wanted to assassinate Padshah Khan Zadran is arrested', *Hewaad*, 19 December 2006; Declan Walsh, 'Kandahar under threat, war raging in two provinces and an isolated president. So what went wrong?', *Guardian*, 16 September 2006.

12 Human Rights Watch (2006), pp. 39–41; interview with Afghan security officer, Kandahar, January 2006; Jason Burke, 'Taliban rising', *India Today*, 1 December 2003; 'Taliban issues warning to people of southern Afghan province', *RFE/RL*, 6 March 2007.

13 Human Rights Watch (2006).

14 Tom Coghlan, 'Taliban use beheadings and beatings to keep Afghanistan's schools closed', *Independent*, 11 July 2006; Human Rights Watch (2006), pp. 39–41, 50–1; interview with Afghan journalist returning from the south, Kabul, October 2006; Jason Straziuso, 'New Taliban rules target Afghan teachers', *Associated Press*, 9 December 2006; Suzanna Koster, 'Taliban fighters talk tactics – while safe in Pakistan', *Christian Science Monitor*, 9 November 2006; Michael Evans *et al.*, 'Aid effort fails to impress war-weary Afghans', *The Times*, 27 January 2007; Noor Khan, 'Taliban to open schools in Afghanistan', *Associated Press*, 21 January 2007; Javid Hamim, Saeed Zabuli and Samad Rohani, 'A turn from burning to learning', *Pajhwok Afghan News*, 21 January 2007; 'Schools face murderous challenge', *Afghan Recovery Report*, no. 241 (9 February 2007); personal communication with UNICEF official, Jalalabad, February 2007; Laura King, 'Afghans try to stop attacks on their schools', *Los Angeles Times*, 11 February 2007; 'Militant attacks at Afghan schools killed 85 students, teachers last year, minister says', *Associated Press*, 29 April 2007.

15 Geoffrey York, 'Taliban rising', *Globe and Mail*, 29 May 2006; Guy Dinmore and Rachel Morarjee, 'To a second front? How Afghanistan could again be engulfed by civil war', *Financial Times*, 22 November 2006; Victoria Burnett, 'Afghan officials see Taliban resurgence', *Boston Globe*, 25 September 2003; Talatbek Masadykov of UNAMA, quoted in April Witt, 'Afghan political violence on the rise'; Ahmed Rashid, 'Afghanistan and Pakistan, safe haven for the Taliban', *Far Eastern Economic Review*, 16 October 2003; Françoise Chipaux, 'Dans le plus complet dénuement, la province afghane de Zabul mène la lutte contre les talibans', *Le Monde*, 24 December 2003; interview with Maulana Obeidullah, Peace Strengthening Commission, Kandahar, January 2006; Talatbek Masadykov, quoted in James Rupert, 'Corruption and coalition failures spur Taliban resurgence in Afghanistan', *Newsday*, 17

June 2006; personal communication with UN official, Jalalabad, February 2007.

16 See the example of Lizha (Khost) in Paul Watson, 'On the trail of the Taliban's support', *Los Angeles Times*, 24 December 2006.

17 David Rohde and James Risen, 'C.I.A. review highlights Afghan leader's woes', *New York Times*, 5 November 2006; Schiewek (2006), p. 161.

18 Syed Saleem Shahzad, 'Taliban raise the stakes in Afghanistan', *Asia Times Online*, 30 October 2003; personal communication with UN official, Kabul, October 2006; Cordesman (2007); UNDSS weekly reports, February 2007.

19 Scott Peterson, 'Taliban adopting Iraq-style jihad', *Christian Science Monitor*, 13 September 2006; Senlis Council (2006a), p. 9; Lee Greenberg, 'Renewed Afghan fighting comes amid signs of Taliban buildup', *Ottawa Citizen*, 30 October 2006; Owais Tohid, 'Taliban regroups – on the road', *Christian Science Monitor*, 27 June 2003; Syed Saleem Shahzad, 'Taliban raise the stakes in Afghanistan'; Jason Straziuso, 'Outgoing Gen. sees more Afghan battles', *Associated Press*, 30 December 2006; Ron Synovitz, 'Afghanistan: are militants copying Iraqi insurgents' suicide tactics?', *RFE/RL*, 17 January 2006; 'Afghanistan blames blasts on Taliban and al-Qaeda', *AFP*, 21 January 2006; 'New U.S. commander in Afghanistan predicts more suicide attacks this year', *Associated Press*, 30 January 2007.

20 'L'activisme recule en Afghanistan (général américain)', *Xinhuanet*, 7 March 2005.

21 Tom Coghlan, 'Taliban train snipers on British forces', *Daily Telegraph*, 23 July 2006; Scott Baldauf and Ashraf Khan, 'New guns, new drive for Taliban', *Christian Science Monitor*, 26 September 2005; 'Canadian troops cite evidence of rift among Afghan insurgents', *RFE/RL Newsline*, 29 June 2006.

22 Rubin (2007); International Crisis Group (2003a); Mirwais Atal, 'US hearts and minds cash goes to Taliban', *Afghan Recovery Report*, no. 236 (28 November 2006); *Pajhwok Afghan News*, 6 June 2006; Syed Saleem Shahzad, 'Rough justice and blooming poppies', *Asia Times Online*, 7 December 2006; Syed Saleem Shahzad, 'Taliban line up the heavy artillery'.

23 One execution in Daikundi province is mentioned in 'A geographical expression in search of a state', *The Economist*, 6 July 2006.

24 Elizabeth Rubin, 'In the land of the Taliban', *New York Times Magazine*, 22 October 2006; Syed Saleem Shahzad, 'Taliban raise the stakes in Afghanistan'; 'Taliban makes gains against Afghan government', *Stratfor*, 7 August 2003; Sami Yousafzai and Urs Gehriger, 'A new layeha for the Mujahideen', *Die Weltwoche*, 29 November 2006, <http://www.signandsight.com/features/1071.html>; Declan Walsh, 'Beaten, robbed and exiled: life on the frontline of someone else's war', *Guardian*, 20 June 2006; Senlis Council (2006a), p. 11; 'Armed men abduct doctor, driver in S Afghanistan', *Xinhua*, 25 February 2007; James Bays, 'Taliban "in control" in Helmand', *Al Jazeera*, 25 February 2007; Schiewek (2006), p. 161.

25 *Pajhwok Afghan News*, 21 April 2006; interview with Massoud Kharokhel, Tribal Liaison Office, Kabul, October 2006; Borhan Younus, 'Taliban call the shots in Ghazni'; Elizabeth Rubin, 'Taking the fight to the Taliban', *New York Times Magazine*, 29 October 2006; David Rohde, 'Afghan symbol for change becomes a symbol of failure'; Victoria Burnett, 'Afghan officials see Taliban resurgence'; interview with UN official, October 2006, Gardez; personal communication with UN official, Gardez, October 2006; Senlis Council (2006a), p. 9.

26 Eric Schmitt and David Rohde, 'Taliban fighters increase attacks', *New York Times*, 1 August 2004 (interview with General Barno); Daniel Cooney, 'General: hard-hit Taliban recruiting kids', *Associated Press*, 24 July 2005 (interview with General Kamiya); 'Neo-Taliban says it won't attack polling stations, but will disrupt elections', *RFE/RL Newsline*, 23 August 2005; Borhan Younus, 'Taliban hit and run, and come back for more', *Afghan Recovery Report*, no. 185 (10 September 2005); personal communication with British diplomat, Kabul, February 2005; personal communication with Joint Election Management Body logistical officer, May 2004; *BBC News* reporters' log – Afghan vote, 9 October 2004.

27 Erben (n.d.). Although there were as many as two dozen attacks on election day, they do not seem to have been targeted at voters: see Akram Gizabi, 'Landmark Afghan parliamentary election goes smoothly', *Eurasia Daily Monitor* (Jamestown Foundation), vol. 2, no. 178 (26 September 2005).

28 Also according to the RAND-MIPT Terrorism Incident Database, as reported in Jones (2006), p. 113.

29 As argued in Akram Gizabi, 'Landmark Afghan parliamentary election goes smoothly'.

30 Gregg Zoroya, 'Afghanistan insurgents extremely resolute and fought to the last man', *USA Today*, 16 November 2005; Naylor (2006); Akram Gizabi, 'Landmark Afghan parliamentary election goes smoothly'; Nivat (2006), pp. 81–2; 'A geographical expression in search of a state', *The Economist*, 6 July 2006; Tim McGirk, 'The Taliban on the run'; personal communication with diplomats and UN officials in Kabul, January 2006.

31 As noted in Kemp (forthcoming), p. 7.

32 Carlotta Gall, 'Despite years of U.S. pressure, Taliban fight on in jagged hills'; Sara Daniel, 'Afghanistan: "Résister aux talibans? À quoi bon!"', *Le Nouvel Observateur*, 10 August 2006; Françoise Chipaux, 'Dans le plus complet dénuement, la province afghane de Zabul mène la lutte contre les talibans'; 'Excuses des talibans pour une "petite erreur" ayant fait 16 morts', *Reuters*, 6 January 2004; Paul Watson, 'On the trail of the Taliban's support'.

33 Greg Grant, 'Emboldened Taliban emerging', *Army Times*, 3 July 2006; Wright (2006a); Ángeles Espinosa, 'La OTAN lucha en territorio talibán', *El País*, 14 September 2006; Kathy Gannon, 'Taliban comeback traced to corruption', *Associated Press*, 24 November 2006; Sami Yousafzai and Urs Gehriger, 'A new layeha for the Mujahideen'; Christopher Dickey,

'Afghanistan: the Taliban's book of rules', *Newsweek*, 12 December 2006; Graeme Smith, 'Inspiring tale of triumph over Taliban not all it seems', *Globe and Mail*, 23 September 2006; Carlotta Gall, 'Despite years of U.S. pressure, Taliban fight on in jagged hills'.

34   On this see Trives (2006).

35   Elizabeth Rubin, 'In the land of the Taliban'; Kate Clark, 'Cash rewards for Taliban fighters', *File On 4, BBC Radio 4*, 28 February 2006; interview with Massoud Kharokhel, Tribal Liaison Office, Kabul, October 2006.

36   Syed Saleem Shahzad, 'Taliban line up the heavy artillery'; Syed Saleem Shahzad, 'Afghanistan's highway to hell', *Asia Times Online*, 25 January 2007.

37   Bill Graveland, 'Canadians battling Taliban propaganda', *CNews*, 4 December 2006; Graeme Smith, 'The Taliban: knowing the enemy', *Globe and Mail*, 27 November 2006; Sami Yousafzai, 'Afghanistan: want to meet the Taliban? No prob', *Newsweek*, 25 December 2006; Syed Saleem Shahzad, 'How the Taliban prepare for battle', *Asia Times Online*, 5 December 2006; Syed Saleem Shahzad, 'The vultures are circling', *Asia Times Online*, 13 December 2006; 'Taliban military commander Mullah Dadallah: we are in contact with Iraqi mujahideen, Osama bin Laden and Al-Zawahiri', *MEMRI Special Dispatch Series*, no. 1180 (2 June 2006).

38   Tom Coghlan, 'Karzai questions NATO campaign as Taliban takes to hi-tech propaganda', *Independent*, 23 June 2006.

39   B. Raman, 'Al Qaeda and India', South Asia Analysis Group Paper no. 1498 (13 August 2005); Syed Saleem Shahzad, 'Taliban's call for jihad answered in Pakistan', *Asia Times Online*, 16 June 2006; Senlis Council (2006b), ch. 6; Bill Graveland, 'Canadians battling Taliban propaganda'; 'Propaganda masters: the Taliban is using emotionally-charged video discs in Afghanistan that play on ethnic and religious pride to recruit potential sympathizers', *AFP*, 17 July 2006; Elizabeth Rubin, 'In the land of the Taliban'.

40   'Propaganda masters ...', *AFP*, 17 July 2006. See <http://www.siteinstitute.org/>.

41   Rothstein (2006), p. 117.

42   This hypothesis is favoured by some high-ranking UN officials (personal communication, Kabul, October 2006).

43   Tim McGirk, 'The Taliban on the run'; 'Menace taliban dans le Sud', *AFP*, 20 February 2004.

44   'Canadian, American killed in Afghanistan firefight', *CBS News*, 29 March 2006.

45   Michael Smith, 'Key strike puts Taliban to flight', *Sunday Times*, 17 September 2006; Tim Albone, 'Amid the thud of artillery, soldiers stormed into a Taliban stronghold', *The Times*, 14 September 2006; personal communication with military attaché, Kabul, October 2006; personal communication with European Union official, 3 October 2006; personal communication with UN official, Kabul, October 2006; Carlotta Gall, 'After Taliban battle, allies seek advantage', *New York Times*, 2 October

2006; Murray Brewster, 'Taliban to be pushed into the mountains and marginalized: Canadian commander', *Canadian Press*, 7 February 2007.

46 This was implicitly admitted by NATO itself when its spokesman said that more attention should have been paid to sparing civilian lives: 'NATO laments Afghan civilian dead', *BBC News*, 3 January 2007.

47 Ahmed Rashid, 'Musharraf: stop aiding the Taliban', *Daily Telegraph*, 6 October 2006.

48 Bill Graveland, 'Taliban shows little resistance', *Canadian Press*, 24 December 2006; Syed Saleem Shahzad, 'Afghanistan's highway to hell'; 'Les taliban annoncent une offensive de printemps en Afghanistan', *Reuters*, 22 November 2006; 'A growing threat in Afghanistan', *Spiegel Online*, 4 December 2006; Jason Burke, 'Taliban plan to fight through winter to throttle Kabul', *Observer*, 29 October 2006; David Wood, 'Afghan war needs troops', *Baltimore Sun*, 7 January 2007; personal communication with ISAF source, Kabul, 7 December 2006; Ahto Lobjakas, 'Afghanistan: NATO seeks to preempt Taliban offensive in Helmand', *RFE/RL*, 31 January 2007; personal communication with Niamatullah Ibrahimi, Crisis States Research Centre, Kabul, January 2007; Alastair Leithead, 'Helmand seeing insurgent surge', *BBC News*, 11 February 2007; Sami Yousafzai and Ron Moreau, 'The mysterious Mullah Omar'; *Afghanistan*, 19 April 2007.

49 Syed Saleem Shahzad, 'Taliban raise the stakes in Afghanistan'; Marie-France Calle, 'Les talibans auraient infiltré les grandes villes', *Le Figaro*, 30 December 2003.

50 Shahin Eghraghi, 'Hekmatyar: the wild card in Afghanistan', *Asia Times Online*, 7 January 2004; Romesh Ratnesar, 'In the line of fire', *Time*, 8 September 2002; Syed Saleem Shahzad, 'Afghanistan strikes back at Pakistan', *Asia Times Online*, 9 November 2006; Syed Saleem Shahzad, 'Taliban line up the heavy artillery'; 'Interview with Afghan Islamist leader on jihad against U.S.', *MEMRI Special Dispatch Series*, no. 455 (6 January 2003); Abdul Qadir Munsif and Hakim Basharat, 'Conflicts keep away Taliban, Hizb-i-Islami', *Pajhwok Afghan News*, 12 December 2006; 'Hezb-E Islami claim to have taken control of Wormami district', *Arman*, 10 December 2006; ANA sources, January 2007; 'Afghan warlord wants "joint front" with Taleban', *AFP*, 10 March 2007; Zarar Khan, 'Afghan warlord sends mixed signals', *Associated Press*, 9 March 2007; Isambard Wilkinson, 'Warlord claims alliance with Taliban over', *Daily Telegraph*, 9 March 2007; Rahimullah Yusufzai, 'Hekmatyar denies offering unconditional talks to Karzai', *News International*, 9 March 2007.

51 Cordesman (2007); Noor Khan, 'NATO forces recapture Afghan territory', *Associated Press*, 12 September 2006; interview with police officers, Teluqan, May 2006; personal communication with UN source, Kunduz, March 2004; 'North is becoming unstable', *Anis*, 5 November 2006; Shoaib Tanha, 'Herat: distribution of statement by Hezb-e Eslami', *Pagah*, 10 October 2006; Kunduz governor rejects militants' comeback', *Pajhwok Afghan News*, 22 November 2006; *Pajhwok Afghan News*, 19 December 2006.

52 'New armed group announces "jihad"', *Pajhwok Afghan News*, 12 October 2006; van der Schriek (2005); Syed Saleem Shahzad, 'Osama back in the US crosshairs', *Asia Times Online*, 17 May 2006; Schiewek (2006), p. 163.

53 Syed Saleem Shahzad, 'Pakistan makes a deal with the Taliban', *Asia Times Online*, 1 March 2007; Claudio Franco, 'In remote Afghan camp, Taliban explain how and why they fight'; translation of biography of Arab jihadist, in *Global Terror Alert*, January 2006.

54 Michael Scheuer, 'Awakening Afghanistan's "old mujahideen"', *National Post*, 15 November 2006; Graeme Smith, 'The Taliban: knowing the enemy'; personal communication with UN official, Kabul, October 2005; personal communication with UN official, Kabul, March 2007.

55 Guy Dinmore and Rachel Morarjee, 'To a second front? How Afghanistan could again be engulfed by civil war'; 'Rocket attack on Maimana city', *Pajhwok Afghan News*, 10 December 2006.

56 Personal communication with UN official, Kabul, October 2003; Syed Saleem Shahzad, 'US turns to the Taliban', *Asia Times Online*, 14 June 2003; Victoria Burnett, 'US backs Afghan proposal to woo moderate Taliban', *Financial Times*, 31 December 2003; Rahim Faiez, 'Karzai says he has met with Taliban', *Associated Press*, 6 April 2007.

57 Saeed Ali Achakzai, 'Taliban says might join Afghan tribal peace talks', *Reuters*, 9 December 2006; 'Taliban says want no part of tribal peace talks', *Reuters*, 11 December 2006.

58 Fisnik Abrashi and Jason Straziuso, 'Deepening insurgency puts Afghanistan on brink', *Associated Press*, 8 October 2006; interview with Zaif, ex ambassador of Taliban in Pakistan, Kabul, October 2006.

59 Ismail Khan, 'Omar threatens to intensify war: talks with Karzai govt ruled out', *Dawn*, 4 January 2007; *Daily Times*, 28 October 2006; Muhammad Saleh Zaafir, 'Kabul against holding of one peace jirga', *The News*, 12 December 2006.

60 See 'Taliban military commander Mullah Dadallah: we are in contact with Iraqi mujahideen, Osama bin Laden and Al-Zawahiri', *MEMRI Special Dispatch Series*, no. 1180 (2 June 2006).

5
MILITARY TACTICS OF
THE INSURGENCY

Taliban tactics have been described as 'ingenious'[1] and there is certainly an element of truth in that. However, this applies to their use of available technology as well as to their tactics, as the Taliban were trying to make up for their shortage of both technology and skills.

5.1 MILITARY TECHNOLOGY OF THE INSURGENCY

Confronted with a far more technologically advanced enemy, the leadership of the Taliban seemed to have been well aware that motivation, commitment, determination, popular support and a sound strategy might not suffice to wear out the foreign contingents. In the early stages of the insurgency advanced weaponry was not necessary. However, as the Taliban escalated their activities in 2005–7, in order to inflict significant casualties an adequate military technology was required. Despite claims that the rebels were 'well armed' and had 'excellent weapons', throughout 2002–6 the weapons used by the Taliban were largely the usual Kalashnikov assault rifle (AK-47, -74, AKM) and RPG-7 rocket launcher, as well as primitive models of field rockets (BM-1) and machine guns, including a few heavy DShK. They also used hand-made IEDs of rather primitive design and antiquated types of land mines. 'Well armed', therefore, can only have meant that the Taliban have not just been using left-over Kalashnikovs and RPGs, but have also been purchasing brand new ones. By the standards of the early twenty-first century, these are quite obsolete weapons when the enemy being confronted is a state-of-the-art Western army, the more so since the ammunition available to the insurgents was mostly standard. Some improved penetration bullets, better able to pierce bullet-proof vests, were reportedly found in the Taliban's hands on a few occasions, while the Taliban seemed to be aware of the weakest spots in the body armour of US soldiers, but the ability to inflict mortal wounds on foreign troops seems to have been only marginally affected. The RPG-7 proved ill suited to inflict serious damage on the armoured troops transports commonly used by the foreign contingents in Afghanistan. Particularly in flat areas, the mobility awarded to the foreign troops by all-terrain transport and helicopters contrasted with the Taliban's reliance on foot soldiers, unable to move quickly and to counter enemy re-deployments effectively. In engagements taking place over large areas, the gap in communications technologies was also a major handicap for the Taliban.[2]

Although there are clear indications that the insurgents were trying to improve the quality of the equipment used, such desire clashed with the limited availability of advanced weaponry on the regional black market. Nonetheless, some progress was recorded in the arsenal of the Taliban. Two key weapons were non-conventional: IEDs and suicide bombers. There is no doubt about the rapidly increasing use of both, as shown in Graphs 1 and 3, but the ability of the Taliban to manage the technology also improved dramatically after 2002. Although the Taliban always lagged behind the sophistication of their Iraqi colleagues in the manufacturing of IEDs, the gap was estimated to have narrowed from an initial twelve months to six months during 2006, despite the alleged capture of 250 bomb-makers by foreign and government forces. In the spring of 2006 the Taliban were already making experiments in stacking anti-tank mines together, while during 2006 linking together IEDs to improve the targeting of moving vehicles was also becoming common. Government forces and ISAF/CFC-A (until November 2006) were also improving their skills, though, and in January 2007 about half of all IEDs were identified and neutralised before exploding. Similarly, the technology used in suicide bombings improved, as did the skills of the suicide bombers. In 2004 suicide attacks were still estimated to have a failure rate of around 60–70 per cent. In 2005 the failure rate was down to 10–15 per cent, showing a dramatic improvement in the skills of the Taliban's 'bomb craftsmen' and of the suicide volunteers. Experts disagree on whether the improvement was the result of imported skills from the insurgents active in the Iraqi theatre or the result of local developments, but the Taliban themselves claim to have received help from the Arabs starting from no later than 2004. Certainly some technology seems to have come from abroad: in September 2006 fifteen 'highly sophisticated' bombs were seized by police in a mosque in Kabul, and they were thought to have been imported into Afghanistan.[3]

In terms of weaponry, most of the remaining progress achieved by the Taliban after 2002 was a matter of expanding the range available, rather than upgrading the technology used. The use of mortars was already reported in 2002 in attacks against US and Afghan bases. Since mortars require a relatively high degree of training to be used effectively, and are rather cumbersome on the battlefield for non-motorised infantry, it is perhaps not surprising that they started being employed in open engagements only in 2006 and even then played only a relatively limited role. The largest use of mortars took place during the most violent fighting of the conflict to date, in September 2006 in Pashmul (Kandahar), when it is estimated that the Taliban fired 1,000 shells, along with 2,000 RPG rounds and 400,000 rounds of automatic weapons. In general, NATO officers had disparaging views of the ability of the Taliban to use mortars effectively.[4]

The difficulty of the Taliban in dealing with armoured vehicles was by 2006 proving to be a major shortcoming, as they had started closing in on Kandahar and had made the decision to contest the mainly flat ground surrounding the city. The Taliban apparently referred to armoured vehicles as 'monsters' or 'beasts'. Although recoilless guns started being used in July 2006, because of being so cumbersome they were only used in engagements fought within the Taliban's strongholds of Helmand and Zabul and were not reported to have been used against armour. Anti-tank mines have been used by the Taliban since at least 2003,[5] but these were old models and often ineffective. More effective types were reportedly in use in 2005, but only occasionally. Moreover, the impact of mines on the battlefield can only be limited to defensive operations or to occasional ambushes. The Taliban tried to cope with the problem by organising ambushes in which salvos of several RPG grenades were fired at a single target (or kill zone), but again there are obvious limitations to the impact of these tactics. Foreign advisors to the police and officers of various foreign military contingents acknowledged that the Taliban were actively seeking heavier anti-tank weapons, with little success. During the autumn of 2006 there were unconfirmed reports of Chinese-made anti-tank weapons of more advanced types than the RPG-7 being found in Uruzgan, but it is not clear what models these would be.[6]

There were some other efforts by the Taliban to upgrade the technological content of their arsenal, but these too were limited. The capture of Russian-made silencers and night-vision equipment was reported as early as September 2003 in Paktika, and similar equipment was also employed in Uruzgan in 2004, but does not seem to have been commonly used. They might have been old devices captured during the anti-Soviet jihad, or small quantities of equipment belonging to individual volunteers, probably from Chechnya. For years rumours circulated that the Taliban were obtaining advanced equipment such as anti-aircraft guided missiles, including claims by the Taliban themselves. However, according to US and ISAF sources these had never been used in combat until late 2006. In 2006 rumours surfaced that Mullah Obeidullah, one of the leaders, had travelled abroad looking for anti-aircraft missiles to purchase. According to Taliban and UN sources, copies of Russian Strela 1 or 2 shoulder-fired missiles were first obtained in 2005, but the Taliban faced serious difficulties in training their fighters to use them and had to involve 'Arabs' in order to employ them on the battlefield or to receive appropriate training. At least two such missiles were fired against ISAF planes at the end of 2006 and another in early 2007, all of which missed their targets. In 2006 the Taliban also claimed to be trying to acquire more precise and powerful field rockets than the light Chinese and North Korean version they had been using since 2002, but it is not clear how they would have been able to move this heavy equipment around Afghanistan. The aiming and success rate of the field rockets undoubtedly improved in 2002–6, but this appears to have been due to the greater skills of those firing them than to the adoption of more advanced models.[7]

Given the features of the Afghan conflict and the low marksmanship levels of the Taliban rank-and-file, an obvious option to improve the ability to inflict casualties would have been the widespread deployment of snipers. Although laser pointers seem to have been utilised relatively often, they were rarely put to good use. In August 2005 the effective deployment of snipers by the Taliban was reported in the fighting at Mari Ghar, but the tendency among US officers was to attribute sniping skills to foreign volunteers, particularly Chechens. In any case, there was little report of appearances of skilled snipers after Mari Ghar. Taliban sources announced in July 2006 the ongoing training of teams of snipers and the acquisition of Russian Dragunov rifles as a major innovation. The case of sniper rifles is a confirmation of the Taliban's limited access to black market sources of advanced weaponry and of their dependence on Arab allies and sympathisers for the supply of more advanced military technology. All they could do was to hope that the Arabs' promises of bringing in more advanced equipment from the Middle East would be fulfilled.[8]

Some of the most important innovations in the Taliban's arsenal were not weapons. Reports that the Taliban were buying many hundreds of motorcycles during the summer of 2003, mainly 125cc Hondas, were later confirmed when these motorcycles started being used extensively inside Afghanistan as means of transport, reconnaissance, communications and battlefield coordination and also to carry out attacks against road-blocks. Substantial resources were also invested in improving telecommunications. Already during the summer of 2003 the insurgents were spotted using satellite phones in large numbers, presumably for long-distance communications. The motorcycles were usually all fitted with phone chargers, a fact which suggests that motorcycle-mounted reconnaissance scouts played an important role in the insurgents' operations at least for some time. Field radios made their first appearance during the summer of 2005, although it was not until 2006 that the Taliban started using them proficiently on the battlefield to coordinate groups of more than 100 combatants. However, the radios used by the Taliban up to the end of 2006 were always commercial types, not frequency-hopping military models. Precise US artillery and air bombardment, combined with advanced radio monitoring techniques, often resulted in the quick elimination of Taliban scouting teams. After some disastrous incidents involving radios and satellite phones, the Taliban became increasingly aware of the fact that their enemies were constantly monitoring their communications and started using them more carefully, resorting to coded messages or even dropping radios in favour of low-technology techniques like torch-signalling.[9]

5.2 MANOEUVRABILITY AND COORDINATION

As highlighted earlier, in order to upgrade their challenge to the enemy, the Taliban increasingly needed to concentrate larger numbers of fighters on the battlefield (see 4.8 *The third phase: 'final offensive'?*). This posed a number of problems. The first was how to command and control their men during the fighting. When the number reached over a hundred, shouting lost its effectiveness. The introduction of radios gave the Taliban the potential to manage the larger concentrations and the tactic appears to have been used effectively. NATO and US sources tend to agree that by 2005–6 the ability of the Taliban to quickly gather large numbers of men and to respond rapidly on the battlefield improved considerably. The insurgents also demonstrated an ability to split into small groups of four or five, as well as to scatter when ambushed and then reorganise. Some Taliban sources explain the improvement in operational capabilities in part with the cooperation between Jalaluddin Haqqani and other Taliban commanders less experienced in guerrilla warfare, as well as cooperation between Hekmatyar's Hizb-i Islami and the Taliban. While it is likely that Haqqani might have had a role, there is little evidence of any effective cooperation between Taliban and Hizb (see 4.9 *Alliances*), but former members of Hizb-i Islami absorbed by the Taliban could have played that role.[10]

The Taliban also placed great emphasis in establishing a thick network of informers, able to advise them of the movements of the enemy and enabling their forces to set up ambushes quickly. They also created their own motorcycle-mounted reconnaissance units, tasked with following NATO/US patrols and other potential targets, as well as with field reconnaissance. The use of Icom scanners to monitor radio and phone calls has also been reported.[11]

5.3 TACTICAL SKILLS

If tactical coordination was an area of evident improvement in 2005–6, other major shortcomings in the training of the insurgents remained. Initially at least, the training imparted to the new recruits was limited to forty days of 'physical and spiritual' instruction, including mainly lectures about the need for jihad and technical training on explosive devices and rockets. In practice, ideological training had pre-eminence over technical in many training camps. This did not always have negative repercussions on the tactical ability of the fighters, as at least it helped the Taliban to instil in them a strong determination. NATO and US officers were generally quite impressed by their resolution, particularly after 2004. Until 2004 the insurgents would normally break off contact as soon as air support was called in. Once ordered to stand and fight even while under air attack, however, the Taliban demonstrated the courage to do it. In a number of fights in 2005 and 2006 the Taliban did not even break contact after having been targeted by 2000lb bombs, often fighting to the last man, actually an odd tactic in guerrilla warfare. However, the stress on ideological indoctrination and on the formation of group comrade-ship came at the expense of tactical skills. Often in the early times of the insurgency little military training was imparted at all, resulting in disastrous outcomes on the battlefield. While this problem was at least in part resolved (see 5.2 *Manoeuvrability and coordination*), others were not. Particularly in the south, the aiming skills of the insurgents were very bad and they were often missing their targets even at very short distances, such as ten to fifty feet. US sources estimated that the Taliban only had a 5 per cent chance of killing an American soldier in the average engagement. Another shortcoming derived from poor training was weak radio discipline, despite the awareness that NATO/US forces were constantly monitoring the insurgents' communications. Poor training might have reflected the shortage of skilled cadres, which derived from the rapid expansion of the ranks, the extremely weak recruitment of educated individuals and the limited experience in guerrilla warfare. US forces on the ground also reported the preoccupation of Taliban units with protecting their leaders, even at the cost of high casualties, a fact which might be a reflection of this shortage of cadres. The loss of a commander could lead to permanent damage to the effectiveness of the insurgents. However, the lack of experience and training was evident when Taliban commanders would mistake mortar fire for air bombardment, or when they would underestimate the reconnaissance and communication abilities of the opponent, hiding in unsafe places.[12]

There were efforts to improve the situation. In 2005 some members of the Taliban reportedly started training in Iraq. Eight Afghans were allegedly part of a first group to travel there through Baluchistan and presumably Iran, to spend three months training. On their return to Pakistan, the trainees would impart to other Afghans the same training. However, the courses were mainly based on handling explosives and remote control detonators and while they might well have improved the insurgents' skills with IEDs, it is unlikely that they significantly affected their battlefield performance.[13]

The biggest tactical problem for the Taliban was how to avoid air strikes. They identified three basic options. The first was to split into small groups and flee. This was in fact the soundest option, but given the near omnipresence of air support, it would have amounted to forsaking any major offensive operation against international troops, ANA and from 2005 even Afghan police. Moreover, splitting into small groups and disappearing into the countryside was not always easy for non-local guerrillas who did not know the region where they were operating. A source close to the US military alleges that most losses among the Taliban ranks in the summer of 2006 were Pakistani volunteers, unable to melt in an unknown countryside.[14]

The second option was to seek cover whenever it was available once air power intervened on their enemy's side. Engagements were often refused when aircraft were present on the scene. Whenever possible the insurgents exploited the rugged terrain to avoid the superior firepower of US and NATO troops. In their own strongholds of northern Helmand, for example, the Taliban would dig ditches and channels or use existing ones and every other type of cover available.[15] The choice of Pashmul as a stronghold-to-be near Kandahar also appears to have been due to similar characteristics (see 4.8 *The third phase: 'final offensive'?*). The Taliban developed the ability to calculate the exact flight time of helicopters from their bases to the target area, preparing themselves to go into hiding with the arrival of the helicopter. However, the use of UAVs meant that US forces could survey an area of suspected Taliban concentration virtually indefinitely, often without the insurgents even realising it. Nonetheless, during the first few months of 2007 signs emerged that the Taliban were becoming increasingly proficient in avoiding offering easy targets to air attack. The US and allied air forces were being forced increasingly to rely on expensive guided missiles to eliminate small teams of insurgents, often as small as two or three individuals.[16]

The third option, adopted when it was deemed necessary to confront the adversary on the open ground or to attack its bases, was to carry out human wave attacks in order to close in as rapidly as possible. The tactic was first used as early as 2005 in the south-east, where the level of training and the skill of Taliban cadres were higher. They usually abstained from resorting to this tactic in flat areas or where the enemy had strong artillery support, or whenever the target was not worth it. The tactic later spread to the south, but was still used parsimoniously. In Kandahar province during 2006 there was a reduction in the number of ambushes and IED attacks by the insurgents compared to 2005, but a strong increase in 'outbreaks of open warfare', from twelve to twenty-eight, although many of these clashes were started by NATO troops. In terms of tactical effectiveness, human waves were clearly counterproductive. In Kandahar province estimates of casualties on both sides for the first five months of 2006 saw a much greater increase in civilian casualties and even more so in insurgent casualties than in the ranks of Afghan security forces and of the foreign troops. Moreover, the Taliban never succeeded in taking any objective defended by foreign troops, or inflicting large casualties on the foreigners. During 2005–6 the improved communication equipment of police and district headquarters meant that they were often able to appeal to ISAF for air support rather quickly, raising the cost of the Taliban's raids. In many cases, despite problems in USAF–US Army and US–British coordination, it might have taken as little as twenty minutes for air support to be deployed on the battlefield, making the task of closing in quickly enough a very demanding one for the Taliban field commanders. The political impact of the intense battles of 2006, however, was a different matter (see 2.7 *Changes in recruitment patterns*).[17]

The Neo-Taliban also demonstrated a fierce concern for the evacuation of casualties, including dead, and developed the ability to carry out this task efficiently.[18] Starting in no later than 2006, field hospitals were built in close proximity to enemy outposts and equipped with medical supplies.[19]

From late 2006 the Taliban began paying much greater attention to fighting off the infiltration attempts of the intelligence agencies of the government and of its external allies. As the insurgents moved closer to the cities and increased recruitment inside Afghanistan, they became increasingly vulnerable to the information gathering of their enemies. While Western officials recognised that penetrating the core of the Taliban remained almost impossible, their presence in many inhabited areas and the travels of the leaders across vast regions offered opportunities for villagers to supply key information to the Taliban's enemies. Searching individuals and in particular 'strangers' became routine for the Taliban and executions of 'informers' and 'spies' were constantly being reported in early 2007.[20]

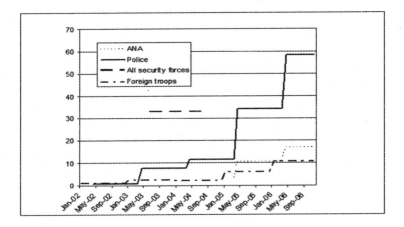

Graph 6. Combat losses suffered by Afghan armed forces and foreign contingents, 2002–7 (killed in action). 'All security forces' includes militias.

Sources: <www.icasualties.org/oef>, Ministry of Defence of Afghanistan press releases, Ministry of Interior of Afghanistan press releases, Law and Order Trust Fund—Afghanistan, press reports.

NOTES

1 Captain McKenzie, quoted in Christina Lamb, 'Have you ever used a pistol?', *Sunday Times*, 2 July 2006.

2 British officers quoted in Thomas Harding, 'Paras strike deep into the Taliban heartland', *Daily Telegraph*, 19 June 2006; McCaffrey (2006); *AFP*, 22 July 2006; Nick Allen, 'Sticks and carrots sway wayward Afghan town', *DPA*, 18 December 2006; David Rohde, 'G.I.s in Afghanistan on hunt, but now for hearts and minds', *New York Times*, 30 March 2004; 'Les talibans cherchent à se procurer des armes plus puissantes', *Afghan.org*, 8 May 2006, <http://www.afghana.org/html/article.php?sid=2092>.

3 'Increasing Afghan IED threat gives forces cause for concern', *Jane's Intelligence Review*, 1 August 2006; personal communication with UNAMA official, Kabul, May 2005; ANSO sources, quoted in Françoise Chipaux, 'En Afghanistan, des rebelles mieux organisés infligent de lourdes pertes aux forces américaines', *Le Monde*, 22 August 2005; Elizabeth Rubin, 'In the land of the Taliban', *New York Times Magazine*, 22 October 2006; 'Taliban military commander Mullah Dadallah: we are in contact with Iraqi mujahideen, Osama bin Laden and Al-Zawahiri', *MEMRI Special Dispatch Series*, no. 1180 (2 June 2006); Anna Badkhen, 'Foreign jihadists seen as key to spike in Afghan attacks', *San Francisco Chronicle*, 25 September 2006; 'Taliban seen adjusting tactics', *Reuters*, 13 February 2007; Kevin Dougherty, 'NATO and Afghanistan: a status report', *Stars and Stripes* (Mideast edition), 18 February 2007; UNDSS weekly presentation, 26 January–1 February 2007.

4 Tim McGirk and Michael Ware, 'Losing control? The U.S. concedes it has lost momentum in Afghanistan, while its enemies grow bolder', *Time*, 11 November 2002; Ron Synovitz, 'Taliban launches "spring offensive" with attack on Helmand base', *RFE/RL*, 30 March 2006; Peter Bergen, 'The Taliban, "regrouped and rearmed"', *Washington Post*, 10 September 2006; Christina Lamb, 'Have you ever used a pistol?'; Ahmed Rashid, 'Musharraf: stop aiding the Taliban', *Daily Telegraph*, 6 October 2006; Bill Roggio, 'Taliban losses in Afghanistan, gains in Pakistan', blog, *Fourth Rail*, 25 June 2006, <http://billroggio.com/archives/2006/06/taliban_losses_in_af.php>.

5 Owais Tohid, 'Arid Afghan province proves fertile for Taliban', *Christian Science Monitor*, 14 July 2003.

6 'Increasing Afghan IED threat gives forces cause for concern', *Jane's Intelligence Review*, 1 August 2006; Peter Bergen, 'The Taliban, "regrouped and rearmed"'; Tim Albone, 'Pathfinders on a four-day mission fight off eight-week Taliban siege', *The Times*, 27 September 2006; Nick Meo, 'In Afghanistan, the Taliban rises again for fighting season', *Independent*, 15 May 2005; 'Les talibans cherchent à se procurer des armes plus puissantes', *Afghan.org*, 8 May 2006, <http://www.afghana.org/html/article.php?sid=2092>; personal communication with researcher Armando Geller,

London, November 2006.

7   Carsten Stormer, 'Winning hearts, minds and firefights in Uruzgan', *Asia Times Online*, 6 August 2004; *AFP*, 21 September 2003; Scott Baldauf and Ashraf Khan, 'New guns, new drive for Taliban', *Christian Science Monitor*, 26 September 2005; Bill Roggio, 'Observations from southeastern Afghanistan', <http://counterterrorismblog.org/2006/06/observations_from_southeastern.php>; Graeme Smith, 'The Taliban: knowing the enemy', *Globe and Mail*, 27 November 2006; Tom Coghlan, 'Taliban train snipers on British forces', *Daily Telegraph*, 23 July 2006; 'Increasing Afghan IED threat gives forces cause for concern', *Jane's Intelligence Review*, 1 August 2006; 'Taliban claims it used surface-to-air missile to down helicopter', *Adnkronos International*, 22 February 2007; personal communication with UN official, Kabul, March 2007; Syed Saleem Shahzad, 'Pakistan makes a deal with the Taliban', *Asia Times Online*, 1 March 2007; 'Coalition strikes Taleban linked to anti-aircraft weapons', *AFP*, 10 March 2007.

8   David Rohde, 'G.I.s in Afghanistan on hunt, but now for hearts and minds'; Sean D. Naylor, 'Outnumbered and surrounded by Taliban, the Spartans came out on top in 54-hour fight', *Army Times*, 26 June 2006; Declan Walsh, 'In the heartland of a mysterious enemy, US troops battle to survive', *Guardian*, 5 December 2006; Tom Coghlan, 'Taliban train snipers on British forces'.

9   Ahmed Rashid, 'Safe haven for the Taliban', *Far Eastern Economic Review*, 16 October 2003; *AFP*, 21 September 2003; Andrew Maykuth, 'An Afghan rebuilding takes shape', *Philadelphia Inquirer*, 6 October 2003; Scott Baldauf and Ashraf Khan, 'New guns, new drive for Taliban'; Sean D. Naylor, 'The waiting game. A stronger Taliban lies low, hoping the U.S. will leave Afghanistan', *Army Times*, February 2006; Carsten Stormer, 'Winning hearts, minds and firefights in Uruzgan'; Wright (2006a); Elizabeth Rubin, 'Taking the fight to the Taliban', *New York Times Magazine*, 29 October 2006.

10 Sean D. Naylor, 'The waiting game. A stronger Taliban lies low, hoping the U.S. will leave Afghanistan'; Christina Lamb, 'Have you ever used a pistol?'; 'Taliban fighting with more sophistication: US-led coalition', *AFP*, 22 July 2006; Wright (2006a); Tom Coghlan, 'Taliban train snipers on British forces'; Claudio Franco, 'Islamic militant insurgency in Afghanistan experiencing "Iraqization"', *Eurasianet*, 8 November 2005.

11 Phil Zabriskie, 'Dangers up ahead: how druglords and insurgents are making the war in Afghanistan deadlier than ever', *Time*, 5 March 2006; Wright (2006a).

12 Owais Tohid, 'Taliban regroups – on the road', *Christian Science Monitor*, 27 June 2003; Sean D. Naylor, 'The waiting game. A stronger Taliban lies low, hoping the U.S. will leave Afghanistan'; Gregg Zoroya, 'Afghanistan insurgents "extremely resolute and fought to the last man"', *USA Today*, 16 November 2005; Scott Baldauf, 'Small US units lure Taliban into losing battles', *Christian Science Monitor*, 31 October 2005; Scott Baldauf, 'Taliban

play hide-and-seek with US troops', *Christian Science Monitor*, 12 October 2005; Christina Lamb, 'Have you ever used a pistol?'; Declan Walsh, 'In the heartland of a mysterious enemy, US troops battle to survive'; Tom Coghlan, 'Taliban train snipers on British forces'; Sean D. Naylor, 'Outnumbered and surrounded by Taliban, the Spartans came out on top in 54-hour fight'. For an example of the impact of poor training as described by a militant see Philippe Grangereau, 'Comment le Pakistan redonne des forces aux talibans afghans', *Libération*, 4 September 2003; Cordesman (2007).

13 Sara Daniel and Sami Yousufzai, 'Ils Apprenent en Irak les secrets du Djihad Technologique', *Le Nouvel Observateur*, 3 November, 2005.

14 James Dunnigan, 'The secret war in Afghanistan', *Strategy Page*, 1 January 2007.

15 Wright (2006a).

16 Anthony Loyd, 'It's dawn, and the shelling starts. Time to go into the Taleban maze', *The Times*, 14 February 2007; personal communication with Declan Walsh, who was embedded as a journalist with British forces in Helmand, April 2007.

17 Nick Meo, 'In Afghanistan, the Taliban rises again for fighting season'; Lee Greenberg, 'Renewed Afghan fighting comes amid signs of Taliban buildup', *Ottawa Citizen*, 30 October 2006; Senlis Council (2006c), pp. 32, 37; 'Afghan firefight kills 55 militants', *Associated Press*, 30 October 2006; on some problems of USAF–US Army coordination in the use of close air support, see Greg Jaffe, 'Getting U.S. forces together poses challenge for war plan', *Wall Street Journal*, 11 February 2003. For a more detailed analysis see Pirnie (2005).

18 'A double spring offensive', *The Economist*, 22 February 2007.

19 Laura King, 'Taliban offensive expected in spring', *Los Angeles Times*, 18 February 2007.

20 'Informer killings show growing Taleban control', *Afghan Recovery Report*, no. 243 (26 February 2007).

6

THE COUNTER-INSURGENCY EFFORT

In the beginning neither the Americans nor the Afghan government took the Neo-Taliban insurgency very seriously, although for different reasons. The United States had other places in the world in their sight and the Afghan campaign was left without much political or strategic direction. The Afghans were relying on what they perceived as the United States' overwhelming power to rid them of their enemies in the remote countryside and across the Pakistani border and did not invest much energy or resources in the counter-insurgency effort or in seeking to prevent the conditions which made the spread of the insurgency possible. In fact, Karzai and his circle continued to busy themselves with building a power system without paying any consideration to the effects these efforts would have either on the ongoing insurgency or on the popularity of the government. When criticism of the Karzai administration's conduct started to surface among Afghans and expatriates alike, opinion polls were produced showing very high popularity ratings for Karzai (on the reliability of polls see 2.1 *How strong are the Taliban?*). Those travelling around the country during the early years of the insurgency had different feelings about the popularity of the government, but were not listened to by the over-confident Americans and pro-Karzai Afghans. By 2006, when reality struck back with a vengeance, the insurgency was already well past the incubation stage.

The military counter-insurgency effort in Afghanistan was the work of several different components. At the top, in terms of combat potential and decisional power, ranked the US Task Force assigned to the Afghan theatre. Until 2006 the only other foreign contingents to see significant fighting were a 200-man detachment of French special troops based in Spin Boldak and a Romanian battalion based in Kandahar as well some Australian special troops. From 2006 British, Canadian, Australian and Dutch troops were also actively involved. On the Afghan side, until 2004 the only forces active against the insurgents were various Afghan militias, the police and Afghan units directly recruited by the Americans. This section focuses mainly on the Afghan component of the counter-insurgency, in part because of its neglected importance and in part because the qualities and limitations of the Western armies involved are better known.

A very important component of the counter-insurgency effort which is not discussed at length is the National Security Directorate (NSD), Afghanistan's intelligence service. Due to its inevitably secretive character, not much is known about its activities and capabilities. Its strength is variously estimated at 15–20,000, to which a large number of informers should be added. Starting from 2004 the NSD tried to expand its network of informers, aiming to have at least one in each village, but it is doubtful that it succeeded, at least in the insurgency-ridden regions of the south. The Directorate certainly contains a comparatively large number of professionally-trained officers, largely coming from the Soviet school. What is of particular concern to the scope of this book is that the NSD's methods of information gathering remain to date largely 'traditional' and technologically primitive. One of the consequences of having a relatively limited network of informers is that cross-checking information is often difficult, a fact which makes the NSD vulnerable to 'bad tips'. Many former jihadi fighters and former Taliban seem to believe that the NSD's Soviet-trained officers are deliberately targeting them for revenge purposes, but it is likely that misreporting and false accusations might derive from the limitations of the informers' network, which can be easily exploited by information suppliers to pursue personal feuds. There are also indications that in order to recruit informers in sensitive areas and in specific sectors of the population the NSD might resort to harassment and intimidation. The other main source of information apart from informers is the interrogation of suspects. Beatings and torture appear to be used routinely for this purpose. Since many of those arrested are then released, if for no other reason than a lack of capacity in NSD's prisons, these practices are likely to have driven many into the hands of the insurgency.[1]

6.1 INTERNATIONAL ACTORS

As far as the foreign contingents involved in the counter-insurgency are concerned, suffice it to say that they were all composed of professional troops, with a strong presence of Special Operations Forces (about 2,000 in late 2006) and élite troops such as paratroopers and others. The equipment did not include tanks until the arrival of fifteen Canadian ones at the end of 2006, but it did include armoured troops transports. Artillery was available at the main bases. Air support was available through A-10s, F-16s and AH-64s based in Bagram, Kandahar and Kabul, as well as plenty of UAVs and B-52s and B-1s flying from distant US bases and circling over Afghanistan waiting for a call. The actual number of troops increased from some 15,000 in 2002 to around 47,000 in March 2007. While the numbers were far too small to secure all or even a substantial part of Afghanistan, in terms of tactical potential these troops far outclassed anything the Taliban could field (see also 5.1 *Military technology of the insurgency*). Based on released figures, in direct engagements the average casualty rate (including dead and wounded) would appear to be as high as ten or twenty to one, although the overall rate (including military victims of road bombs, suicide attacks and Afghan government forces) was significantly lower at maybe three to one. Criticism vented at the foreign contingents involved in the counter-insurgency has focused on a reliance on massive firepower, mostly delivered from the air, a lack of attention for developing local knowledge and familiarity and a failure to maintain whatever knowledge was accumulated through the successive rotations of personnel.[2]

Another weakness of the foreign contingents was found in their relations with the local population. The AIHRC registered forty-four complaints against the behaviour of US forces in June 2003–June 2004[3] and 113 in June 2004–May 2005,[4] of which at least eighty were from southern Afghanistan. These ranged from lack of respect for local customs to arbitrary arrest and killings. Unauthorised access to homes was a major source of discontent, to the extent that it soon forced US forces to rely on Afghan militias and security forces rather than their own troops. Using Afghan troops was not always possible or even seen as desirable by some US commanders, so that house searches continued even if at a diminished pace. Efforts by the local authorities to restrain such activities by US troops were sometimes at least partially successful, such as in Khost province, but the 'disrespectful' attitude towards house searches would then resurface elsewhere, for example in Nangarhar. Smaller incidents, such as the 'recreational' looting of agricultural fields, also contributed to generate a climate of resentment towards the foreign troops. In general, there was little understanding among the population for US security requirements, such as the ban on drivers overtaking US convoys. This background helps to explain how simple road accidents could spark whole riots, as happened in Kabul in May 2006. Even officials of the reconciliation commission established by the government (see 6.8 *Reconciliation efforts*) tried to stay clear of US representatives, fearing that meeting them would reflect negatively on their popularity. Other foreign contingents were not necessarily welcome either, in part because the rural population failed to distinguish between them and in part because of historical memories. The heritage of two nineteenth-century wars against the British was still felt in southern Afghanistan, where the British are often described in 'derogatory' terms.[5]

As the counter-insurgent force took an increasingly multinational character during 2006, issues related to the unity of intents and to the formulation of a common strategy became paramount. The rift within ISAF during 2006, pitting in particular Germans against Americans and British, concerned exactly the unity of intents and contributed to create a climate of uncertainty, which was perceived by the Afghan population too.[6] Tension had been simmering throughout 2004–6 as

NATO struggled to organise its takeover of the international security effort in Afghanistan and to ensure a greater presence of its member countries. It started boiling over during 2006 as British and Canadian troops were stretched thin in the south and other countries showed little solidarity. According to British MPs, German commanding officers refused to commit their reserves to help Canadian troops in southern Afghanistan despite a request for assistance. However, high-ranking British officers in Afghanistan expressed reservations about the value of having half-committed and casualty-shy troops in the south.[7] The idea that an under-equipped Polish battalion would be able to replace a US battalion in eastern Afghanistan in 2007 also aroused criticism. The tension within NATO, however, was wider than a simple divide between 'gung-ho' and 'battle-shy' nations and concerned the diverging strategies adopted by the foreign contingents deployed to the south. Only the Australians seemed inclined to accept whatever approach the lead country in their area of operations (Uruzgan) would take. The Dutch found themselves quite apart from the other countries (see 6.5 *Strategy*), and a rift emerged between the Americans and the British concerning the role of truces in Helmand, the administrative line-up there (see 6.7 *Improving 'governance'*), the attitude towards Pakistan and the approach towards poppy eradication. The attitude of General Richards, the British commander of ISAF in Afghanistan, was judged to be 'too political' by some partners, in particular the Americans. Different attitudes towards key problems also contributed to prevent the shaping of a coherent strategy. While for example in Helmand British troops carefully avoided interfering with the eradication effort, even abstaining from seizing opium when coming across it, in Kabul US officials were lobbying the government to start spraying the poppy fields in 2007. A decision in this sense was taken in December 2006, irritating British, Canadian and Dutch diplomats who reacted by trying to prevent the adoption of aerial eradication, eventually forcing the Afghan government at least to postpone the plan to spray the crops and rely instead on 'traditional' techniques.[8]

In terms of the impact of foreign intervention against the insurgency, the picture is a blurred one. It certainly did not lead to increased security in the south, nor to a strengthening of government presence. Quite the contrary, the situation rapidly deteriorated in Helmand and Kandahar at least. Numerous districts were lost by the government, while violence escalated. Was it a nationalistic or xenophobic reaction to the presence of large numbers of foreign troops? Definitive evidence in this regard was lacking at the time of completing this book. However, it is more likely that the main factor in the deterioration of the situation was the perception of a threat to the *status quo* from communities and powerful individuals, for example those active in the narcotics business.

6.2 AFGHAN MILITIAS

At the outset of the insurgency in 2002 the main component of the Afghan counter-insurgent effort consisted of a range of militias, including the so-called Afghan Military Forces (AMF), under the orders of the MoD, some private militias mainly referring to provincial governors, village militias and US-recruited local militias called ASF. The ASF started developing in late 2001, as US Special Forces formed and trained their first militias. Their role in the war was completely subordinated to the requirements of US units; they had no autonomy. Deployed in units of 100–150 men at US firebases, they would provide external security to those bases and accompany US troops on missions. Their most valuable contribution was as screens protecting US troops and in tasks such as house searching and information gathering, which were problematic for the Americans. At their peak they must have numbered no more than 3,000 men distributed among twenty-six US firebases. The ASF were gradually disbanded from 2005 as the existence of militias was drawing a lot of flak from NGOs and the UN, but were provided incentives to join the ANA or the ANP.[9]

Of greater impact were the AMF, due to their larger numbers and to their more widespread presence across the territory. In early 2002 the various anti-Taliban militias and guerrilla armies coalesced in part into a 'transitional' army, later dubbed 'Afghan Militia Forces' or 'Afghan Military Forces' (AMF), formally under the command of the MoD. The new central government legitimised the commanders of these non-state armed groups by appointing them officers and assigning to their formations names of military units. It could be described as a form of privatisation of security reminiscent of the feudal model. Some 200,000 militiamen were included in the personnel charts of the AMF. Some of their units had been receiving cash payments from the CIA to fight against the Taliban, but starting from the early months of 2002 such transfers of cash were limited to *ad hoc* payments whenever a militia was mobilised to accompany US troops in some operation against the remnants of the Taliban and Al Qaida. As the militiamen were not being paid significant sums and the commanders did not need to keep large numbers mobilised any more, the AMF began to shrink. UNAMA estimated during 2002 that there were some 75,000 active militiamen in the AMF, but over the following year the size of the mobilised AMF constantly declined, mainly due to the failure of the MoD to pay salaries; often even food allowances were paid late. By the end of 2003 they did not exceed 45,000 active militiamen, although many more were still included in the personnel charts, despite having been demobilised.[10]

The AMF suffered from a number of problems. The Minister of Defence in 2002–4, Mohammed Fahim, was mainly interested in turning it into a patronage machine for his own political ambitions. Hence an inflation in military ranks which resulted in the existence of 2,500 officially recognised generals on the payroll of the Ministry of Defence by the end of 2002. In order to expand the number of high-ranking officers and incorporate more militias into the system, even as the AMF personnel strength was shrinking, the number of units continued to rise. By the spring of 2002 the AMF boasted over forty divisions, with a few more being established later in the year. In other words, the AMF were anything but a meritocracy. Initially that did not bother too many within the government or within the diplomatic corps, as the war was assumed to be essentially over. Once the insurgency began to spread, however, the AMF's indiscipline, lack of a clearly defined chain of command and primitive organisation were soon recognised as serious problems. The Ministry of Defence never succeeded in bringing under its control the militias that nominally answered to it. In practice the chain of command remained very weak and the commanders of the largest units maintained a nearly complete autonomy in running what were still their private armies. When new commanders were appointed by the MoD to lead AMF units, they proved unable to control them.[11] In turn, unit commanders had difficulties in maintaining the discipline of their own troops. Most units had to be ordered out of cities and towns, in order to contain episodes of looting and violence targeting the urban population. While the order was obeyed in many towns and cities, in Kabul many troops continued to hang around and were reported to be behind a crime wave hitting the capital. Outside Kabul, patrolled by ISAF troops and Afghan police, several AMF units were maintained in active service—and sometimes issued with uniforms—with the task of trying to collect weapons from the population. The remaining units of the AMF were gathered in improvised garrisons and asked to hand over their weapons, in order to have them registered and stored.[12]

With some isolated exceptions, little effort was made to re-train these soldiers or their officers, mainly because of a lack of funding, since most international help in the security sector was directed at forming a new army from scratch. Under international pressure, plan after plan was proposed to reorganise the AMF:

- summer 2002: an MoD plan to assess the current level of education and preparation and then train the officers and soldiers of the AMF's forty-plus divisions, which did not succeed in attracting any funding;
- summer 2002: a plan to modify the organisational chart of the AMF according to the effective personnel strength of the units rather than the political connections of their commanders, which was never implemented;

- beginning of March 2003: a plan to bring in line the ranks of the commanding officers of the transitional army with the type of units they were actually commanding; many of the thousands of Afghan generals would have faced demotion, but it was never implemented;
- spring 2002: a proposal by the Ministry of Defence to appoint professional deputies to the untrained commanders of the old private militias was partially implemented;
- first half of 2003: a plan to reform the AMF was circulated, envisaging the incorporation of a greater number of former regular army officers and their appointment to more senior positions, but it was never adopted;
- a plan to transfer commanders away from their strongholds for training and other purposes, with the effect of weakening their hold over their 'private armies', was partially implemented in 2003–4.[13]

By the end of 2003 the US command had given up any prospect of reforming the AMF as a whole. However, being increasingly worried about the deterioration of security in the country and the slow start of the ANA, by the end of the year it was toying with the idea of 're-forming' and retraining at least some AMF units and using them as a mobile reserve to provide security during the forthcoming elections, scheduled for June 2004. This 'interim security force' or 'National Guard' was to number 5,000 men, but again it never saw the light of day.[14]

Most of these plans were intended by the MoD to meet criticism of the AMF from international sources and were not implemented because in the end the Coalition and external donors were more interested in pushing for the dismantling of the existing military structures, mainly through the plan to demobilise former mujahidin fighters incorporated in the MoD (DDR). Their disarmament was completed nationwide in 2005 and even sooner than that in the south, where AMF units were already in a state of particularly advanced decline. Lack of government support and in some cases of local resources affected the AMF nationwide, besides which in the south the resurgent Taliban had been targeting them since 2002. By 2003 the ragtag southern AMF militias were wholeheartedly demoralised and unable to oppose a significant resistance to the Taliban except in their own strongholds in Popolzai, Barakzai, Achakzai, Alkozai and Alizai villages (see 4.3 *Demoralisation of the enemy*). Their role was limited to occasionally accompanying US troops in 'clear and sweep' operations, but their services were in decreasing demand because of their ineffectiveness and unreliability. In the south-east and east the AMF was in better shape and somewhat more effective. The 25th Division in Khost, for example, succeeded in keeping the insurgents at bay until it was disbanded in 2005. It had been established with former professional army officers in Khost with local funding thanks to the efforts of the governor of Khost. Insurgent activity in the area started increasing and penetrating deeper after its disbandment, although whether there was a causal connection between the two developments is not clear (see 2.6 *Recruiting local communities*).[15]

The third type of militia fighting the Taliban was the private armies of various strongmen and governors. The Karzai administration endorsed and encouraged the practice of allowing governors to maintain small private armies to consolidate their hold over their provinces, but several of them did not have the means to recruit significant numbers. In comparatively poor Zabul, for example, the local strongmen appointed by President Karzai to run the province did not have a sufficient revenue base to maintain a large force in the face of Taliban opposition. Where the resources existed, the private armies survived their role of 'governor's militias'. In Helmand, for example, Sher Mohammed maintained a militia even after his removal from the governorship. In any case, given the extreme weakness of the government security forces, having a private army was often a matter of survival for governors. Even the new governor of Helmand, Eng. Daoud, who did not have a past in the militias and had not fought in the war, before accepting the post at the beginning of 2006 insisted that he be allowed to form his personal militia. The government imposed, however, a formal limit of 500 men to such militias, which also existed at least in Ghazni, Kunar, Daikundi and Farah.[16]

Those hired by private contractors, such as private security companies, for the protection of specific activities were a fourth type of militia/security force in evidence. The largest contractors were two American companies, USPI and Dyncorp, but tens of others existed, including several Afghan ones. These forces were involved in the fighting mainly as the object of attacks from insurgents. For example, one Afghan security company (NCL) had lost seven of its 250 guards by early 2007. However, such militias would generally refuse to play an active role in the conflict.[17]

As violence seemed to spin out of control in the south during the spring of 2006, President Karzai once again tried to promote private armies as one at least partial solution to the security problem. At the beginning of the summer of 2006 he announced the formation of highly-paid mobile militias in four southern provinces, to be led by local strongmen and former governors. In Helmand such a militia was established immediately by Sher Mohammed, without even waiting for a formal decision. By October reports of corruption and of commanders pocketing the pay of ghost militiamen had already surfaced.[18] The plan was soon vetoed by the British and replaced with an alternative proposal to recruit an 'auxiliary police' (see below). Nonetheless, even without official status the Sher Mohammed militia continue to exist and to operate alongside government and British forces, often drawing accusations of abuses against the population. In Uruzgan both Jan Mohammed and Matiullah maintained militias after their sacking, but the Dutch refused to cooperate with them. Jan Mohammed's militia withdrew from the battlefield in protest, but Matiullah's continued to fight on its own and alongside the US Special Operations Forces.[19]

This leads us to the fifth and last type of militia involved in the counter-insurgency effort, that is village militias. They first re-emerged as tribal militias in 2002 in south-eastern and eastern Afghanistan, where local tribes have a tradition of organising so-called *arbakai*, tribal militias, at the orders of the elders. This was a reaction of tribal elders to both the insurgency and the ineffectiveness of the government's law enforcement. Despite the opposition of Minister of Interior Jalali, several such formations were created and by the end of 2003 several thousand tribal militiamen existed. In terms of protecting local installations and individuals, they did their job. Although there were fears in some quarters that creating militias of this kind might re-ignite tribal rivalries and in the end push some other tribes into the arms of the Taliban and other opposition groups, this had not yet happened by 2006. Because the role of the *arbakai* in the conflict was mostly judged positively, it might have contributed to the formulation of a proposal to create the 'auxiliary police', initially described as a village-based militia to be deployed in the provinces most affected by the insurgency. In October 2006 President Karzai approved a plan for the deployment of more than 11,000 such 'auxiliary police' to strengthen the weakened ANP. They were to be quickly trained in ten-day courses, to be topped up by four additional weeks of training once operational, and operate under the orders of district CoPs. The pay would be the same as regular police, but they were to be on yearly contracts. The candidates were to be screened by a committee of district officials and local elders and then vetted by the CoP. The rationale of having village militias was presented as providing an income for young men in the villages and motivating them to actively defend their communities against the encroachment of the insurgents, but in the end the auxiliary police was not deployed in the villages. However, as the programme was just starting, it immediately drew criticism because of the low recruitment standards and the little training provided. Drop out rates were high. Even with such low standards the recruiters were forced to reject many volunteers because they did not meet the requirements, mostly because of drug use. Quite a few of those left in the ranks looked suspicious too and infiltration by the Taliban was seen as a possibility by those involved in training and monitoring.[20]

If it is accepted that a major problem of counter-insurgency in Afghanistan is the inability to control the villages, a logical conclusion would be that the formation of village militias is a necessity. Neither police nor ANA would ever have been available in numbers large enough to be deployed everywhere. The formation of militias aroused passions in Afghanistan, as people tended to associate the term with the formations which fought the civil war, which were undisciplined and had an inclination towards abusing the civilian population. Certainly, the record of mobile militias, able to operate away from their villages, had been a negative one even after 2001. Village-bound militias could do better as the incentive to misbehave diminishes if an armed formation operates in its own village, but much would depend on the ability of the National Police to supervise them.

6.3 AFGHAN POLICE

The police force was involved in the counter-insurgency effort from the very beginning and bore the brunt of it from the implementation of DDR in 2004–05 until 2006, when the ANA was deployed in greater numbers to the south. The Afghan police force was not very different in its origins from the AMF. It too had been created out of the factional militias in 2002, with militia commanders becoming chiefs of police at the district or provincial level and their sub-commanders being appointed as officers. As such, the police force was almost completely untrained and unskilled, with the exception of a sprinkling of professionals appointed here and there, mainly in investigative, administrative and logistical tasks.[21] While the AMF was being disbanded, in most provinces the police continued to exist with little improvement, except that the replacement of commanders by the MoI in many cases weakened its *esprit de corps* and broke the relationship between the strongmen and their old militiamen. There was also some mixing of former militiamen from different districts and provinces, particularly in Kandahar. In Zabul, the police force had been to some extent professionalised after the top authorities in the province had been replaced in 2005. In Kandahar the first signs of an attempt to discipline the police surfaced in early 2007. However, Uruzgan and Helmand police, as well as Kandahar's border police, were still *de facto* mostly homogeneous militias, often coming from a single tribe. As such, they were somewhat more effective fighting forces, but at the same time were liable to keep creating conflictual situations with other communities. The presence of the Achakzai-dominated border police behind the Taliban contributed not only to create a conflict with the Noorzais in Panjwai, but also to maintain it even after the battle of Pashmul and the occupation of the area by Canadian and Afghan troops (see 2.6 *Recruiting local communities*).[22]

The heritage of the factional militias was reflected in the performance of the police. Where the police force was relatively well trained and well led, it did better in terms of containing the Taliban. In Zabul, for example, after the appointment of a professional CoP of good reputation in 2006 and his personally led reform of the unit, the ANP was at least able to control the main highway and contain losses. Elsewhere it might have been more a liability than an asset. A long-term training programme organised by the German authorities only started to produce, slowly, professional policemen in 2003 and its impact on the provinces by 2007 had been minimal. The short-term training programme run by US private security company Dyncorp in 2004–5 had little impact too as it was based on very short courses (two to eight weeks), so that the capabilities of the police in terms of enforcing law and order would at best have been limited in any case.[23] Because of the high staff turnover, the number of trained police was actually declining in 2006 and a substantial percentage of policemen serving in the south in 2006 had not received any training at all. During 2006 Afghan police units received policing and military training from British and Canadian advisors and appear to have improved some of their skills, for example with regard to their ability to identify and neutralise IEDs.

In terms of the direct impact of the police on the counter-insurgency effort, there is plenty of evidence to suggest that the indiscipline and corruption of Afghan security services, including police, was a contributing factor to the insurgency (see 2.6 *Recruiting local communities*). The MoI compounded the situation by usually paying police units their meagre salaries (US$16–70) months late. Sometimes policemen would not be paid for as long as a year, while police chiefs often had to buy fuel and supplies on credit. Inevitably this encouraged the police to impose their own 'taxes' on the population. Although President Karzai tried to diminish the importance of corruption in fuelling the insurgency, allegations of police corruption were already flourishing in 2003.[24] Some examples of the police's illegal activities include:

- in November 2003 a district governor accused his own chief of police of being involved in the narcotics trade;
- in 2006 sources within the AIHRC pointed out that the practice of arresting people in order to extract bribes from them was common in Helmand province;
- the practice of releasing prisoners on payment of a bribe was reported as widespread in Ghazni in 2006;
- Nangarhar's border police reportedly allowed smugglers and insurgents to cross the border during 2006;
- widespread bribing of police to save the poppy fields was also reported in 2006;
- in a rare case of police being brought to account, the authorities confirmed arrests of corrupt police in Helmand in 2006;
- ANA sources alleged that the police of Gereshk (Helmand) were taking money from drivers in early 2007;
- the involvement of the police in the drugs trade was recognised by expatriate anti-narcotics officers in 2007;
- looting of private property in Musa Qala in 2006;
- use of hashish, marijuana and opium was also reported in 2006–7, resulting in the need to squeeze even greater amounts of cash from the population;
- police would sometimes vent their frustration against civilians, as in one case in Kandahar at the beginning of 2007, where they

started shooting traders in the bazaar accusing them of complicity with the Taliban;

- a seizure of 500kg of opium in Helmand in 2007 was divided between police and ANA and only 15kg handed over to foreign troops.[25]

Even US Ambassador Neumann accepted that the Afghan police force was widely viewed as corrupt by the population. Its reported abuses include not only taking bribes, but also more malign ones, including the arrest of relatives and of unarmed civilians in villages where the presence of Taliban had been reported, torture and extrajudicial executions.[26] While the AIHRC does not distinguish between different security agencies when releasing statistics about

2004–5	South-east	West	East	Kabul region	South	All Afghanistan
Illegal detention	464	49	132	47	336	942
Destruction of property	6	9	9	17	17	76
Torture	54	59	19	73	141	439
Extra-judicial killings	31	30	44	33	63	261
Extortion	35	38	40	139	19	410
Other violations	318	281	146	179	304	1,683

Table 7. Abuses by Afghan security agencies as reported by AIHRC's offices in regions affected by the insurgency.

Source: AIHRC, 2004–5 report.

2005–6	South-east	West	East	Kabul region	South	All Afghanistan
Illegal detention/imprisonment	320	19	34	37	127	602
Property destruction	5	12	8	11	3	71
Extortion	15	17	24	54	12	210
Torture and rape	8	24	44	71	36	290
Extra-judicial Killings	11	11	23	11	7	147
Violations of women's rights	289	76	134	39	50	1,041
Other violations	268	105	129	187	126	1,193
Total	916	264	396	410	361	3,554

Source: AIHRC, 2005-6 report.

human rights abuses, it is likely that most abuses were the work of the police (see Table 7).

The potential impact of police's abusive behaviour in turning the population towards the Taliban seems obvious to this author. In any case, this opinion was shared by both UN and Afghan officials, as well as common Afghans. In Panjwai, UN sources explicitly reported that the abusive behaviour of national and border police seemed to have been a key contribution to turning part of the local population towards the Taliban.[27] Demoralised and corrupt police units were often reported refusing to enforce law and order, forcing locals to rely on the Taliban. In Zabul the new, reformist CoP confirmed the presence of widespread corruption within his force, to the extent that the population was forced to turn to the Taliban to resolve disputes and obtain law enforcement. He also alleged that salaries for the police were being embezzled before reaching their destination. The inhabitants of Musa Qala were so unhappy about the exactions of the ANP and ANA that they felt better off once the town had been transferred to the control of the local elders.[28]

Apart from impacting negatively on the feelings of the population towards the government, corruption and low pay ended up corroding the will and ability of the police to oppose the Taliban. The average district in the south would have a force of forty policemen (in fact ranging between fifteen and fifty). Even when the insurgency was not yet a major problem, only about fifteen out of forty would be available to patrol and act as an intervention force. Typically another ten would serve as escort to the district governor, five as escort to the Chief of Police, five as prison guards and five as garrison. As a result, real patrolling was very rare and police would not venture into villages unless tipped off about the presence of anti-government elements. Even in provinces where the threat of the Taliban was not so strong, like Farah before 2006, the police hardly ever visited the villages. Unsurprisingly, the situation worsened once the Taliban became a more fearsome presence. As Taliban strength grew, escort requirements for the local authorities absorbed an ever greater percentage of available resources. In the once safe district centres surrounding Kandahar city, most government officials were relying on the protection of just a couple of policemen until 2005. By 2006 they were being escorted by as many as twenty. Consequently, and because of the increased risk, police would stop patrolling altogether. Hence, the Taliban were able to visit houses and villages next to the district centre without risking the intervention of the police. In general, whenever possible the police would try to avoid confronting the Taliban and would avoid actively pursuing them. Even when manning roadblocks, policemen were often reported to be failing to act on spotting Taliban around the area. In some cases, police units fled their barracks even before the Taliban managed to mount their attacks. The ability of the police to operate with effectiveness was weakened even more by the constant replacement of chiefs of police. Some police stations saw their commander change every fifty days.[29]

The weakness or non-existence of reserve forces able to intervene in support of district centres under attack contributed to demoralise the police, which would often flee when faced with a threat.[30] For a time in Kandahar under CoP Hashem Khan two well trained ANP units were deployed, but were later withdrawn. Afghan police units would also often complain about not receiving help from either the ANA or the foreign contingents and of being left alone to fight off the insurgents despite heavy casualties and bad equipment. Weekly visits by the foreign troops and repeated, unfulfilled promises of new and better equipment only added to the frustration. During 2005 police detachments started receiving communications equipment that enabled them to communicate with US forces and request help, including in the form of air strikes. Previously, Afghan police detachments had been unable to communicate even with each other. This to some extent helped the police to become more resilient against the Taliban, but it did not always work and often police requests of support would not be answered positively. Losses were heavy. In Maiwand district (Kandahar), where the Taliban arrived in 2005, by mid-2006 a quarter of the sixty local policemen had already been killed. During six months of intense fighting in Sangin district (Helmand) fifty-two policemen were killed. In Kandahar province, during less than two months in winter–spring 2006 forty-one policemen were killed. During the Pashmul battle in September 2006 the ANA lost a single soldier, but twenty police were killed. Official figures on total losses (see Graph 6) might even be underestimated if it is true, as stated by unofficial sources within the ministry, that during just March–September 2005 325 policemen were killed throughout Afghanistan. Almost all these losses had occurred in fighting the insurgents. In January 2007 about eighty-five police casualties were reported nationwide by UNDSS.[31]

Demoralisation and rising risk also resulted in large-scale desertions, or in the failure to re-enlist. In Kandahar, out of 6,000 policemen who were trained in 2003–6, half had left the force by June 2006. Seventy of 350 policemen in a Helmand unit deserted in 2006. Kandahar and Helmand were not the worst spots in this regard: in Zabul's Dai Chopan district the local police had already evaporated entirely by the end of the summer of 2003. Sometimes whole units were defecting, as in the case of forty highway policemen in Ghazni province in March 2006, who according to their commander quit because of a delay in the payment of their salaries. Some of these defectors were to join the Taliban, although the numbers were small. However, cooperation between the police and the Taliban seems to have been more widespread. Such instances were already reported in Khost in 2004. In Kandahar, sources within the police force reported that even within Kandahar city the officers of several police stations were in contact with the Taliban. In some cases, police units were accused of collaborating with the Taliban and even of fighting against foreign troops, not only in northern Helmand, but also in Gereshk, a district close to the centre of the province.[32] To a smaller extent such cases were reported also in other parts of Afghanistan. These attitudes towards the Taliban are likely to have been at least in part the result of deep-rooted hostility towards the presence of foreign troops among some members of the Afghan police, as well as of their involvement in the narcotics trade and in their desire to avoid being attacked by the insurgents. The foreign contingents were aware of that, but their reaction often contributed to stoke hostility further, or to undermine the ability of police to work among the population. In at least one instance, US forces confiscated team weapons (machine guns and RPGs) from a government police station in Helmand in 2004, presumably in order to prevent them from falling into the hands of the Taliban. In other cases the Americans, desperate to staff police stations in Taliban strongholds, would make odd choices. Two Hazara militia commanders were appointed as CoPs in the districts of Khakeran and Arghandab Zabul. Although they could certainly be expected not to collaborate with the Taliban, they were also hardly able to communicate with the population or win the sympathy of the very conservative Pashtun villagers, both because of being Shi'as and because of their ethnicity.[33]

For all its weaknesses, the Afghan police force did on some occasions put up a decent fight against the Taliban, particularly when the policemen came from communities or militias that had rivalries with those supporting the insurgents. This is particularly true when the weak equipment of the police is taken into consideration. Its standard included mainly Kalashnikovs, light machine guns and RPG-7 rocket launchers, usually with a limited supply of ammunition. Some of these 'militias in police clothes' fought to the end against the Taliban, particularly in northern Helmand. When this is considered, it is not surprising that the Americans resisted attempts by people like Eng. Daoud, with British support, to terminate their activities (see 6.5 *Strategy* and 6.6 *Tactics*). Ongoing plans to reform the MoI had limited impact in the provinces, although a proposed salary increase to $100 a month seemed to be close to approval as of May 2007. A number of professional provincial chiefs of police had been appointed in the south in early 2006, but faced much resistance in reforming local police forces. During 2007 the MoI seemed intent on replacing them with former militia commanders, who it expected to be more effective in battling the insurgents. The MoI seemed once again to be giving precedence to counter-insurgency over actual policing, oblivious to the great demand for law enforcement in the villages.[34]

6.4 AFGHAN NATIONAL ARMY[35]

The new national army created from May 2002 was a substantially different force from both the various militias and the police. It was in fact the only Afghan security force to be created from scratch on a professional basis. It was widely touted as one of the few success stories of post-2001 Afghanistan, and compared to abject failures such as the formation of a police force worth the name it was indeed a success. However, from the beginning the ANA showed intrinsic limitations, which would later affect its ability to engage the insurgency successfully. Some analysts criticise the ANA model as based on the US light infantry unit model, suitable for presence patrols and 'clear and sweep' operations, rather than non-conventional ones. However, given the human resources available, it is doubtful whether an ANA modelled after the Special Forces would ever have been a realistic option. There is some evidence that initially the ANA was essentially intended by its financial supporters (the US government) to become in the short and medium terms little more than an auxiliary force accompanying US forces in the field, rather than an army capable of autonomous action.[36] This created some friction with both the government and the MoD. The latter objected, for example, to the involvement of ANA battalions in raids deep into Taliban territory and would have preferred to secure more control over ANA units by concentrating them around the main population centres. President Karzai tried to claim greater control over the activities of the ANA, but without success. As disengagement from Afghanistan became an issue for the Bush Administration in 2006, the need for an ANA capable of autonomous operations became obvious, but up to then little had been done to create it. From January 2003 the ANA was heavily dependent on embedded US (and later also Canadian, British and others) 'mentors', who were present down to the company level. The initial neglect of logistics and communications made it impossible for ANA units to operate independently and as a rule each ANA battalion would be attached to a US or NATO unit. Until then the ANA did not even have vehicles to move autonomously and trainees had to be taken to the training centre every day with trucks hired from the bazaar. Even as the ANA started developing some logistical capabilities in mid-2006, its deployment was still subject to the 'dual key' system, which implied negotiations between the government and the Coalition before any deployment or mission. As of September 2005 ANA units were still unable to operate in units larger than a company.[37]

Initially formed by US, British and French trainers, and then by specifically trained Afghan officers under foreign supervision, the basic training course was ten weeks, which later oscillated between eight and fourteen weeks. The creation of fully trained and disciplined units was expected to take six months. The development of the ANA, however, proceeded much slower than first expected and by April 2003 the army had far fewer than the 12,000 men initially planned. The reorganisation and rationalisation of the training process, together with improvement in the living conditions of the troops and the injection of additional funding into the training, led to an acceleration of the process from early 2004 (see Graph 7). However, this rapid and on-target expansion of the personnel charts was not matched by a similar rise in effectively deployable troops, which constantly lagged well below. The initial inflow of recruits was insufficient to staff the battalions fully, which moreover suffered high attrition rates during training due to the low quality of the recruits, itself a consequence of the lack of commitment to the ANA within the MoD. Under the pressure of US political and military authorities, a new system of recruitment, virtually autonomous from the MoD and like the rest of the ANA *de facto* under American control, was introduced in the summer of 2003. This led not only to a rapid increase in the inflow of recruits from the end of 2003, but also to a significant improvement in their quality, which in turn resulted in the reduction of the training attrition rate.[38]

This was not the end of the early problems experienced by the ANA, as the newly trained battalions suffered throughout 2002–3 from a very high desertion rate, although it was positive that desertions were mostly concentrated among private soldiers and were proportionally much lower among NCOs and almost non-existent among officers. A study carried out under the aegis of the Coalition's Office of Military Cooperation-Afghanistan (OMC-A) discovered that low wages and problems accepting military regulations figured among the prominent reasons for deserting, a fact confirmed by anecdotal evidence. Hazing and other abuses also reportedly contributed to high desertion rates, at least until abusive NCOs and officers were relieved by late 2003. Moreover, many among the fist batches of ANA trainees were not genuine volunteers, as they had been sent to the Army by the village elders. That desertions were not politically motivated is confirmed by the fact that until at least 2006 hardly any ANA soldier ever deserted to the Taliban. A number of measures were taken to address the problem, including pay rises from US$50 a month to US$70 for private soldiers plus field deployment indemnities, and the situation improved from the end of 2003 (see Graph 8). However, the ANA never really resolved the problem. The post-2003 improvement was in part a statistical reflection of the fact that most desertions occurred just after the completion of the training and of the lenient attitude adopted towards AWOL troops, who were allowed to return to their units without punishment. This in turn led to the routinisation of the practice of going on unauthorised leave on pay day or whenever needed, which contributed to ANA battalions being permanently below strength (300–400 men instead of 600). There are clear indications that the attractiveness of a long-term ANA job was still limited in 2005–6. The desertion rate started increasing again once ANA units were deployed in battle. This was the result of casualties and of threats by the insurgents against the families of the soldiers hailing from areas affected by the conflict.

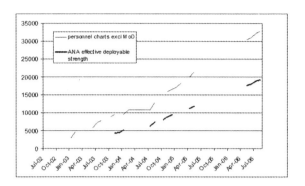

Graph 7. Personnel charts of ANA and deployable ANA strength.
Sources: MoD, Coalition, press reports.

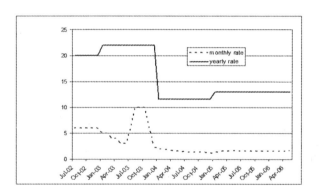

Graph 8. Desertions in the ANA (per cent), 2002–6.

Sources: elaboration from MoD, Coalition and press reports.

Note: the yearly rate takes into account soldiers who returned to their units after having gone AWOL and therefore it is not consistent with monthly rates.

Moreover, when the first battalions reached the end of their three-year contract in spring 2005, re-enlistment rates were a mere 35 per cent. Intimidation and threats by the Taliban might also have contributed to lower recruitment and retention. Captured ANA soldiers were routinely tortured and executed.[39]

Until the beginning of 2005 the ANA had seen only marginal deployment to the battlefield. Its casualties were consequently low, with only about thirty servicemen killed up to March 2005. These deployments were, however, sufficient to push the desertion rate back up, as most soldiers now resented being based away from home and unable to visit their families often (see Graph 8). Over the following year the ANA's involvement in the counter-insurgency grew significantly, even if only a minority of battalions were deployed in conflict-affected areas at any given time. Casualties rose to 130 killed over the March 2005–March 2006 period, corresponding to a rate of about 15 per cent (killed and wounded) for the two corps deployed on the frontline, but the impact was reduced by the rotation of the battalions, with the six permanently deployed in the south and south-east being relieved periodically. For the period March 2006-7, ANA losses rose to 200 killed. However, it has to be considered that the number of battalions deployed to the southern region increased dramatically from the spring of 2006. The desertion rate climbed much higher as far as the units deployed in the areas of operations were concerned. Several detachments in Paktika lost more than half of their men, while Corps 205 in Kandahar in September 2004–June 2005 lost between 1,200 and 1,500 men out of a personnel chart of 2,400, and desertions continued later in the year. Because of the long distances and difficulty in travelling home, AWOL rates increased further for units deployed in the conflict area, shooting up to as high as 50 per cent. As a result, one of the ANA units in the south operated with only 27 per cent of its personnel chart in November 2006. Retention rates also dropped further and by the second half of 2006 were down to just 20 per cent.[40]

The deployment of embedded mentors allowed ANA battalions to take up an operational role from February 2003, although battalion-size operations started only in 2004, almost two years after the training had started. Although the initial plan was to maintain embedded trainers in each unit for a period of two years, until at least the end of 2006 no ANA unit had ever been deployed without embedded advisors, even in the case of the two-dozen battalions which in early 2007 were claimed to be able to operate 'on their own with minimal support'.[41] In practice mentors often served as commanding officers in the place of Afghans, to the extent that occasional displays of initiative by ANA officers were seen as major events. The best units, able to operate in relative autonomy, were soon overworked. Most reports suggested that ANA soldiers fought bravely in small units, although there are also examples of officers avoiding contact with the enemy. However, that ANA officers were not allowed to grow professionally by a mentoring programme which worked more like nursing is shown by the fact that even the more combative ANA officers maintained the tendency not to plan operations and to seek immediate contact with the enemy, forcing their mentors to restrain them. After an initial show of enthusiasm, ANA units would often scatter under enemy fire, forcing the 'mentors' to intervene and re-group them. These difficulties in forming the officer corps are not surprising when it is considered that due to the recruitment policies adopted at the outset, and to the limited attractiveness of ANA service, the illiteracy rate remained very high among officers. For example, as late as February 2006 50 per cent of the officers of Army Corps Kandahar were illiterate. Bearing witness to the dissatisfaction with the capabilities of the ANA, in 2006 the training process was revised once again to shift the focus of training away from 'quantity' and towards 'quality'.[42]

Another problematic aspect of the ANA was its ethnic composition, which became a serious issue once battalions started being deployed against the insurgency. Patronage politics at the centre resulted in an over representation of Tajiks, particularly among officers. When the MoD came under pressure to resolve this issue, a vetting system was introduced to re-balance the higher ranks of the Ministry, while the new recruitment system introduced in 2003 addressed the problem among the rank-and-file with provincial quotas.

However, among field officers the imbalance largely remained (see Table 8). Allegations continued to surface that the training staff, by then completely Afghan and mostly Tajik, was trying to weed out non-Tajiks from the army by pressurising them and forcing them to quit the training courses, or by discouraging selected recruits from joining the army altogether in ethnically mixed provinces. Ethnic differences were reported to affect sometimes the functionality of units, as in the case of one unit where the pay clerk was not filling out the pay forms. Other instances of ethnic tension in the ANA were reported in the press. Apart from the existence of ethnic tensions within the ANA, which are also demonstrated by the fact that punishment existed for soldiers using ethnic slurs, the presence of so many Tajik officers led to difficult relations with the local authorities and population in the conflict-ridden south. For example, the Tajik commanders of the ANA battalions deployed in Kandahar in early 2005 refused to speak Pashto to the local authorities and entertained bad relations with the local police. Problems between the Tajik component of ANA units and the Pashtun population were reported by

	Troops	NCOs	Officers
Pashtuns	52.7	35.8	32.0
Tajiks	36.8	52.9	55.9
Hazaras	5.1	7.2	6.5
Uzbeks	2.7	3.2	3.4
Others	2.7	0.9	2.2
Total	100.0	100.0	100.0

Table 8. Ethnic breakdown (per cent) of ANA by rank, summer 2004.
Source: elaboration based on Coalition sources.

US sources as well, again in part due to the refusal of some ANA officers to speak Pashto.[43]

One of the main selling points of the ANA was originally its human rights and no-corruption record. While there is no doubt that these are much better for the ANA than they are for the AMF or ANP, as

ANA units came under pressure in the south and south-east, much of what had been taught by their trainers in terms of respect for human rights appears to have been readily forgotten. Canadian soldiers intervened at least twice to stop summary executions of suspected Taliban fighters. Accusations of abuses against the civilian population, accused of supporting the Taliban, also surfaced. At least one case of beating of UN national staff was confirmed. In Ghazni villagers were complaining in 2006 of ANA soldiers robbing their homes and of brutal behaviour.[44]

Although the reputation of the higher ranks of the ANA and MoD was never very good, allegations of corruption among field officers too started surfacing in 2006, when even some trainers were convinced that officers were pocketing part of the soldiers' wages. There were reports of military equipment being sold, which resulted in shortages on the frontline, and rumours abounded about the involvement of some ANA units in the narcotics trade. Consumption of hashish in the ranks was also reportedly common. At least one report exists concerning a police seizure of narcotics in an ANA vehicle and there are allegations of a much wider involvement. Reports started to emerge that ANA soldiers too, like the police, indulged in 'taxing' road travellers when manning checkpoints, even in the presence of foreign troops, although whether the latter were aware of such activities is not clear. As a result of this as well as a lack of contact with the population and a lack of any public relations efforts, among the southern and south-eastern population the reputation of the ANA was being eroded during 2006.[45]

At least the ANA does not seem to have suffered significant desertions to the Taliban. In the summer of 2006 it was reported that the Taliban had started offering ANA soldiers three times their pay to switch sides, but it is not clear whether this had any impact. To most soldiers it would of course have meant abandoning their family, an unlikely option. The offer, if true, was probably meant to demoralise ANA troops rather than attract any serious number. Some sources allege that many who quit the police or ANA in 2002–3 later joined the Taliban, particularly in Zabul province, but even if true this is more likely to refer to rejected volunteers. More recently, the Taliban claimed that a number of ANA soldiers defected to them in late 2006, but there is no independent confirmation of this.[46]

6.5 STRATEGY

Following the successful campaign to remove the Taliban regime from power, the US armed forces restructured their military commitment to Afghanistan. During 2002 the roughly 500 US Special Forces that had been the main presence on the ground during Operation Enduring Freedom were integrated into conventional US troops. Their main task was to hunt down the remnants of the Taliban and particularly Al Qaida, leaving to the multi-national contingent known as ISAF the task of securing the government and stabilising the country. Throughout the first four years of its existence, ISAF was mainly based in Kabul, successfully preventing a coup against President Karzai, but had little presence in the provinces, including those where the insurgency was beginning to emerge. Only in 2006 did ISAF contingents start being dispatched to the south in any strength, under NATO command.

With the US regular army taking the lead in 2002, an attitude prevailed that was radically different from that initially adopted by the Special Operations Forces in the search for the remnants of the Taliban and their Arab allies. Rather than operating in small units and spending weeks in the same location trying to forge links with the local population, the new arrivals carried out large sweeps covering many districts with large concentrations of force ('clear and sweep'). The conventionalisation of the US campaign in Afghanistan was the result of the creation of Combined Joint Task Force 180 under the command of a regular army general, a development which marginalised the Special Operations Forces. Several analysts argued the ineffectiveness of 'clear and sweep' operations in rooting out the insurgents and some regular army officers seem to have agreed. In practice, there are some doubts concerning the viability of an alternative model in Afghanistan, since covering the territory affected by the insurgency would have required not only more Special Operations Forces than were in Afghanistan at that time, but even more than were available anywhere. One estimate is that 200,000 troops would be required to control Afghanistan's territory.[47] This figure might have been lower for Special Operations Forces, but with only around 17,000 troops available to the Special Operations Command worldwide, sufficient numbers could never have been mustered for Afghanistan. Moreover, as some of the analysts mentioned above admit, Special Operations Forces too changed their tactics in 2002–4, abandoning operations focused on occupying and pacifying the villages (and establishing local security forces) and shifting instead to raiding suspected enemy hideouts. As the conventional troops lacked specific training on how to handle counter-insurgency, reports rapidly surfaced of their heavy-handed behaviour, in particular with regard to violating the privacy of Afghan homes and of Afghan women. Moreover, the difficulty of the Americans to identify the Taliban among the population often deprived them of the ability to make arrests. Quite the contrary, it often led to the arrest and harassment of the wrong people. Journalists and analysts who spoke to Special Forces members found that they were very critical of the approach adopted by the regular troops. Already during 2002 there were signs that this behaviour was one of three main factors beginning to turn local opinion against the United States (see 6.1 *International actors*), and complaints were still being reported in early 2007. The other two factors were civilian casualties of air strikes (see 6.6 *Tactics*) and the reliance on anti-Taliban local strongmen for their insurgency effort, even when these had a reputation for abusing the population (see 1.2 *'Rebuilding' the Afghan state* and 6.2 *Afghan militias*).[48]

An interesting and involuntary 'counter-factual' experiment took place in Orgun district (Paktika) during 2002, when a single Special Forces detachment continued to use population control tactics while the rest of the Special Forces were focusing on hunting 'terrorists'. The Special Forces in Orgun sidelined a corrupt militia commander who was alienating the local population and proceeded to establish a relationship with the local elders, start a local development programme and recruit an ASF militia. As a result the detachment was able to gather much local intelligence from the population. This limited effort was, however, abandoned in September 2002, after just three months, under pressure from the Task Force command. The main problem, however, was that conducting the experiment in a single district, which had not even been a major focus of opposition activities, made it all too easy for the insurgents to move to another area of operations. How successful the same approach would have been if the insurgents had opposed a stronger resistance is not clear. It is also important to consider that not all was necessarily well with the SOF either, as reports of severe abuses against the civilian population have been emerging since at least 2005.[49]

US Army regular troops were not totally oblivious of hearts and minds tactics when carrying out their operations, but these were implemented in a mechanical and ultimately ineffective way. A typical conventional counter-insurgency operation would involve rapidly occupying a village, rounding up the men, interrogating them, arresting a few and then proceeding with hearts and minds deliveries, such as providing medical services for humans and animals, hygiene kits and medicines, and bringing in some local authorities so that the villagers could vent their grievances. In such operations, the hearts and minds component was compromised by the aggressive entry into the village and by the fact that the troops would soon withdraw, leaving the village to its fate. Similarly, reconstruction and development work in the Pashmul area was compromised by what the farmers perceived as the threat of being expelled again from their villages if the foreign troops were attacked, even if the evacuation of the civilians was meant to be for their own safety.[50]

By 2003 the Task Force command had concluded that this approach was counter-productive, probably helped by the change at the top with the end of Gen. McNeill's tour of duty in August and his replacement by Lieutenant General Vines. The Task Force had by then been renamed Combined Joint Task Force 76. While the lack of permanent presence in the villages had turned out to be a major limitation of counter-insurgency operations, better results were achieved around the US Forward Operating Bases (FOBs), because the Americans were permanently based there and could afford some protection to the villagers. As a result, and for other reasons, US forces were spread wider over Afghanistan, with the number of bases increasing from eleven in 2003 to twenty-six in 2004 and to twenty-nine in 2005. A softer attitude was adopted, involving communicating with the local population, building schools, digging wells and clinics. Platoon-size US units were dispatched to spend time in the villages in order to forge ties with village elders and to gather information about the insurgents' activities. During 2004 US forces reported a marked improvement in the cooperation of locals, who turned to the US military more than a hundred arms caches, compared to just thirteen in 2003. Discoveries of arms caches continued to increase in later years regardless of the strategy adopted by the United States or ISAF and by early 2007 about 600 of them had been found. However, this might well have been the result of more caches being there in the first place. Furthermore, it is likely that much of the cooperation enlisted by the troops was the result of handsome cash payments, as opposed to a vaguely friendly inclination of the villagers.[51] By the spring of 2005 US forces were reporting further increases in cooperation among local villagers at least in areas such as Kandahar and provinces, compared to six months earlier. According to US troops, the idea was that engaging people, by distributing aid and providing jobs in the reconstruction effort, would turn them against the Taliban/Al Qaida and into pro-government informers. An alternative explanation is that anti-Taliban elements already present in the villages might have felt that coming out was no longer so dangerous. In any case, a number of US garrisons had discretionary funds for US$6 million to spend yearly, with larger amounts for critical areas such as Zabul. The total 2004 budget for these operations was US$40 million. On top of that, US FOBs would allow locals access to army clinics six days a week and 7,300 people were treated by November 2005. Later, a similar benefits-for-information approach was also adopted by the British when they deployed in Helmand (2006), and by other contingents as well, often with a greater dose of cash injected into their counter-insurgency strategies; for example the Turkish PRT in Wardak was planning to spend US$24 million when it was set up in early 2007. At the roots of the new approach was the claim that what the military called 'development' (and in fact rather resembled patronage) was the best counter-insurgency strategy and that the Americans 'like the Romans' wanted to leave behind something which would last. The traditional lull in the fighting during winter was seen as a window of opportunity for advancing the reconstruction process, so that in spring the returning Taliban would find a hostile population. One such scheme was the Temporary Work for Afghans, which in September 2005 was employing 11,000 Afghans in reconstruction projects. Initially there seemed to be signs that this could work. There were, however, problems in the implementation of the strategy: Special Troops operating in Afghanistan told an analyst that there was a 'disconnect between aid programs and military operation'. Despite the lack of cooperation of villagers in providing information, 'military commanders remain[ed] unable to stop the flow of aid to them'. Where local security was established, it often seemed to the villagers to be coming from the pro-government strongmen's militias rather than from US troops. More important, once again it was to be proved that counter-insurgency is much easier when insurgents are not around. Possibly because they sensed that the Americans were making some inroads, the Taliban quickly developed counter-measures to the benefits-for-information approach. By 2006 it was widespread knowledge in the Afghan countryside that the Taliban would retaliate against anybody supplying information to their enemies (see also 4.2 *Rooting out government presence*). The attempt to rehabilitate the Kajaki dam, which used to supply electricity to much of southern Afghanistan, was similarly hampered by the dogged determination of the Taliban to keep harassing the British troops deployed to protect the area.[52]

Although other factors might also have contributed to turn the population against the foreign presence, the Taliban's countermeasures seemed to be working. Rapidly, a dark shadow started being cast over the viability of the patronage-based counter-insurgency. Often foreign troops would face the steadfast refusal of the villagers to even accept help such as building bridges or schools, although it is not clear to what extent this was due to fear of Taliban reprisals or to genuine distrust of the foreigners. Anecdotal evidence suggests that there was genuine hostility towards the foreign presence in Kandahar, where it was often interpreted as part of a wider attempt to dominate the Muslim world. In some cases, and certainly in Ghazni, local villagers, following the instructions of their mullahs and fearful of retaliation, handed over to the Taliban cash help provided by US forces for reconstruction projects. Reportedly the Taliban often entered the villages just after a visit by US forces, confiscating and destroying any goods or propaganda material left behind.[53]

The shift away from big 'clear and sweep' operations and towards more village-focused ones reached its apex in the first half of 2005. Soon, however, a backlash followed, with yet another new command of Combined Joint Task Force 76 assessing that the local focus of military operations was leaving the enemy unaffected in most areas, allowing it to reorganise. During the second half of 2005, therefore, US forces changed tack again and started pursuing the Taliban more aggressively into their sanctuaries, leading to more intense fighting and heavier casualties on both sides. With the appointment of British General Richards to lead an expanded ISAF in 2006, there was once again a return to a more patronage-based strategy. The Bush Administration seemed to have come around to supporting similar concepts and in early 2007 it announced an increase in its support for Afghanistan, to the tune of US$10.6 billion for the following two years. If approved by Congress, it would bring the rate of US transfers to Afghanistan to over US$5 billion a year, up from less than US$3 billion a year in 2002–6. Although most of this money was meant for the security sector, a substantial part of it (US$2 billion) was targeted at reconstruction.[54]

The actual impact of different strategies is difficult to assess, not least because changes occurred so frequently that there was no time for the outcome of a particular approach to become obvious. Task Force and ISAF commanders were rotated as often as every nine months, although some stayed longer. However, it is clear that US/ISAF forces struggled to achieve one of the stated main aims (particularly by the British), that is to 'separate the insurgent either physically or psychologically from the populace'. US officers were well aware that this task would have required the presence of troops in every village within the area of activity of the Taliban, but such troops were not available.[55] The strategy of occupying territory permanently, therefore, might well have been the right one, but it was impossible to apply consistently in practice. Occupying only small portions of the country left the insurgents with the options of moving to different areas or of lying low until the Americans eventually moved on to pacify a different area. The task of occupying territory was therefore left to the ragtag Afghan armed forces, which proved not to be up to the task.

Petty political concerns also often interfered with the formulation of military strategies, particularly once the insurgency started becoming seriously threatening. As non-US contingents started deploying to the area of conflict in the spring of 2006, they came under pressure not only from the United States to actively hunt down the insurgents in large scale operations, but also from the Kabul government to protect government administrative centres in areas where the threat was stronger. The British, in particular, were compelled to split their forces into small units and deploy them in the mountainous districts of northern Helmand. Before that US forces had already been establishing garrisons in several district centres of Zabul, incorporating the administrative centres into the fortified garrisons, but did not try to use them to expand control over the surrounding territory, nor was much of Zabul of the same strategic importance to the Taliban. In combination with deploying forces to protect the districts, British troops would continue staging raids deep into Taliban strongholds, to show that the insurgents did not have firm control over any part of Afghanistan's territory, to prevent them from consolidating their organisation inside Afghanistan, and to provoke them to react and fight against superior firepower. However, British hopes to drive the Taliban out of Helmand by the end of the summer of 2006 turned out to have been mere wishful thinking. Faulty intelligence led British commanding officers to claim that the Taliban were unable to amass forces for a counter-attack and that they had 'fewer and fewer places to go and hide'. When the Taliban reacted and it became apparent that there were at least 1,500–2,000 of them in northern Helmand, as opposed to the few hundreds estimated by US intelligence in early 2006, the small British raiding units were often forced to seek shelter and in some cases ended up being besieged for many days in small villages and towns. Similarly, the small district garrisons came under siege too. By the autumn of 2006 the British decided it was wiser to reduce their commitment to controlling the northern district headquarters.[56]

As the Taliban were beginning to concentrate large forces close to a key city like Kandahar in August 2006, what was by now NATO's strategy had to be adapted once again. It now appeared imperative to clear and hold on to at least key parts of the territory. The new strategy incorporated elements of the patronage-based model of counter-insurgency with the 'clear and sweep' one: some key parts of the territory would be consolidated and occupied and more remote and strategically less significant areas would be kept in check through periodical raids. The first component of the new strategy was evident in the battle of Pashmul, when the plan was to conquer territory, hold it, and turn it into an anti-Taliban stronghold without withdrawing (see 4.8 *The third phase: 'final offensive'?*). A large amount of cash was allocated for distribution to the soon-to-be-displaced population and to rebuild the areas destroyed by air raids. After the Pashmul

fighting, USAID alone rushed US$14 million to southern Afghani-
stan in assistance to displaced people, of which US$8 million was
destined for the Pashmul area, with relatives of dead civilians being
promised US$8,000 in compensation for each victim. The Ministry
for Rural Rehabilitation and Development was given another US$18
million to spend in Kandahar province. Canadian troops re-opened
schools and established medical clinics. Early indications from the
UN about the Pashmul post-battle impact were that hiring young
villagers in the reconstruction effort had positive effects on security.
However, by mid-January 2007 the promised aid, to be delivered
during the 'winter lull', had not yet materialised, with the exception
of a new road which was built on the property of angry locals. By
early March work had started on only sixteen of fifty projects in the
whole province. Lack of coordination between the military and the
civilians in charge of reconstruction projects and the lack of secu-
rity for aid workers were blamed for the failure to deliver. Assessing
compensation claims also proved more complicated than originally
thought. The same problem of missing coordination between civil-
ians and military and of missing reconstruction aid was experienced
in Musa Qala in late 2006 and early 2007. Although British forces
claimed to have completed eighty-three projects in Helmand worth
US$9 million in all by December 2006, the population seemed to
have hardly noticed. Significantly, reports emerged after the battle
of Pashmul that despite the presence of foreign troops, insurgents
remained active in the area with local support and their number was
estimated at 300–400, a relatively large number for just a couple of
districts. In December it was necessary to launch another 'clear and
sweep' operation to purge Panjwai and Zhare districts of Taliban.
After that NATO and Afghan authorities could finally claim that
the locals were cooperating with them and reporting the location
of roadside bombs, but also admitted that re-infiltration was very
likely. Indeed, by March the frequency of IED attacks was rising fast
in Panjwai and Zhare, while the Canadians had to scale down their

ambition to hold positions tens of miles west of Kandahar city due to high risk to the supply convoys.[57]

If in the context of southern Afghanistan (2006) delivering development was problematic, an even greater difficulty was presented by the fact that even a successful delivery might not have impacted on the counter-insurgency effort. One reason is that development and assistance matter little as long as security is not reliably provided. In the Pashmul area, as the reconstruction process was starting, following devastating air strikes in September 2006, the locals often seemed less than impressed and remained wary of finding themselves between two fires. Often villagers and town dwellers alike were unaware of whatever reconstruction aid had effectively been delivered to their localities and in any case were more concerned about the lack of security and the death of relatives at the hands of foreign troops. Another reason was that even when the 'foreigners' could reasonably argue to have delivered something in terms of reconstruction, they stood accused of having catered only for their own self-serving interests. The Kabul–Kandahar highway, for example, was the first highway to be rebuilt with aid money after 2001. However, it was often seen as being intended to facilitate the movement of foreign and government troops to the south rather than to benefit the local economy. A third reason was that the expectations of the villagers, inflated by excessive promises, were hard to meet. The inhabitants of a village endowed with no less than sixteen wells dug by aid agencies were still reported to be complaining about the lack of development aid and about what they considered the unjustified arrest of villagers on allegations of aiding the insurgents.[58]

Some controversy surrounds the role of Dutch troops in Uruzgan and their adoption of a different approach in dealing with the Taliban (the 'Dutch approach'), which they had already 'tested' in Kabul and in Baghlan in 2002–5. Until the autumn of 2006 the Dutch described their own role as establishing contact with the population and privileging support for local government as opposed to focusing on killing insurgents. Secure bases would be established from where stability, security and reconstruction projects would win the trust of the local population and gradually spread elsewhere. In fact, the Dutch were even reported to have insisted on restraining the activities of two detachments of US Special Forces deployed in Uruzgan with them. The appointment of a new governor with a background in the Taliban regime helped to develop informal contact with some groups of insurgents. The Dutch started from negotiating with the local insurgents, before despatching patrols away from their bases. According to their own radio intercepts, they succeeded in delivering the message that a new 'type of foreigner' was now in Uruzgan, more interested in negotiating than fighting. The Dutch troops made a point of paying as many visits as possible to the households of the area to reinforce the message and of offering to mediate between villagers and US military authorities for the release of Afghan prisoners or at least find out about their fate. According to the Dutch, they were also trying to protect villagers from predatory members of the Afghan security forces, taking the controversial militias off the battle front and confining them to guard duties. During the first four months of their presence in Uruzgan, the Dutch suffered only two injured and none killed in action; the level of enemy military activity against them was comparatively modest, standing at seven ambushes and eighteen roadside bombs. British and US officers did not always appear to be fully convinced of the validity of the Dutch approach and objected that they remained confined in the region of Tarin Kwot, sheltered from some of the Taliban's largest concentration of forces by a mix of US and Australian troops. Some Dutch troops, in particular commandos, also complained about not being allowed by the 'politicians' in Amsterdam to hit the Taliban as hard as required to improve local security. It certainly should be considered that the Taliban do not normally prioritise fighting foreign troops, unless ordered to do so by their leadership. Hence, in the absence of aggressive activities from the Dutch side, the Taliban might have had little incentive to mount a major effort against them. The Dutch approach was adopted by the smaller Australian contingent too, which had earlier fought aggressively alongside the American Special Forces in the same province.[59]

From the beginning much tension was reported between the Dutch and the Americans in Uruzgan, with the former pointing out how the latter were very arrogant and focused on destroying the 'Taliban' without even knowing exactly who these were. The US Special Forces were reported by the Dutch as being very gung-ho and all too keen to call in air strikes, which the Dutch opposed as likely to cause much collateral damage. As the end of 2006 approached, in any case, nobody was talking of the 'Dutch approach' any more. Dutch sources attributed the development to the worsening violence in Uruzgan, which prevented the carrying out of any development activities, as well as to the insufficient numbers of ANA and ANP troops. The Dutch were critical of the US approach to delivering aid, for example mentioning schools were built without involving the locals and without follow-up; soon the schools were burnt down. However, reports published in the Afghan press suggested that the Dutch were not doing very well in terms of delivering reconstruction to Uruzgan, even compared to the US. All that was left of the Dutch peculiarity in late 2006 seemed to be the refusal to carry out poppy eradication activities and the insistence on advising the authorities of Uruzgan to do likewise. It is, however, worth noting that the change of 'approach' took place just after the Dutch parliamentary elections of November 2006 and might have been due to the pressure of NATO allies.[60]

General Richards made a strong point to the press that NATO needed to show the Afghans that it was ready to stand and fight when it deployed to southern Afghanistan in 2006. However, his hope that a first round of tough fighting in the summer of 2006 might have been sufficient to deliver the message would later appear quite optimistic. ISAF/US strategy remained largely reactive throughout 2002–6, until in 2007 ISAF started increasingly taking more of a proactive role, committing itself to exercise continuous pressure on the Taliban and to force them to withdraw to the mountains and slowly wither away. It is not clear how successful such a strategy can be in a country like Afghanistan, where mountains represent the largest part of the country. Moreover, divergences continued to exist, as Americans were pushing for increased air strikes and for the targeting of commanders, the British were claiming to be refocusing their efforts in terms of identifying 'tired Taliban' and convincing them to stop fighting.[61]

6.6 TACTICS

At the tactical level, the main problem for the United States and their allies was to draw the insurgents out of their hideouts to fight against their far better armed enemy. Until at least 2003 avoiding casualties remained a major concern of US commanders and US patrols would usually try to break off contacts as soon as possible. However, a radically opposed approach emerged between 2004 and 2005. Small units were deployed in areas of activity of the insurgents in order to lure them into battle and then inflict heavy casualties with the help of air power. Other tricks used included the issuing of provocative statements about the 'cowardice' of the Taliban and provoking them by burning Taliban corpses, even though the latter practice was condemned by the Afghan government who feared its unpopularity. When the Taliban of their own initiative started launching attacks against small NATO and Coalition outposts in 2006, the development was welcomed as an opportunity to inflict heavy casualties on the enemy, despite some apprehension that the small outposts might be somewhat vulnerable. However, as has been pointed out by A. Cordesman, the Taliban displayed a remarkable ability to replace casualties, while these US tactics were not able to inflict losses where the Taliban might have been more vulnerable, that is the cadre structure. The NATO command seems to have realised this weakness and by December it was claiming to have shifted its focus towards targeting Taliban commanders; the killing of Osmani in December 2006, of Dadullah in May 2007 and the alleged capture of Obeidullah in February were attributed to this new approach. It is worth adding that NATO and US commanders appear not to have realised the political impact of the rising violence of the conflict in the south (see 2.7 *Changes in recruitment patterns*). Claims of huge losses inflicted on the Taliban during the spring and summer of 2006, whether accurate or not, backfired as they implicitly demonstrated to the Afghan public that either the Taliban were many more than officially estimated, or many civilians were being killed and branded as Taliban.[62]

The perception that US troops lacked conviction and were afraid of fighting except when strongly supported by air power might have contributed to embolden the resistance, strengthening the feeling that Americans could not stomach a long conflict in Afghanistan. The reliance on air power was particularly accentuated in 2006. Between June and November 2006 alone, the US Air Force conducted more than 2,000 air strikes in Afghanistan, a figure which represented a massive acceleration on previous years. The 2006 monthly rate of aircraft ammunition expenditure was ninety-eight bombs and 14,000 bullets, compared with twenty-two bombs and 3,000 bullets in 2001–4. During early 2007 a further increase in air activity was reported. Reliance on air power led inevitably to significant casualties among the population and to the accusation of excessive force, particularly when 2,000lb bombs were extensively used to deal with small groups of insurgents. In the few cases investigated, civilian casualties were regularly reported to be higher than initial NATO/US estimates. Locals often argued that civilian casualties were underreported by NATO and the United States and that civilians were often mistaken for Taliban and targeted in air raids.[63] Health authorities also tended to disagree with NATO reports of low civilian casualties. UNDSS reported that about one third of the civilian casualties of January 2007 (about sixty) were to be attributed to ISAF and ANA and the rest to the Taliban. Whatever the actual number of civilian casualties, because of the lack of territorial control, Taliban propaganda claims that tended to inflate the number of civilian victims of the bombardments were difficult to dispute convincingly. Such propaganda appeared successful insofar as it led in some cases to local residents fearful of 'collateral damage' asking for a withdrawal of foreign troops from the Panjwai and Zhare areas of Kandahar, in part inspired by the example of Musa Qala and Sangin districts in Helmand. Afghan authorities in Kabul and in the provinces came under pressure to pay at least lip service to these widespread feelings. Even the most pro-US members of the local authorities, like Governor Asadullah Khalid of Kandahar, were forced to complain about excessive use of force by the Americans. It should also be considered that the intense fighting around Kandahar in 2006 led to a negative economic turnaround in the city, compounding the economic problems.[64]

6.7 IMPROVING 'GOVERNANCE'

Once the contradictions of the state-building process in Afghanistan (see 1.2 'Rebuilding' the Afghan state) became increasingly evident, pressure started mounting for a change in the government's approach. Improving 'governance' in Afghanistan became the new motto of the international community. The underlying idea was that by delivering a good and efficient administration, the root cause of grievances would be removed and the political situation would improve. This author takes it that what is meant by governance is that an institutionalised administration replaces a patrimonial one based on the personal power base and attitudes of appointees, although there is rarely any clarity about governance in official documents.[65] According to a UN analysis, in 2005 about one third of 1,500 political killings in Afghanistan and three quarters of all violent incidents were not linked to the insurgency but to land or resource conflicts and to the 'lopsided distribution of power in local administrations'.[66] Hence, improved governance could likely have reduced these types of conflict, thereby possibly contributing to prevent a spread of the insurgency too. As a result, starting from 2004 the Karzai administration was forced to start removing the most controversial governors in the south. The first to fall was Gul Agha Shirzai, governor of Kandahar, whose alliance with the Karzai circle was shakier (see Introduction). In early 2006, faced with British and Dutch ultimatums, Karzai had to sack Sher Mohammed in Helmand and Jan Mohammed in Uruzgan and to replace them with Eng. Daoud in Helmand, who had a reputation as a good administrator, and Abdul Hakim Monib in Uruzgan, who had potential as a mediator with the insurgents. Monib had been Junior Minister for Tribal Affairs under the Taliban and as a Ghilzai he was thought to be well positioned to talk to the insurgents in Uruzgan. At the same time, as an outsider (he hailed from Paktia) he could be seen as an impartial broker by different factions. However, he was not liked by either the Americans or many in the government and, starved of funds, was incapable of exercising a significant role. In early 2007 he offered his resignation in protest of the lack of funding and of the activities of the US Special Forces, which hampered his attempts at negotiations. In Zabul, which had seen a succession of ineffective governors after 2001, Karzai appointed Haji Arman, who also had a reputation as a good administrator. Despite widespread optimism about the impact of these developments, it might already have been too late. The government failed to quickly follow up the appointment of new governors with improvements in policing (except in Zabul) and the judiciary. Moreover, local communities had already been mobilised against the government and 'good governance' was no longer sufficient to appease them. The Taliban were by now well established in most of the countryside and were in a position to sabotage any attempt to deliver better 'governance'. In Zabul the administrative skills of Haji Arman had little impact outside Qalat, as whatever was left of district level administration was barely surviving under the direct protection of the ANA and US forces. Administrative offices were often housed in the same fortified compounds where US troops were based, making interaction with the population very hard. Being associated with the US presence might even have played against the ability of the local administration to interact with the population, not least given the decreasing popularity of foreign troops in the south. Similarly, the hosting of government radio stations within US military compounds in the south-east was seen by many Afghans as a sign of the inability of the government to maintain a degree of autonomy *vis-à-vis* the foreigners. The presence of the administration in the districts was merely symbolic, as district administrators would spend most of their time in the safer environment of the provincial capital.[67]

While the 'better governance' project harvested few positive results due to an already compromised situation and the resistance of elements of the central government, the replacement of the old governors created a vacuum of power, as communities that had sided with the pro-Karzai strongmen were now unhappy and afraid of their forthcoming marginalisation or in any case of losing the privileges and positions they had acquired (see 2.6 *Recruiting local communities*). The fact that the new governors and particularly Eng. Daoud were under pressure to support poppy eradication measures contributed to weaken their hold and prevent them from establishing a working relationship with much of the population. The choice to focus the eradication programme on the south rather than on the north-east, the other main poppy growing area, was seen as controversial and was attributed to the personal interest of Deputy Minister of Interior for Counter-narcotics Daoud Khan. Eng. Daoud's attempt to strike a balance between opposite sources of pressure consisted of avoiding compulsory eradication and trying to convince farmers to give up planting the poppies. The situation, however, had deteriorated to the extent that a reputedly honest administrator like Daoud, trying to resist the arbitrary behaviour of the security forces and to endorse to some extent the eradication agenda, found himself almost completely isolated. Less than a year after his appointment, Daoud became the object of a strong backlash from local allies of former governor Sher Mohammed Akhundzada, who had maintained good relations with Karzai (who appointed him senator) and continued to meet him often in Kabul. Sher Mohammed and his family had assiduously been building their own 'power bloc' in Helmand between 2001 and 2006. Not only had he staffed the police and administration with cronies, but during previous attempts to eradicate the poppies in Helmand, landlords connected with Sher Mohammed had usually been spared, while others were seeing their crops eradicated. Strengthened as it was by powerful connections in Kabul, Sher Mohammed's 'power bloc' proved quite resilient. Some of the Kabul press reported the 'criticism', by former and current government officials from Helmand, of Daoud, whose attempts to restrain and isolate the rogue militias and police forces of Helmand were described in terms of collaborationism with the Taliban. Daoud reacted by accusing the local 'drug mafia' of plotting against him and tried to convince President Karzai to leave him in his post, but not even British Prime Minister Tony Blair's efforts sufficed to save him. Karzai sacked Daoud in the autumn of 2006. His replacement, Asadullah Wafa, was widely seen as a weak figure who for several months even refused to deploy to Lashkargah. Daoud's chief of police, a professional named Muhammad Nabi Molakhel, was also transferred. After the sacking, British sources would blame the United States for having supported the removal of Daoud, while Defence Secretary Des Browne was reportedly very upset. Karzai had adopted a similar strategy in the past, grudgingly accepting to appoint individuals sponsored by the international community only in order to discredit and then remove them at the first sign of difficulty. From the perspective of this book, however, the most salient point is that Daoud's replacement was in line with the continuous change in the military and political strategies adopted to deal with the insurgency. It can be argued that changing strategy every six to twelve months is tantamount to having no strategy whatsoever, particularly if that is not justified by changes in the insurgents' own strategy.[68]

6.8 RECONCILIATION EFFORTS

In early 2002 the Afghan government offered an amnesty to all members of the Taliban regime, except for those 142 listed by the UN as 'leaders'. The original intention of the Karzai administration seems to have been an even wider amnesty which would have included even Mullah Omar, but US objections led to a more careful formulation, first excluding Mullah Omar and then all the 'leaders'. This amnesty had a degree of success in that most 'old Taliban' went back to their villages and stayed quiet there, at least initially. However, harassment by local security forces often pushed them back into the Taliban fold. In April 2003 Karzai, with a public speech, re-opened the door to 'moderate' Taliban, inviting them to join the political process. He reiterated the offer during an interview with the BBC in October of that year and a few days later Chief Justice Mawlawi Fazl Hadi Shinwari stated that talks were already underway with some Taliban. In the end the main prize of the negotiations was former Minister of Foreign Affairs Mutawakkil, who signed a reconciliation deal with the government and later put forward his candidature in the parliamentary elections of 2005. Mutawakkil, however, was in detention at the time of the deal and had never been a military commander. Former field commander Salam Rocketi also made peace with Kabul, but he had never joined the Neo-Taliban and did not bring with him substantial numbers of combatants.[69]

By 2005, after at least two years of efforts to attract 'moderate Taliban' to the government side through secret negotiations, the government had little to show. In an effort to approach the rank-and-file directly, bypassing the leadership, the Peace Strengthening Commission was established in March 2005 in Kabul and at the regional level. As of the summer of 2006 the Peace Strengthening Commission was still trying to expand throughout the country, establishing offices at the provincial level. Working with limited manpower, the Commission led by Segbatullah Mojaddedi relied on tribal and religious notables to establish contact with opposition elements at the local level. After the initial contact, individuals and groups willing to reconcile with the government would meet the provincial governor and the regional representatives of the Commission. In the case of a successful agreement, the reconciled oppositionists would be given a letter in three copies, one to keep and the remaining two to be handed over to NATO or the Coalition and to the government. By October 2006 2,400 individuals had been granted such letters, of whom 700 in the south-eastern region (including Logar).

Government sources showed a strong tendency to overstate the success of the reconciliation programme. When 169 mostly former members of the 'old Taliban' surrendered in western Afghanistan in March 2006, local officials described them as '169 high-ranking Taliban commanders'. This supposedly happened in a region which until then had seen little or no Taliban activity (Herat, Farah, Ghor and Badghis).[70] When asked to identify the most important Taliban commanders who joined the reconciliation process, one of the representatives of the Commission mentioned a number of officials who had not even been active after 2001:

- Abdul Hakim Mojahed, who had been the unofficial representative of the Taliban regime at the UN and later one of the founders of Jamiat-i Khudam-ul Koran (see 3.1 *Cohesiveness of the Taliban*);
- Pir Mohammed Rohani, who had been rector of Kabul University under the Taliban regime;
- Arsala Rehmani, another founder of Jami'at-i Khudam-ul Koran and Deputy Education Minister under the Taliban;
- Abdul Wahid, former Taliban commander in Baghran, who never fought actively against the government or the Coalition after 2001 and moreover was alleged to be maintaining contacts with the Taliban.[71]

UN sources in eastern Afghanistan alleged that many of the applicants to the Commission had never been with the insurgency or with the Taliban and were just refugees trying to return to Afghanistan under privileged conditions. A US officer admitted in 2005 that none of the thirty or so relatively high-ranking Taliban officials to accept amnesty was a former military commander. Moreover, several of them continued to support the Taliban politically even as they enjoyed government protection in Kabul's safehouses. Of the 2,400 who joined the process, about 1,000 were former fighters, with very few recently active commanders of any rank among them. On the whole the reconciliation programme scored some successes in provinces like Paktia, Laghman and Kunar, where even some mid-rank field commanders of the insurgency joined the process, but not much anywhere else. In Kandahar the environment was so far from conducive to reconciliation that local officials of the Commission were just contacting non-active former Taliban in the hope that these could at some point drag in some active fighters.[72]

Although only a handful of those accepting reconciliation then went back to fighting, lack of trust in the genuine character of the government's offer continued to affect the chances of success of the Commission. A number of other problems also existed. The performance of the Commission was allegedly hampered by the sometimes dubious choice of staffing, often responding more to patronage logic than to a concern with the effectiveness of the programme. The appointment of a new and more respected chief of the Commission in Kandahar in September 2006 (Agha Lalai), for example, produced an immediate increase in the number of individuals accepting to support the government, particularly in Agha Lalai's own district of Panjwai, where over 10 per cent of the local insurgents were reported to have quit fighting in just seven months. There were also allegations that some elements in the National Security Council in Kabul, an institution modelled on the US original, opposed reconciliation and tried to sabotage it by mistreating applicants. According to officials of the Commission, another limitation was the lack of resources to provide the reconciled elements with shelter, jobs and protection, except for a few top defectors housed in Kabul under NSD protection. In fact, some former Taliban who expressed their support for the government were assassinated, such as former Deputy Interior Minister Mullah Abdul Samad (January 2006). Allegations also flourished that the Pakistani security services actively tried to prevent Taliban militants from accepting the government's reconciliation offer. The demand that defectors from the Taliban be provided with jobs and housing, however, sounds quite demagogic in a country where unemployment was estimated at 30–40 per cent of the workforce; it would have been seen as rewarding the wrongdoers at a time when the needs of most of the population were being ignored. In the end, it is obvious that as long as the Taliban were thinking that the insurgency was making progress, 'reconciliation' or surrender were not going to be attractive options. Reconciliation was not going to take off until the Taliban would appear militarily defeated. Until the end of 2006 the main role of the reconciliation process was to offer an alternative to former Taliban who were not inclined to fight for their own reasons.[73]

6.9 LOCAL TRUCES

When the focus of the counter-insurgency campaign was not on the south and more on the east and south-east, where Al Qaida elements were present in strength, truces with individual Taliban commanders in the south were well accepted by the Americans. However, these had little lasting positive impact. The case of Rais-e Baghran, alias Mullah Abdul Wahid, the strongman in control of Baghran district (Helmand), who had been aligned with the Taliban since 1995, is illustrative. Negotiations with him had been going on since the fall of the regime in 2001, but integrating him and his supporters within the power system of Sher Mohammed, governor of Helmand, proved impossible. The original deal between the two men was ready in 2002, but had immediately collapsed because of a lack of trust between the two parties. Although after more than three years of truce Sher Mohammed successfully renegotiated Abdul Wahid's 'surrender' in March 2005, allowing him to keep his weapons and his militia, by the end of the year the two were once again at odds.[74] In the end Abdul Wahid continued to linger in a limbo between the government and the Taliban, maintaining contacts with both of them, while Baghran district returned to its old status of a Taliban stronghold.

Other negotiations between provincial authorities and local Taliban commanders took place in Zabul province in 2003, but they seem to have brought no results. Allegedly an informal deal existed in Nangarhar province between Taliban, Hizb-i Islami and governor Din Mohammed, according to which the city and the surrounding districts would be spared violence from both sides, but whether the deal was ever endorsed by Kabul is not clear; it might have been purely informal. Despite some bellicose statements by NATO officers during the summer of 2006, by September the exhaustion of British troops in Helmand following intense fighting forced the British to accept truces in Musa Qala and Sangin districts, negotiated by the local elders. The two truces held until the beginning of December, despite some tension over the terms of the agreement. The deals were supported by UNAMA and were also strongly sponsored by then governor of Helmand, Eng. Daoud, but Afghan officials in Kabul and in Helmand were often unhappy, describing the truces as 'surrender to the Taliban'. Even President Karzai expressed some doubts, while some cabinet members such as Foreign Affairs Minister Spanta openly expressed their opposition. By early 2007 relations between Great Britain and Afghanistan were seriously strained, impacting negatively even within Kabul's government itself. A strong argument against the deals was that it allowed the local elders, whoever they were, effectively to choose the district governor, CoP and even individual policemen, against an established practice of appointments from above. It was feared that similar demands might surface in other districts if fully endorsed from Kabul, endangering the ultra-centralised character of the Afghan state. By contrast, the reaction among the population of Musa Qala town appeared positive, as shown by a burst of reconstruction efforts aimed at repairing and rebuilding houses and shops. In the opinion of cynics, the forthcoming poppy planting season might have contributed to the peace-making mood of the locals. Nobody, however, argued that the Taliban disbanded or disarmed and the elders had only committed themselves to 'try to limit' the number of the insurgents, who continued to be allowed into the town, although without carrying arms. Some locals argued that the elders were not really independent of the Taliban, who were in a position to pressure them.[75]

In early February the truce in Musa Qala collapsed amid recriminations over who was responsible. Sources in the British Army alleged that the truce-breaking airstrike which killed the brother of the local insurgent commander was deliberately intended by the Americans to sabotage the truce. It also appears that pressure from Kabul and from the United States might have pushed the British towards adopting a more aggressive approach. Confirmation that government pressure played a role came from the fact that shortly afterwards the governor of Helmand, Eng. Daoud, who had been instrumental in negotiating the truces, was removed from his post (see 6.7 *Improving 'governance'*). The new governor, Asadullah Wafa, expressed his opposition to such truces. Pressure for more truces had started building up after these initial deals, particularly around Panjwai, a development which must not have been welcome in NATO headquarters. In any case the truces were then re-established under a new plan to hand over to local elders control over the recruitment of police and reconstruction aid in exchange for assurances of loyalty to Kabul. By offering a better financial deal to the elders, while at the same time tying them to specific undertakings to respect the sovereignty of Kabul, it was hoped the aim of separating the insurgents from the population might be made more attainable. As of January 2007 similar deals were being negotiated in Sangin and Garmser, although there were sceptics within the British ranks too, arguing that it was likely too late to drive a wedge between the population and the insurgents. Reports from Musa Qala in February 2007 suggested however that at least in this regard the truces might have succeeded, as a delegation of elders reached Kabul to appeal for help against the repression unleashed by the Taliban. The new deals might not have been welcomed by the Taliban, who argued that they would never negotiate deals in the future. Taken aback, as of February 2007 the British had little option left apart from dropping leaflets in the hope of scaring the non-core Taliban to give up the fight. The situation appeared to be at a standstill, but the new commander of ISAF in Afghanistan, US General McNeill, was widely expected to cancel such deals after taking over that month.[76]

Another unwanted effect of the local truces, together with the deal between militants and the Pakistani government in Waziristan, was the spread of rumours concerning negotiations with the Taliban leadership, stimulated also by the fact that individuals around the increasingly beleaguered Bush Administration had started talking about the possibility or indeed even the need for a political solution. This was most notoriously the case of Bill Frist, Senate Republican majority leader.[77]

6.10 WHAT COUNTER-INSURGENCY?

US counter-insurgency in Afghanistan wavered between the old Cold War approach, targeted at fighting strategies mainly inspired by left-wing ideologies, and an alternative identifying prevention through development and aid as the only possible solution to the 'war of the flea'. The classical approach postulated that would-be Taliban strongholds had to be periodically raided in order to prevent the insurgents from consolidating their presence and developing the means to move on to the next phase of the insurgency. The development-based approach argued that since there was no point in trying to kill off all the 'fleas', the solution was to prevent the 'fleas' from infesting the 'dog' by undermining conditions that would allow the 'fleas' to breed. 'Development' was to clean the country of insurgents in much the same way as good hygiene would rescue the dog from the fleas. 'Fourth generation' counter-insurgency warfare, being a new proposition, had not yet filtered down to policy makers by early 2007 and since it implies a major restructuring of the US armed forces, it might never do so. Nonetheless, the wavering between the first two options resulted in the Taliban still being able to develop their strongholds, if with some delay, during the lulls in the raiding by enemy forces. It also resulted in attempts to combine the dispensation of patronage ('development') with counter-insurgency being patchy, *ad hoc* and implemented on and off. Similarly, the approach towards eradication, combining verbal commitment, strong rhetoric and little and unbalanced action, was sufficient to irritate and scare large sections and the population, without removing what was alleged to be an important source of funding for the insurgency.

This pattern continued well into 2007. While the Americans were actively lobbying in favour of eradication, the British were favouring the targeting of traffickers and of the refining business and the Dutch were communicating their desire to stay out of it altogether.[78]

By 2006 few people in southern Afghanistan were impressed with the benefits of this wavering approach. This author's view, however, is that even if either of the two strategies had been implemented consistently, it is unlikely that they would have resulted in the defeat of the insurgents, although they might have made their life more difficult. Classical counter-insurgency might have been able to further slow the development of Taliban strongholds and therefore the formation of small insurgent 'armies' and the passage to the third phase of the insurgency. This, however, would have been a mixed blessing, because the Taliban would have been forced to drop their risky plans to take Kandahar and focus on the 'war of the flea', spreading it wider and wider into Afghanistan. Classical counter-insurgency would only have succeeded in blocking the development of the insurgency (but not yet defeating it) if it had been possible to wipe out the strongholds entirely, depriving the Taliban of the ability to support infiltration deeper into Afghan territory. This, however, would have demanded a greater concentration of forces and their permanent deployment in the mountainous areas where the strongholds were being established. In the context of 2003–6, this was not possible because of the commitment of almost all US ground forces to Iraq. It is also unlikely that any US government would have wanted to commit a large portion of its armed forces to Afghanistan for long periods of time.

Patronage-based counter-insurgency, combined with extensive use of special troops for population control, could have been useful in the early days of the insurgency, when it was not yet widespread. It might then have been possible to suffocate it before it spread. Once the Taliban became active in tens of districts, there were never going to be sufficient special troops or 'development' funds and workers to cover such large areas. However, during the incubation stage of the insurgency nobody in either Kabul or Washington was taking it seriously, hence the chance of a major investment in resources to suffocate it in its early days never really existed. By the time it actually started being implemented, success in one district would only have meant that the insurgents would move to another one, where the ground had in the meanwhile been prepared by the elusive infiltration teams, and intensify military operations there. This strategy was also confronted with the hard facts of the corruption of the central government. In early 2007 US and British defence officials were reported to have estimated that up to half of all aid to Afghanistan failed to reach 'the right people'. Not only the authorities seemed to be siphoning off much of the aid, but even much of what was delivered by them was hoarded by village elders and notables and not distributed to the villagers. The existence of such attitudes is confirmed by the experience of development workers inside Afghanistan, whose best efforts at providing services for the population, such as deep wells, were often hijacked by local notables for their exclusive benefit.[79]

It has been argued that a better integrated effort would have benefited the counter-insurgency war. While there is truth in this, this is not the main point. Analysts are fond of citing successful British experiences in defeating insurgencies in Malaya, Kenya, Oman and Borneo as models of an 'integrated, coordinated, interagency approach' to be emulated.[80] However in a fashion typical of those who focus on tactics more than on strategy, and on military aspects more than political ones, they miss the main factor in securing victories in those cases: the British wisely chose to fight only wars they could win. If the British had known of some magic formula to defeat any insurgency, they would not have given up their Empire once nationalist mobilisation started building up in India and elsewhere. They dropped struggles which were leading nowhere and looked unsustainable in the long term, even in cases where the military challenge itself looked manageable in the short term. Even the celebrated 'victories' in Malaya, Kenya, Oman and Borneo were in fact a result of the political willingness to compromise and abandon control of those territories, in exchange for guarantees regarding the protection of some vital British interests there. This is exactly the contrary of what the Bush Administration did in Afghanistan and elsewhere. By ideologising the struggle against radical and extremist groups in the Middle East as the 'War on Terror', the American leadership unwittingly trapped itself in a situation where strategic and tactical flexibility could no longer exist. While ideologisation might work in a context of confrontation between states of similar strength, in the post-9/11 context it legitimised the claim of a relatively small nucleus of terrorists to be the leadership of a much larger movement incorporating mainly national and local grievances. When the Bush Administration accepted to be dragged into an ideological war, as the planners of the 9/11 attacks likely wished it would be, it accepted to fight on the ground chosen by the enemy, pitting its weaknesses against the enemy's strengths.

To the extent that the Afghan insurgency was becoming part of a wider jihadist movement, there was little that political and military authorities based in Afghanistan could do, except make a deal which also satisfied the regional powers, including Pakistan, or make a grand attempt to claim political ground from the insurgency in order to marginalise it. Reducing counter-insurgency to a mere technical/technological problem could only lead towards proposing unviable solutions, such as imposing population control through the establishment of a national identification card system.[81] To the extent that local communities were not yet merged into the Taliban and maintained a separate identity and specific grievances, serious progress towards the solution to the conflict in Afghanistan might have been achieved by addressing the outstanding political issues. Given the advanced state of the insurgency, possibly nearing its 'metastasis', mild measures such as slowly improving governance skills seem insufficient, not to mention the fact that the 'power blocs' that had developed in many provinces often opposed reforms and new appointments aimed at improving 'governance'. In this author's opinion, better results might have come from developing new and more institutionalised ways of managing subnational administrations in Afghanistan, more inclusive of local communities, strongmen and interest groups, ensuring at the same time that checks and balances were established to prevent 'bad' authorities from tyrannising large sectors of the population. The provincial councils established in 2005 were powerless entities which could only advise local authorities and were usually paid little or no attention. Any reform moving in this direction should have been packaged as a major political campaign aimed at changing the way the Afghan state behaves in relation to the population and should have recognised past wrongdoings in order to have a significant impact on the areas affected by the insurgency.[82]

NOTES

1   Personal communications with NSD officers, Kunduz, 2003–4 and Pul-i
    Khumri, 2006; personal communications with individuals harassed by the
    security services and their relatives, 2006–7; 'Afghans tortured prisoners
    captured by Canadians', *Pajhwok Afghan News*, 23 April 2007; Lee Carter,
    'Canadian row over Afghan "abuse"', *BBC News*, 24 April 2007.
2   Cordesman (2007).
3   Afghan Independent Human Rights Commission (2004), p. 20. 'Eleven
    of the complaints were related to the bombing of civilians. The other 33
    complaints included cases of beatings, detention of innocent people, and
    damage to houses, injuries to people and a lack of respect for Afghan culture
    during coalition raids', <http://www.aihrc.org.af/mon_inv.htm>.
4   Afghan Independent Human Rights Commission (2005), p. 37.
5   Interview with Afghan security officer, Kandahar, January 2006; Elizabeth
    Rubin, 'In the land of the Taliban', *New York Times Magazine*, 22 October
    2006; Eric Schmitt and David Rohde, 'Afghan rebels widen attacks', *New
    York Times*, 1 August 2004; Chris Sands, 'Afghanistan: battle for hearts
    and minds lost', *PalestineChronicle.com*, 11 December 2005; Amin Tarzi,
    'Afghanistan: Kabul riots appeared spontaneous', *RFE/RL*, 6 June 2006;
    interview with Maulana Obeidullah, Peace Strengthening Commission,
    Kandahar, January 2006; Declan Walsh, 'We'll beat you again, Afghans
    warn British', *Guardian*, 26 June 2006; interview with Haji Mir Khan, MP
    from Khost, Kabul, February 2007; interview with Afghan notable from
    Khugyani, Jalalabad, February 2007.
6   For a summary of the early differences within NATO, see Gallis (2006).
7   Personal communication, Kabul, October 2006.
8   Konstantin von Hammerstein *et al.*, 'NATO chaos deepens in Afghanistan',
    Der Spiegel Online, 20 November 2006; Cordesman (2007); Robert Fox,
    'CIA is undermining British war effort, say military chiefs', *Independent*, 10
    December 2006; Jason Burke, 'Fear battles hope on the road to Kandahar',
    Observer, 25 June 2006; Declan Walsh, 'Afghanistan's opium poppies will
    be sprayed, says US drugs tsar', *Guardian*, 11 December 2006; Murray
    Brewster, 'Canada trying to deter spraying of poppy fields', *Canadian Press*,
    22 January 2007; Raymond Whitaker, 'Opium war revealed …', *Independent*,
    21 January 2007; Syed Saleem Shahzad, 'Afghanistan's highway to hell',
    Asia Times Online, 25 January 2007.
9   See 'Afghan Security Forces demobilize, join ANA, ANP', *Freedom
    Watch* (CENTCOM), January 2006, <http://www.cfc-a.centcom.
    mil/Freedom%20Watch/2006/01-January/Jan%2023.pdf>. For more
    information see Giustozzi (2007a).
10 On the AMF see International Crisis Group (2003b). On the warlords'
    system behind the AMF, see Giustozzi (2003). UNAMA source, Kabul,
    2003; UN sources, Kabul, January 2004.

11 For an example in Herat see *Erada Daily*, 28 October 2003; *RFE/RL Newsline*, vol. 7, no. 140, part III, 25 July 2003; *RFE/RL Newsline*, vol. 7, no. 156, part III, 18 August 2003.
12 Personal interviews with local authorities in various provinces of Afghanistan, October 2003–February 2004.
13 Ministry of Defence of Afghanistan (2002); General Pezhanwai, quoted in *RFE/RL Newsline*, 5 March 2003; General Atiqullah Baryalai, quoted in *New York Times*, 25 January 2003; General Gulad, quoted in *Christian Science Monitor*, 27 March 2002; personal interview with General Nurul Haq Ulumi, May 2003.
14 Personal interview with UNAMA military liaison officer, February 2004.
15 See Giustozzi (2007a); International Crisis Group (2003b).
16 Owais Tohid, 'Arid Afghan province proves fertile for Taliban', *Christian Science Monitor*, 14 July 2003; UN and ISAF sources, Kabul, October 2006; David Rohde, 'Afghan symbol for change becomes a symbol of failure', *New York Times*, 5 September 2006; International Crisis Group (2006a), p. 17.
17 Personal communication with NCL employee, Kabul, February 2007. For the case of Kajaki see 'A double spring offensive', *The Economist*, 22 February 2007. See also Giustozzi (2007a).
18 Interview with Afghan journalist returning from the south, Kabul, October 2006.
19 Tom Coghlan, 'Taliban flee Afghan-led NATO offensive', *Daily Telegraph*, 30 March 2007; *Arman-e Milli*, 11 April 2007; 'Men in uniforms rob civilians in Helmand', *IRIN*, 24 Apr 2007; interview with tribal notable from Chora, April 2007; personal communication with UN officials and foreign diplomats.
20 Trives (2006); Scott Baldauf, 'Key to governing Afghans: the clans', *Christian Science Monitor*, 24 June 2004; Scott Baldauf, 'Outside Kabul, militias bring security to Afghanistan', *Christian Science Monitor*, 24 April 2003; 'Jalali rejects formation of tribal units in Afghanistan', *Pakistan Tribune*, 1 August 2003; International Crisis Group (2006a), p. 17; Pamela Constable, 'A NATO bid to regain Afghans' trust', *Washington Post*, 27 November 2006; Declan Walsh, 'Special deals and raw recruits employed to halt the Taliban in embattled Helmand', *Guardian*, 4 January 2007; Fisnik Abrashi, 'Taliban, criminals may be among militiamen recruited as auxiliary police in Afghanistan', *Associated Press*, 25 November 2006.
21 On the problem of corruption and abuses in the police see Amnesty International (2003). Kandahar police has 120 professionally trained policemen out of a total force of 3,000 in 2003 (p. 9).
22 Graeme Smith, 'Chief cracks down on Kandahar police', *Globe and Mail*, 24 January 2007; personal communications with UN officials, Kandahar and Kabul, January, February and October 2006; Graeme Smith, 'Inspiring tale of triumph over Taliban not all it seems', *Globe and Mail*, 23 September 2006; Graeme Smith, 'The Taliban: knowing the enemy', *Globe and Mail*, 27 November 2006; Pamela Constable, 'A NATO bid to regain Afghans'

trust'.

23 See *Interagency Assessment of Afghanistan Police Training and Readiness* (2006).

24 Interview with Afghan journalist returning from the south, Kabul, October 2006; Phil Zabriskie, 'Dangers up ahead: how druglords and insurgents are making the war in Afghanistan deadlier than ever', *Time*, 5 March 2006; James Rupert, 'Corruption and coalition failures spur Taliban resurgence in Afghanistan', *Newsday*, 17 June 2006; Elizabeth Rubin, 'In the land of the Taliban'; Terry Friel, 'Resurgent Taliban strangles southern heartland', *Reuters*, 16 November 2006; Andrew Maykuth, 'An Afghan rebuilding takes shape', *Philadelphia Inquirer*, 6 October 2003; Kathy Gannon, 'Taliban comeback traced to corruption', *Associated Press*, 24 November 2006; Murray Brewster, 'Kandahar cops making progress says RCMP', *Canadian Press*, 3 February 2007.

25 Jason Burke, 'Stronger and more deadly, the terror of the Taliban is back', *Observer*, 16 November 2003; Kate Clark, 'Cash rewards for Taliban fighters', *File On 4, BBC Radio 4*, 28 February 2006; Sara Daniel, 'Afghanistan: "Résister aux talibans? A quoi bon!"', *Le Nouvel Observateur*, 10 August 2006; Senlis Council (2006d), p. 27; Elizabeth Rubin, 'In the land of the Taliban'; Jason Burke, 'Fear battles hope on the road to Kandahar'; David Leask, 'In some areas of Helmand, the police are your worst enemy', *Herald*, 10 January 2007; Syed Saleem Shahzad, 'Afghanistan's highway to hell'; Harm Ede Botje, 'We zitten darr goed', *Vrij Nederland*, 6 January 2007 (courtesy of J. van den Zwan, Crisis States Research Centre, London); Graeme Smith, 'Chief cracks down on Kandahar police'; Tom Coghlan, 'Profits are vast but only the big fish survive', *Daily Telegraph*, 8 February 2007; 'Living under the Taleban', *Afghan Recovery Report* (IWPR), no. 249 (4 April 2007).

26 David Rohde and James Risen, 'C.I.A. review highlights Afghan leader's woes', *New York Times*, 5 November 2006; Elizabeth Rubin, 'Taking the fight to the Taliban', *New York Times Magazine*, 29 October 2006; Elizabeth Rubin, 'In the land of the Taliban'.

27 Quoted in Graeme Smith, 'Inspiring tale of triumph over Taliban not all it seems'.

28 Senlis Council (2006a), p. 11; Kathy Gannon, 'Taliban comeback traced to corruption'; Syed Saleem Shahzad, 'Rough justice and blooming poppies', *Asia Times Online*, 7 December 2006.

29 James Rupert, 'Corruption and coalition failures spur Taliban resurgence in Afghanistan'; 'ANP don't control the villages', *Arman-e Milli*, 10 December 2006; Kim Barker, 'Taliban flexes renewed muscle', *Chicago Tribune*, 3 July 2006; Phil Zabriskie, 'Dangers up ahead: how druglords and insurgents are making the war in Afghanistan deadlier than ever'; Borhan Younus, 'Taliban call the shots in Ghazni', *Afghanistan Recovery Report*, no. 213 (25 April 2006); Eric de Lavarène, 'La province de tous les dangers', *RFI*, 19 March 2006; interview with Afghan security officer, Kandahar, January 2006; David Rohde, 'G.I.s in Afghanistan on hunt, but now for hearts and minds', *New*

York Times, 30 March 2004; Amir Shah, 'Police flee after Afghan bomb attack', *Associated Press*, 19 February 2007.

30 For the case of Chora district of Helmand, 2006 see Kim Barker, 'Taliban flexes renewed muscle'.

31 Interview with Afghan security officer, Kandahar, January 2006; David Rohde, 'G.I.s in Afghanistan on hunt, but now for hearts and minds'; Paul Watson, 'On the trail of the Taliban's support', *Los Angeles Times*, 24 December 2006; Declan Walsh, 'We'll beat you again, Afghans warn British'; 'Why are Helmand's districts falling to the Taliban?', *Abadi*, 13 December 2006; Hamid Mir, 'The Taliban's new face', *Rediff* (India), 27 September 2005; Murray Brewster, 'Kandahar cops making progress says RCMP'; Jason Straziuso, 'Race is on to prevent Taliban's return', *Associated Press*, 6 February 2007; UNDSS weekly presentation, 2–8 February 2007.

32 For two cases in Helmand see Tim Albone, 'Pathfinders on a four-day mission fight off eight-week Taliban siege', *The Times*, 27 September 2006, and Thomas Coghlan and Justin Huggler, 'A ruthless enemy, a hostile population and 50C heat', *Independent*, 9 July 2006.

33 Françoise Chipaux, 'Les talibans consolident leur emprise dans le sud de l'Afghanistan', *Le Monde*, 9 June 2006; Kathy Gannon, 'Taliban comeback traced to corruption'; Andrew Maykuth, 'An Afghan rebuilding takes shape'; 'Forty Afghan police flee checkpoints with weapons after not paid in full', *Pajhwok News Agency*, 30 March 2006; Scott Baldauf, 'Small US units lure Taliban into losing battles', *Christian Science Monitor*, 31 October 2005; 'Sept policiers afghans tués par des collègues alliés aux taliban', *Reuters*, 5 June 2006; David Rohde, 'G.I.s in Afghanistan on hunt, but now for hearts and minds'; interview with Afghan police officer, Kandahar, January 2006; Elizabeth Rubin, 'Taking the fight to the Taliban'; Kathy Gannon, 'Taliban comeback traced to corruption'; Eric Schmitt and David Rohde, 'Afghan rebels widen attacks'; personal communication with Niamtullah Ibrahimi, Crisis States Research Centre, Kabul, October 2006.

34 Kim Barker, 'Taliban flexes renewed muscle'; Terry Friel, 'Resurgent Taliban strangles southern heartland'; David Rohde, 'G.I.s in Afghanistan on hunt, but now for hearts and minds'; 'Why are Helmand's districts falling to the Taliban?', *Abadi*, 13 December 2006; personal communication with UN officials, Kabul, April and May 2007; personal communication with police advisor, Kabul, May 2007.

35 This paragraph is based mainly on Giustozzi (2007b), where the reader can find more details and data.

36 For an elaboration of this point see Giustozzi (2007b).

37 Dyke and Crisafulli (2006), pp. 9, 10; Naylor (2006); Michael A. Fletcher, 'Bush rebuffs Karzai's request on troops', *Washington Post*, 24 May 2005; *C4I News*, 17 February 2005; Carlotta Gall, 'U.S.–Afghan foray reveals friction on antirebel raids', *New York Times*, 2 July 2006.

38 Giustozzi (2007b).

39 Interview with former ANA soldier, January 2007; Giustozzi (2007b);

'Taliban tortures two kidnapped Afghan soldiers to death', *Xinhua*, 1 September 2006; personal communication with US military advisor in Afghanistan, May 2007.

40 Giustozzi (2007b); interview with Afghan journalist returning from the south, Kabul, October 2006; Dyke and Crisafulli (2006), p. 10; Cordesman (2006), p. 4.

41 Tim Kilbride, 'As Afghan troops build capacity, decisive battles loom', *American Forces Press Service*, 2 March 2007.

42 Giustozzi (2007b); 'A double spring offensive', *The Economist*, 22 February 2007.

43 Cordesman (2006), p. 5; Kemp (forthcoming), p. 10; drug trader interviewed in Elizabeth Rubin, 'In the land of the Taliban'; interview with Afghan journalist returning from the south, Kabul, October 2006; Giustozzi (2007b).

44 Mirwais Atal, 'US hearts and minds cash goes to Taliban', *Afghan Recovery Report*, no. 236 (28 November 2006); Giustozzi (2007b).

45 Aryn Baker, 'Can the Afghans defend themselves?', *Time*, 3 January 2007; 'Narcotics found in Afghan army vehicle', *UPI*, 29 March 2006; Syed Saleem Shahzad, 'Afghanistan's highway to hell'; David Loyn, 'On the road with the Taliban', *BBC News (BBC Radio 4)*, 21 October 2006; interview with former ELJ commissioner, Kandahar, 26 January 2006; interview with Afghan security officer, Kandahar, January 2006; interview with Alkozai notable and Sufi leader from Dand district, Kandahar, January 2006; Giustozzi (2007b); Tom Coghlan, 'Profits are vast but only the big fish survive'.

46 Kathy Gannon, 'Taliban comeback traced to corruption'; Senlis Council (2006b), ch. 6, pp. 13–14; Giustozzi (2007b).

47 Jones (2006), who bases his estimate on James T. Quinlivan, 'Force requirements in security operations', *Parameters*, vol. 25, no. 4 (winter 1995–6), pp. 59–69 and Dobbins (2003); Dobbins *et al.* (2005).

48 Kemp (forthcoming), pp. 12–14; Rothstein (2006), pp. 113, 129; Dyke and Crisafulli (2006), pp. 8–9; Charles Heyman, 'Special forces and the reality of military operations in Afghanistan', *Jane's World Airlines*, 5 November 2001; John Simpson, 'US special forces are worried because they are leaving', *Sunday Telegraph*, 15 September 2002; Françoise Chipaux, 'Les talibans font régner leur loi dans les provinces pachtounes du Sud', *Le Monde*, 7 October 2004; Sher Ahmad Haidar, 'Residents flay home-search in Ghazni', *Pajhwok Afghan News*, 21 January 2007; Elizabeth Rubin, 'In the land of the Taliban'.

49 Dyke and Crisafulli (2006), pp. 55–7; Kevin Sack and Craig Pyes, 'Cloak of secrecy hides abuse in Afghanistan', *Los Angeles Times*, 26 September 2006; R. Jeffrey Smith, 'Army files cite abuse of Afghans', *Washington Post*, 18 February 2005.

50 Elizabeth Rubin, 'Taking the fight to the Taliban'; Rothstein (2006), p. 141; Murray Brewster, 'Afghan villagers told they'll be expelled again if

Canadian troops attacked', *Canadian Press*, 13 February 2007.

51 For an example of offers of rewards to the villagers see a flier reproduced at <http://www.huffingtonpost.com/h-candace-gorman-/why-i-am-representing-a-_b_29734.html>.

52 Eric Schmitt and David Rohde, 'Afghan rebels widen attacks'; David Rohde, 'G.I.s in Afghanistan on hunt, but now for hearts and minds'; Tim McGirk, 'The Taliban on the run', *Time*, 28 March 2005; Eric de Lavarène, 'La fin des Taliban?', *RFI*, 1 March 2005; 'A geographical expression in search of a state', *The Economist*, 6 July 2006; Naylor (2006); Patrick Bishop, 'Taliban or tractor? British try to win over peasants', *Daily Telegraph*, 16 September 2006; Ahmad Khalid Mowahid, 'PRT to spend $24m in Maidan Wardak', *Pajhwok Afghan News*, 18 January 2007; 'Afghanistan: le manque d'Etat nourrit la rébellion des talibans (armée US)', *AFP*, 22 September 2005; Carlotta Gall, 'Despite years of U.S. pressure, Taliban fight on in jagged hills', *New York Times*, 4 June 2005; Rothstein (2006), p. 115; Bill Graveland, 'Canadians battling Taliban propaganda', *CNews*, 4 December 2006; Anthony Loyd, 'It's dawn, and the shelling starts. Time to go into the Taleban maze', *The Times*, 14 February 2007; Anthony Loyd, 'Missiles drive US staff from dam that Royal Marines fought to save', *The Times*, 15 February 2007; Tom Coghlan, 'British "quick fix" aid for Afghans brought to halt by insurgents', *Daily Telegraph*, 19 February 2007; Kevin Dougherty, 'NATO and Afghanistan: a status report', *Stars and Stripes* (Mideast edition), 18 February 2007.

53 Elizabeth Rubin, 'Taking the fight to the Taliban'; Senlis Council (2006c), p. 34; Mirwais Atal, 'US hearts and minds cash goes to Taliban'.

54 Naylor (2006); Michael Evans and Anthony Loyd, 'I will build more and kill less, says NATO's Afghanistan general', *The Times*, 1 November 2006; Michael Abramowitz, 'Bush plans new focus on Afghan recovery', *Washington Post*, 25 January 2007.

55 Naylor (2006).

56 Christina Lamb, 'Have you ever used a pistol?'; Alastair Leithead, 'Unravelling the Helmand impasse', *BBC News*, 14 July 2006; Thomas Harding, 'Paras strike deep into the Taliban heartland', *Daily Telegraph*, 19 June 2006; Tim Albone, 'Pathfinders on a four-day mission fight off eight-week Taliban siege'.

57 Les Perreaux, 'NATO urges Afghans to vacate volatile Panjwaii district', *Canadian Press*, 31 August 2006; David Rohde and James Risen, 'C.I.A. review highlights Afghan leader's woes'; Pamela Constable, 'A NATO bid to regain Afghans' trust'; Carlotta Gall, 'NATO's Afghan struggle: build, and fight Taliban', *New York Times*, 13 January 2007; Declan Walsh, 'Special deals and raw recruits employed to halt the Taliban in embattled Helmand'; Akram Naurzi, Najib Khilwatgar, 'Expectations go unfulfilled in Helmand', *Pajhwok Afghan News*, 24 December 2006; Murray Brewster, 'A ride through Taliban country', *Canadian Press*, 17 January 2007; Graeme Smith, 'Inspiring tale of triumph over Taliban not all it seems'; Graeme

Smith, 'The Taliban: knowing the enemy'; Bill Graveland, 'Taliban shows little resistance', *Canadian Press*, 24 December 2006; Gethin Chamberlain, 'Afghan army takes fight to Taliban's heartland', *Sunday Telegraph*, 17 December 2006; 'At site of NATO's largest Afghan ground battle, race is on to prevent Taliban return', *Associated Press*, 30 January 2007; Jason Straziuso, 'Race is on to prevent Taliban's return'; John Cotter, 'Increased roadside bombs, rocket attacks in Afghanistan', *Canadian Press*, 25 March 2007; Damien McElroy, 'Afghan hearts and minds refuse to be won', *Daily Telegraph*, 26 March 2007.

58 Pamela Constable, 'A NATO bid to regain Afghans' trust'; Michael Evans *et al.*, 'Aid effort fails to impress war-weary Afghans', *The Times*, 27 January 2007; Elizabeth Rubin, 'In the land of the Taliban'; Senlis Council (2006c), p. 34; Fisnik Abrashi and Jason Straziuso, 'Deepening insurgency puts Afghanistan on brink', *Associated Press*, 8 October 2006; Tom Coghlan, 'British "quick fix" aid for Afghans brought to halt by insurgents'.

59 Karimi (2006), pp. 148–9, 154, 168ff (courtesy of J. van den Zwan, Crisis States Research Centre, London); Harm Ede Botje, 'We zitten darr goed'; Graeme Smith, 'Doing it the Dutch way in Afghanistan', *Globe and Mail*, 2 December 2006; personal communication with high-ranking NATO officer, Kabul, October 2006; Joeri Boom, 'Martelende gesprekken', *De Groene Amsterdammer*, 24 November 2006; Vik Franke, author of documentary on the Dutch in Uruzgan ('De Wereld draait door'), interviewed on *Vaara TV*, 20 November 2006 (courtesy of J. van den Zwan, Crisis States Research Centre, London); Cordesman (2007); Paul McGeough, 'Winning hearts and minds is keeping the Taliban at bay', *Sydney Morning Herald*, 22 February 2007.

60 Harm Ede Botje, 'We zitten darr goed'; Marina Brouwer, 'Geen zachte aanpak meer in Afghanistan', *Radio Nederland*, 22 December 2006; 'Vredemissie verliest het van wapengeld', *NRC Handelsblad*, 16 November 2006 (courtesy of J. van den Zwan, Crisis States Research Centre, London); 'Reconstruction of Uruzgan is proceeding slowly', *Paktia Ghag*, 18 December 2006; 'Dutch troops won't participate in destruction of poppy crops in Afghanistan', *Associated Press*, 30 January 2007; 'Dutch scale back strategy in southern Afghanistan', *DPA*, 16 February 2007.

61 Michael Evans and Anthony Loyd, 'I will build more and kill less, says NATO's Afghanistan general'; David Wood, 'Afghan war needs troops', *Baltimore Sun*, 7 January 2007; Murray Brewster, 'Taliban to be pushed into the mountains and marginalized: Canadian commander', *Canadian Press*, 7 February 2007; Richard Norton-Taylor, 'Britain switches tactics to undermine the Taliban', *Guardian*, 27 February 2007.

62 'Sud-est de l'Afghanistan: "Ici, c'est la guerre!"', *AFP*, 20 September 2003; Scott Baldauf, 'Small US units lure Taliban into losing battles'; 'SBS shows troops burning Taliban bodies', *Australian Associated Press*, 20 October 2005; Ghufran (2006), pp. 85–94; Cordesman (2006), pp. 15–16; Sardar Ahmad, 'Forces in Afghanistan shift focus to Taliban leaders', *AFP*, 2 January 2007;

Matthew Pennington, 'Afghanistan body count raises skepticism', *Associated Press*, 15 September 2006.

63 For some of these allegations see Senlis Council (2006a), pp. 10 and 43.

64 Syed Saleem Shahzad, 'The vultures are circling', *Asia Times Online*, 13 December 2006; David S. Cloud, 'U.S. airstrikes climb sharply in Afghanistan', *New York Times*, 17 November 2006; David Rohde and Taimoor Shah, 'Strike killed 31 Afghans, NATO finds', *New York Times*, 14 November 2006; Ángeles Espinosa, 'La OTAN lucha en territorio talibán', *El País*, 14 September 2006; 'Civilian casualties trigger anti-govt sentiments', *Pajhwok Afghan News*, 21 August 2006; Cordesman (2006), pp. 15–16; 'Some in southern Afghan province call for ISAF's withdrawal', *RFE/RL Newsline*, 8 November 2006; Kathy Gannon, 'Taliban comeback traced to corruption'; Graeme Smith, 'Inspiring tale of triumph over Taliban not all it seems'; Tom Vanden Brook, 'Bombing campaign intensifies in Afghanistan', *USA Today*, 8 February 2007; UNDSS weekly presentation, 2–8 February 2007.

65 Katzman (2006); Sedra and Middlebrook (2005); for a critical discussion of the governance concept as used by international organisations and diplomats, see Allan (2003).

66 Schiewek (2006), pp. 156–7.

67 Harm Ede Botje, 'We zitten darr goed'; Kate Clark, 'Cash rewards for Taliban fighters'; interview with Afghan journalist returning from the south, Kabul, October 2006; personal communication with foreign diplomat, Kabul, February 2007; Philip G. Smucker, 'Afghanistan's eastern front', *U.S. News & World Report*, 9 April 2007.

68 Senlis Council (2006d), pp. 18, 21; Smith (2005), pp. 7–8; Raymond Whitaker, 'Opium war revealed ...'; 'Why are Helmand's districts falling to the Taliban?', *Abadi*, 13 December 2006; 'Key Afghan governor supports spraying of opium poppies, reaching out to Taliban', *Associated Press*, 5 January 2007; Christina Lamb and Michael Smith, 'Sacked Afghan leader blames opium mafia', *Sunday Times*, 10 December 2006; Jeremy Page and Tim Albone, 'Blow for Britain as Helmand's "cleanest" governor is sacked', *The Times*, 9 December 2006; Robert Fox, 'CIA is undermining British war effort, say military chiefs'; Kim Sengupta, 'Helmand governor escapes blast as he battles for job', *Independent*, 13 December 2006.

69 Clark (2002); Bradley Graham and Alan Sipress, 'Reports that Taliban leaders were freed shock, alarm U.S.', *Washington Post*, 10 January 2002; Vernon Loeb and Bradley Graham, 'Rumsfeld says no amnesty for Taliban leader', *Washington Post*, 7 December 2001; Elizabeth Rubin, 'In the land of the Taliban'; Tim McGirk, 'The Taliban on the run'; 'Afghan administration reportedly opens negotiations with Taliban', *RFE/RL Afghanistan Report*, vol. 2, no. 35 (9 October 2003).

70 Interview with Habibullah Mangal, head of Peace Strengthening Commission for Paktia, Gardez, October 2006; interview with Afghan security officer, Kandahar, January 2006; Peter Bergen, 'The Taliban,

"regrouped and rearmed"', *Washington Post*, 10 September 2006; '169 Taliban commanders surrender to gov't in Afghanistan: official', *Xinhuanet*, 28 February 2006.

71 Interview with Habibullah Mangal, head of Peace Strengthening Commission for Paktia, Gardez, October 2006; interview with Afghan security officer, Kandahar, January 2006.

72 Personal communication with UN official, Jalalabad, February 2007; Tim McGirk, 'The Taliban on the run'; interview with Habibullah Mangal, head of Peace Strengthening Commission for Paktia, Gardez, October 2006; interview with Afghan security officer, Kandahar, January 2006; Peter Bergen, 'The Taliban, "regrouped and rearmed"'; Kemp (forthcoming), pp. 12–14; interview with Maulana Obeidullah, Peace Strengthening Commission, Kandahar, January 2006.

73 Peter Bergen, 'The Taliban, "regrouped and rearmed"'; Elizabeth Rubin, 'In the land of the Taliban'; Tim McGirk, 'The Taliban on the run'; interview with Maulana Obeidullah, Peace Strengthening Commission, Kandahar, January 2006; Pamela Constable, 'Afghan city's rebound cut short. Battles between NATO forces, resurgent Taliban make ghost town of Kandahar', *Washington Post*, 19 August 2006; 'Former Deputy Interior Minister killed in S. Afghanistan', *Xinhua*, 15 January 2006; Doug Schmidt, 'Buy Taliban weapons, tribal leader proposes', *Windsor Star*, 8 February 2007.

74 See Giustozzi (2006).

75 'Afghan government opens talks with Taliban in troubled south', *AFP*, 1 September 2003; Syed Saleem Shahzad, 'Taliban deal lights a slow-burning fuse', *Asia Times Online*, 11 February 2006; Les Perreaux, 'NATO urges Afghans to vacate volatile Panjwaii district'; 'ISAF clarifies position on Sangin', *Pajhwok Afghan News*, 27 October 2006; Rahimullah Yusufzai, 'Taliban warn UK troops to vacate Musa Qala district', *The News*, 4 October 2006; Alastair Leithead, 'Can change in Afghan tactics bring peace?', *BBC News*, 17 October 2006; speech of Minister Dadfar Spanta at Chatham House, London, 1 February 2007; Carlotta Gall and Abdul Waheed Wafa, 'Peace accord in provincial Afghanistan dividing opinion', *New York Times*, 2 December 2006; Amin Tarzi, 'Governor of southern Afghan province proposes talks with Taliban', *RFE/RL Newsline*, vol. 11 no. 28 (13 February 2007); personal communication with UN official, Kabul, March 2007.

76 Samad Rohani, 'Whodunit? Violation of truce in Musa Qala', *Pajhwok Afghan News*, 5 December 2006; Ahmed Rashid, 'Britain out of step with NATO allies', *Daily Telegraph*, 6 January 2007; Michael Evans *et al.*, 'Aid effort fails to impress war-weary Afghans'; Declan Walsh, 'Special deals and raw recruits employed to halt the Taliban in embattled Helmand'; James Bays, 'Afghan tribes negotiate with NATO', *Al Jazeera*, 16 November 2006; Tom Coghlan, 'Afghanistan: local leaders offered the chance to recruit their own police force', *Daily Telegraph*, 23 January 2007; Syed Saleem Shahzad, 'Afghanistan's highway to hell'; Carlotta Gall and Taimoor Shah, 'Afghan town is overrun by Taliban', *New York Times*, 3 February 2007; 'Taliban

appears to reverse position on deal over southern Afghan', *Afghan Islamic Press*, 6 February 2007; Murray Brewster, 'Taliban to be pushed into the mountains and marginalized: Canadian commander'; Christina Lamb, 'Karzai bids for peace in furore with London', *Sunday Times*, 11 February 2007; Abdul Waheed Wafa and Carlotta Gall, 'Town's elders plead for help with Taliban', *New York Times*, 26 February 2007; personal communications with UN and British officials.

77 Shaheen Sehbai, 'Bush adopts Musharraf's policy in Afghanistan', *The News*, 4 October 2006.

78 Tim Albone and Claire Billet, 'Ruined poppy farmers join ranks with the Taleban', *The Times*, 27 February 2007; Richard Norton-Taylor, 'Britain switches tactics to undermine the Taliban'.

79 Gethin Chamberlain, 'US military: Afghan leaders steal half of all aid', *Sunday Telegraph*, 28 January 2007; personal communications with NGO and UN staff, Afghanistan 2003–6.

80 See for example Hammes (2006), p. 230, who is, however, one of the most articulate and sophisticated of these analysts.

81 Long (2006), pp. 72–3.

82 On the current debate concerning this topic, see Lister and Nixon (2006).

CONCLUSION

It has been argued that excluding the Taliban from the negotiations in Bonn was a mistake which is at the roots of the subsequent insurgency.[1] Whether there was ever a real chance of including the Taliban in the Bonn process is not clear. The Movement was in a state of disarray at the end of 2001 and it would not have been in a position to win significant representation in the new Transitional Administration, the more so given the strenuous opposition of other Afghan parties and groups. The emergence of a hard-core Taliban opposition, therefore, was probably inevitable. It has also been argued, particularly within the UN,[2] that if the Karzai administration had been keener to cultivate the support of the clergy, large sections of it would not have supported the Taliban. Indeed, President Karzai at times took initiatives aimed in that direction, such as when he appointed ultra-conservative Mawlawi Fazel Haq Shinwari as head of the Supreme Court in 2002, when he sponsored plans by the Council of Ulema to launch its own television station, when he announced the creation of a 'moral police' in 2006, or when he created 500 positions within the Ministry of Hajj and Endowments for Ulema to be on the government's paybook. However, in the context of international intervention in Afghanistan and given the very conservative leanings of the majority of the clergy, it is unlikely that Karzai could ever have gone far enough to appease the latter without deeply upsetting some of his foreign allies. In the absence of a political strategy to bring the clergy closer to the government, the only alternative would have been a massive investment in patronage. Given the sheer size of the clergy (200,000–300,000), including all or most of them on the government payroll might only have been feasible with large-scale support from abroad. Then, elders and tribal leaders too would also have demanded government support, with obvious consequences in terms of financial burden. The resulting inflationary process would have forced the government periodically to increase hand-outs and state salaries, in a vicious cycle which inevitably would have tested the patience of even the most committed donor. Finally, reaching out to the village clerics and incorporating them in a state-sponsored patronage system would probably have resulted in government-sponsored clerics moving to the towns and once again leaving a vacuum in the villages, which could have been filled by the opposition.[3]

Although the insurgency cannot be described in terms of a rural jacquerie against changes imposed from an urban-based government, there are elements of rural revolt which contributed to make the insurgency possible. The foreign-educated élites that made up part of the Afghan cabinet and much of the top ministerial staff were not well equipped to communicate with the remote countryside, or to understand the processes going on there. The reverse is also true, as the rural population had little understanding of the processes going on in Kabul and of the rationale and technicalities of foreign intervention. Nonetheless, it was more than simply a cultural and communication gap. Different and often opposed interests were at stake. The Kabul-based élites wanted to bring the countryside back under some form of central control and used a number of approaches to obtain that, including allying with local strongmen and empowering them as administrators. This attitude was in line with the policies of the Afghan state since at least the nineteenth century, but in the context of the post-2001 period it proved to be hardly sustainable. The emergence of an increasingly politically conscious and ambitious clergy and its attempts to mobilise dissatisfied villagers had been going on amid many ups and downs for over 150 years, dating back to the First Anglo-Afghan War. The crisis of Afghan rural society has not been the subject of many studies, but it can be assumed that the doubling of the population between 1978 and 2002 and the loss of much agricultural land and livestock during the wars of that period intensified it. Hence the rural population and recent immigrants in the cities were likely to become receptive to criticism of the government, of its foreign backers and of their local allies once the original expectations of generous hand-outs and rapid development were not met. Finally, the consensus on the value of Afghanistan as a buffer state among regional powers had been in crisis since 1947 and was well defunct by 2001, creating the conditions for external support to internal opposition. The old model of the Afghan state could hardly survive in the new conditions.

If a clergy-supported and Pakistan-based insurgency was probably inevitable in practice, what could possibly have been avoided was the mobilisation of large constituencies by the remnants of the 'old Taliban' in many parts of southern and south-eastern Afghanistan. In 2002–3 a de-patrimolialised subnational administration could probably have removed one of the main causes of the alliance between the clergy, the militants and the villagers, that is abusive and factionalised local authorities. This could have been a key contribution to preventing the insurgency from escalating from a nuisance to a major problem. The situation, of course, was different at the end of 2006, as the Taliban had by then firmly established themselves in many areas. The alliance between the insurgents and sections of the village population was also favoured by the foolish promises initially made by officials of international organisations, NGOs and government development agencies, who went much beyond what could realistically be offered and even more so beyond what could be delivered, given the conditions of the infrastructure and of the administration. As a result international intervention in Afghanistan was caught between a 'revolution of rising expectations', which they unwittingly encouraged, and the inability to even remotely match them (see 6.5 *Strategy*).

The option of ending the war through negotiations still existed in 2007, although the negotiating leverage of the Taliban had dramatically increased by then, while that of their adversaries had greatly declined. Despite the claims by diplomats and military commanders that no negotiations were possible with the Taliban,[4] contacts seem to have occurred and might occur again in the future, although an eventual success appears a tall order, given the huge disparity of views and ideologies between would-be partners in the negotiations. However, if it was true, as this author has speculated (see 1.3 *The role of Pakistan*), that Pakistan has control over the delivery of support to the Taliban, then Islamabad might play a key role in successful negotiations by simply threatening to cut off the Taliban's lifeline. The Pakistani authorities, of course, would demand to be rewarded with substantial concessions. For the Pakistani leadership the loss of influence over Afghanistan was a major blow both psychologically and in terms of image, given how much had been invested in establishing control over Afghanistan as Pakistan's best (first?) success story in foreign policy. After a half-hearted and ill-fated attempt to create a 'Taliban party' as a vehicle for obtaining some power-sharing in Kabul (see 3.1 *Cohesiveness of the Taliban*), the temptation to exploit Kabul's obvious weaknesses and force the northern neighbour to the negotiating table in a position of inferiority must have been strong in Islamabad. The Durand Line has been mentioned often during 2006 as a key bone of contention between Afghanistan and Pakistan,[5] but recognising the Durand Line would be very costly for any Afghan government and would not necessarily suffice to appease the Pakistanis, as a future Afghan government might still raise the issue again. In the end, any agreement will have to revolve around Pakistan's implicit demand of a significant stake in Afghan government, which likely implies control over at least a key ministry by trusted partners. Such a demand might be difficult to swallow for a government, like Karzai's in 2006, partly built around Pashtun nationalist circles. It would certainly have been unacceptable in 2002, when the Transitional Administration exuded self-confidence and was certain of US support. During 2006 the emergence of many former members of Hizb-i Islami as one of the key components of the cabinet and more in general in the state structure appeared to hint at the direction of a possible solution to the dilemma. Hizb-i Islami maintained good relations with both Pakistan and Iran, but some of its former members incorporated in Karzai's entourage had also accumulated a substantial dose of credibility among Karzai's foreign patrons. However, if the Pakistanis were granted such a stake in Kabul, other regional powers such as India, Iran and Russia would likely also demand similar concessions. If a balance could be stricken, Afghanistan would return to its old status of buffer state.

As long as time is not ripe for a negotiated solution, and short of some major change in the counter-insurgency approach, or in the structure of the Afghan state, the war might go on indefinitely. As of March 2007 the strategic situation was one of stalemate, with a slight advantage for the Taliban. The insurgents were still unable to challenge the ISAF and the US forces on the battlefield, but the latter were unable to check the Taliban's spread across Afghanistan's territory and were failing to maintain control of the population, the most important aim in counter-insurgent warfare. If the Taliban and their allies succeed in spreading to the northern half of Afghanistan, then the ISAF would face a strategic conundrum. Unable to muster larger numbers of troops and given the doubtful inclination to fight of many of its member contingents, the ISAF might turn out to be unable to cope. The main risk for the Taliban seemed one of failing to stand up to the claims made during 2006, that a countrywide jihad was starting and that the war had progressed to a new stage of strategic challenge or even of 'final offensive'.

In terms of mounting a credible insurgency in Afghanistan, the Taliban faced major challenges in 2002. Their original rank-and-file was largely demoralised by the unexpectedly quick collapse of the regime under the attack of the United States and the internal opposition. Moreover, they had little experience in organising a large scale insurgency. Finally, and perhaps most important, the population was tired of war and wanted peace and was also buying into promises of rapid reconstruction and development once Afghanistan rejoined the international community. Despite these constraints, whether by their own efforts or more likely with the help of international jihadists and of at least some elements of the Pakistani state, after a slow start in

2002 they succeeded in mounting a credible threat to the government in Kabul. By skilfully exploiting local grievances against the government and against local authorities, they successfully mobilised much of the southern population against the government and foreign contingents and forced a collapse of the structure of government in whole provinces. Their human losses were heavy but although precise figures will never be available they do not seem to have been out of line with the casualty rates experienced by other insurgent movements in the 1950s–1990s when fighting against superior armies supported by locally recruited troops. For what this type of statistic is worth, according to available figures in Vietnam (1963–75) the casualty ratio was around one to one, when losses from all actors and killed and wounded are included. During the Malayan emergency, it was two to one in favour of the British and their local allies. In Algeria it might have been closer to four to one, while for the Taliban this author estimates it at three to one in favour of their adversaries (see 6.1 *International actors*). Insurgencies can do much worse than that, as shown by the Mau-Mau in Kenya, where the ratio was around fifteen to one against them. The Taliban performed particularly badly in direct engagements, where their casualty ratio might have been similar to that of the Mau-Mau, but managed to reduce greatly the casualty ratio through the use of relatively new insurgency techniques such as IEDs and suicide bombing.

The Taliban subordinated tactics to a strategy. The latter also happened to be mostly sound and consistent in identifying the weaknesses of the enemy and focusing on those. The Taliban did commit a number of blunders, but these were the result of the need to test new tactics and potential weaknesses of the enemy. In other words, the Taliban showed that they could learn from their mistakes, or at least that they had good advisors and were listening to them. However, the Taliban's struggle was also marked by clear differences from the 'classic' insurgencies of the 1940–1980s, Maoist or otherwise. If it is true, as argued in section 4.11, that the Neo-Taliban's strategy was turning into a global jihadist one, then what the leadership wanted was not to expel the 'foreigners' as quickly as possible, but keep them in and wear them out, as was being done in Iraq. That is the opposite of what a classic 'war of national liberation' would have tried to do. Victory was to be achieved at the global level or not be achieved at all.

If they had been fighting a war of national liberation, the greatest strategic limitation of the insurgents would have been their confinement to a single portion of the country, at least until 2006. However, as a global jihadist insurgency, the Neo-Taliban were not affected as much by this limitation. Outside the southern region, the Taliban and their advisors relied only partially on direct infiltration to establish their presence, often opting to use various incentives to mobilise local insurgents, particularly in areas remote from the border. Hence the importance of creating a 'Tet effect' with highly visible initiatives such as the intensified fighting around Kandahar in the summer of 2006, hoping that this would help them mobilise new allies. Undoubtedly, they did succeed in attracting the attention of the Afghan public and in shaking the faith in the ability of the foreign contingents to maintain control of the situation. A substantial number of pragmatically minded but small 'conflict entrepreneurs' seem to have responded to the call of the Taliban, generating low-level violence in many areas. As of March 2007, however, it was still difficult to say whether this would suffice to convince major new players to enter the conflict on the Taliban's side. Indirect mobilisation is cheap and implies little risk-taking for the centre of the insurgency, but it comes at a price. Whether joined by a multitude of small conflict entrepreneurs or by a few large military-political leaders, the insurgency would face a challenge in terms of coordination and control. If the insurgency continues to spread both geographically and politically, it will likely start to resemble more and more the Afghan jihad of the 1980s, which was a chaotic movement with no effective overall leadership. The main tool of control will increasingly become the monopoly over sources of funding, which in turn could be successfully maintained only if endorsed and actively supported by the Pakistani authorities and other regional players. Difficult command and control would, however, not prevent the spread of chaos and insecurity throughout the country.

Although their tactical skills remained weak throughout 2002–6, they made 'creative' use of the modest human resources available. Indeed, compared to the 'old Taliban' of 1994–2001, the insurgents of 2002– deserve to be described as *Neo*-Taliban. If the Kuran and the Kalashnikov continued to describe well the ethos of the Movement, as they did for the old Taliban, the Neo-Taliban developed a passion for the new technologies completely at odds with the ostracism showed in the old days. It is not clear whether the top ranks of the Movement, who played a key role in 1994–2001 too, also personally adopted the new technologies or whether they only allowed their subordinates to use them. The first, shy attempts to court educated constituencies also seemed to hint at the fact that the Taliban might be willing to amend their earlier stance. The internationalisation of the Taliban is a third feature marking the Movement as '*neo*'. The influence of the Arab jihadists was evident in this case. But does the adoption of new technologies and of international jihadist rhetoric imply a more substantial change? What we have been seeing in 2002–6 is probably a process of transition, from an ultra-orthodox and narrowly focused interpretation of Islam towards an ultra-conservative but more 'political' and 'internationalist' interpretation. However, the 'ideological' dimension of the Neo-Taliban does not seem well defined yet. After all, the jihadist component started emerging strongly only in 2005 and it is unlikely that it found deeper roots within the old leadership, who might have adopted it somewhat pragmatically. This pattern of adaptation could still take different paths. The Neo-Taliban could become fully radicalised and incorporated into a global jihadist perspective, or in the event of a negotiated deal their evolution could boil down towards something resembling the Islamic parties of Pakistan, which combine 'reactionary' attitudes with, for example, the acceptance of electoral competition.

The counter-insurgency effort by contrast has been characterised by the extremely inefficient use of the considerable financial and technological resources available. Continuous changes in the military strategy prevented the achievement of durable results, while the high expenditure on strengthening Afghan forces had yielded comparatively modest results by 2006. By all standards the formation of the ANA was a slow process: almost five years after the start of the training programme, the army still had a deployable force of less than 20,000 men (see 6.4 *Afghan National Army*). Just to mention a single example, in a similar situation of having (or choosing) to rebuild an army from scratch and immediately facing an insurgency, the Sandinista government in Nicaragua organised an army of 18,000 men in less than a year (1979–80), without receiving much help from outside. Although the effectiveness of this army was limited, once it started receiving substantial help from abroad (Cuba and Soviet Union) in 1982, it became able to control the insurgency of the Contras in just one year, over which period its strength rose to 24,000.[6] Moreover, the Sandinista army was fighting without embedded mentors or trainers and without the help of foreign military contingents or air forces.

Intelligence gathering and analysis was also far from being up to the task. There was little consistent effort at identifying the weak spots of the enemy and focusing on those. The approach to counter-insurgency was mainly reactive and defensive. The government showed little interest in what was going on in remote parts of the country, being mainly concerned with securing the cities, their surrounding areas and the highways. Understandably US and Afghan officials often issued propaganda statements, as happens in any war, announcing continuous defeats of the Neo-Taliban and imminent victory. These statements were likely often motivated by career and image concerns, exacerbated by the short rotation time and by President Karzai's habit of frequently reshuffling government positions. What is worrying, however, is that often they seemed inclined to believe their own propaganda. Only once the Taliban had started approaching Kandahar and the highway linking it with Kabul and Herat did the government start taking the insurgency seriously. The efforts of both the Karzai administration and its international sponsors could be characterised as 'too little, too late':

- when in 2006 Karzai proposed Peace Jirgas to mobilise tribal leadership against the Taliban, the tribal elders which the jirgas were supposed to mobilise had already lost much power and control to the insurgents, as well as faith in the government;
- concern for governance issues emerged only at a stage where the situation on the ground had already been compromised;
- the half-hearted formation of village militias (auxiliary police), which could have prevented the infiltration of the Taliban at an earlier stage, was only proposed in the south in mid-2006, when the Taliban already had sufficient military strength to threaten to overwhelm them; it was never implemented;
- the decision to bring more development and aid to the southern regions was only taken once the insurgency had taken control of the countryside, greatly complicating the task.

It is also worth noting that patronage-based counter-insurgency and improved governance were at odds, as were reconstruction and fighting tactics heavily reliant on firepower. In the end, whereas the Taliban leadership was doggedly pursuing a strategy of destabilisation, neither the United States nor the Afghan government ever had a consistent strategy lasting more than a year. There was evidently a problem of weak political leadership: the Bush Administration was not interested in Afghanistan and left the direction of its local political affairs to its Ambassador, Zalmay Khalilzad, and of military affairs to the fast-rotating commanders of Task Force 180 or 76. While the US military controlled the ANA, they did not control most militias or the police, a fact which led to weak coordination. The government, apart from not having a military policy, did not have much of a political strategy either. The various initiatives were the result of much talking and lobbying by various actors, chiefly UN agencies, a few foreign embassies, NATO and the US armed forces.

The complex and flawed decisional process resulted in delays and in inconsistent policy making. In some cases, the lack of political will in Kabul to go along with external requests led to the implementation of agreed decisions being further delayed, often by many months. Worse still, under pressure the government would often approve policies and reform initiatives and then pay only lip service to them.

At the beginning of 2007 there were still scant signs that a radical change of direction was about to happen either in Kabul or in Bagram (the US HQ), except for an increased military aggressiveness. The talk was still of separating the mass of 'mercenary' fighters from an isolated leadership and of the virtues of 'development' in healing insurgencies. It was not clear, however, how the 'misled' fighters of southern Afghanistan would be made to see the light, or how patronage was going to be delivered to villages outside government control. From the standpoint of May 2007, the omen was not good; during the first three months of 2007 1,000 insurgency-related deaths were reported, that is twice as many as during the corresponding period of 2006.[7]

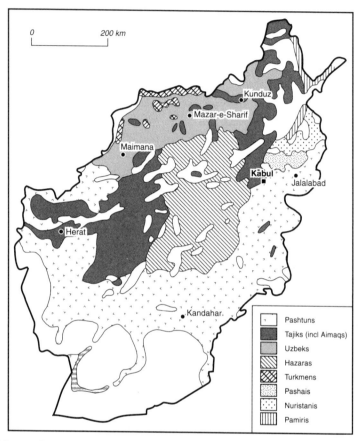

Map 9. Geographical distribution of ethnic groups.

Source: based on maps included in *Le Fait Ethnique en Iran at en Afghanistan*, CNRS 1988.

CONCLUSION

NOTES

1 See, among others, former Indian diplomat M.K. Bhadrakumar, 'The Afghan exit strategy', *Asia Times Online*, 19 January 2006.
2 Several times I took part in discussions concerning this issue when serving in UNAMA in 2003–4.
3 Tom Coghlan, 'Fury as Karzai plans return of Taliban's religious police', *Independent*, 17 July 2006; 'Ulema plan to launch TV in Afghanistan; Ulema Council plans to launch Islamic television channel to balance "immoral and un-Islamic" current programs', *Dawn*, 3 May 2005; Amin Tarzi, 'President orders creation of new Afghan Ulama posts', *Radio Free Europe/Radio Liberty*, 8 July 2006.
4 Mike Blanchfield, 'NATO needs to negotiate with some Taliban', *Ottawa Citizen*, 18 December 2006.
5 Rubin (2007); Middlebrook and Miller (2006).
6 Horton (1998), pp. 121–2.
7 Denis D. Gray, 'NATO pushes to improve Afghan army', *Associated Press*, 25 April 2007.

BIBLIOGRAPHY

Afghan Independent Human Rights Commission (2004), *Annual Report 2003/4*, Kabul.

—— (2005), *Annual Report 2004/5*, Kabul.

Allan, Nigel J.R. (2003), 'Rethinking Governance in Afghanistan', *Journal of International Affairs*, vol. 56, no. 1.

Amnesty International (2003), *Afghanistan: Police Reconstruction Essential for the Protection of Human Rights*, ASA 11/003/2003, London.

Baily, John (2001), *Can You Stop the Birds Singing?*, Copenhagen: Freemuse.

Barno, David W. (2006), 'Challenges in Fighting a Global Insurgency', *Parameters*, summer.

Belasco, Amy (2006), *The Cost of Iraq, Afghanistan, and Other Global War on Terror Operations since 9/11*, Washington, DC: Congressional Research Service.

Cassidy, Robert M. (2003), *Russia in Afghanistan and Chechnya: Military Strategic Culture and the Paradoxes of Asymmetric Conflict*, Carlisle Barracks, PA: Strategic Studies Institute.

Clark, Gen. Wesley (2002), 'An Army of One? In the War on Terrorism, Alliances are not an Obstacle to Victory. They're the Key to it', *Washington Monthly*, September.

Clutterbuck, Richard (1985), *Conflict and Violence in Singapore and Malaysia: 1945–1983*, Boulder, CO: Westview.

Coll, Steve (2004), *Ghost Wars*, New York: Penguin.

Connell, Michael and Alireza Nader (2006), *Iranian Objectives in Afghanistan: Any Basis for Collaboration with the United States?*, A Project Iran Workshop, Alexandria, VA: The CNA Corporation, <http://www.princeton.edu/~lisd/publications/

finn_Iran_Afghanistan.pdf>.

Cordesman, Anthony (2006), 'Press Briefing on Afghanistan', Washington, DC: The Center for Strategic and International Studies.

—— (2007), *Winning in Afghanistan: The Challenges and the Response*, Washington, DC: The Center for Strategic and International Studies.

Davis, Anthony (2002), 'Recent Violence Obscures Deeper Threats for Afghanistan', *Jane's Intelligence Review*, October.

—— (2003), 'Afghan Opposition Gains Coherence', *Jane's Terrorism & Security Monitor*, May.

Dixit, Aabha (n.d.), *Soldiers of Islam: Origins, Ideology and Strategy of the Taliban*, New Delhi: Institute for Defence Studies and Analysis, <http://www.idsa-india.org/an-aug-2.html>.

Dobbins, James (2003), *America's Role in Nation-building: From Germany to Iraq*, Santa Monica, CA: Rand.

Dobbins, James *et al.* (2005), *The UN's Role in Nation-building: From the Congo to Iraq*, Santa Monica, CA: Rand.

Dorronsoro, Gilles (2000), *Pakistan and the Taliban: State Policy, Religious Networks and Political Connections*, Paris: CERI, <http://www.ceri-sciencespo.com/archive/octo00/artgd.pdf>.

—— (2005), *Revolution Unending*, London: Hurst.

Dyke, John R. and John R. Crisafulli (2006), *Unconventional Counter-Insurgency in Afghanistan*, Monterey, CA: Naval Postgraduate School.

Erben, Peter (n.d.), *Election Assessment: 2005 Elections – A Milestone for Afghanistan*, Washington, DC: IFES, <http://www.ifes.org/ctpcg-project.html?projectid=afghanmilestone>.

Gallis, Paul (2006), *NATO in Afghanistan: A Test of the Transatlantic Alliance*, Washington, DC: Congressional Research Service.

Gerges, Fawaz A. (2006), *Journey of the Jihadist*, Orlando, FL: Harcourt.

Ghufran, Nasreen (2006), 'Afghanistan in 2005: The Challenges of Reconstruction', *Asian Survey*, vol. 46, no. 1.

Giustozzi, Antonio (2003), 'Military Reform in Afghanistan' in M. Sedra (ed.), *Afghanistan: Assessing the Progress of Security Sector Reforms*, Bonn International Center for Conversion.

—— (2004), *'Good' State vs. 'Bad' Warlords? A Critique of State-Building Strategies in Afghanistan*, Working Paper 51, London: Crisis States Research Centre.

—— (2006), *'Tribes' and Warlords in Southern Afghanistan, 1980–2005*, Working Paper Series 2, no. 7, London: Crisis States Research Centre.

—— (2007a), 'The Privatizing of War and Security in Afghanistan: Future or Dead End?', *The Economics of Peace and Security Journal*, vol. 2, no. 1.

—— (2007b), 'Auxiliary Force or National Army? Afghanistan's "ANA" and the Counter-Insurgency Effort, 2002–2006', *Small Wars and Insurgencies*, vol. 18, no.1 (March).

—— (forthcoming), 'The Inverted Cycle: Kabul and the Strongmen's Competition for Control over Kandahar, 2001–2006', *Central Asian Survey*, forthcoming.

Hammes, Thomas X. (2005), 'Insurgency: Modern Warfare Evolves into a Fourth Generation', *Forum* (National Defense University), no. 214.

—— (2006), *The Sling and the Stone*, St Paul, MN: Zenith.

Harpviken, Kristian Berg *et al.* (2002), *Afghanistan and Civil Society*, Bergen: CMI.

Horton, Lynn (1998), *Peasants in Arms: War and Peace in the Mountains of Nicaragua, 1979–1994*, Athens, OH: Ohio University Centre for International Studies.

Human Rights Watch (2006), *Lessons in Terror Attacks on Education in Afghanistan*, vol. 18, no. 6.

'Increasing Afghan IED Threat Gives Forces Cause for Concern', *Jane's Intelligence Review*, August 2006.

Interagency Assessment of Afghanistan Police Training and Readiness (2006), Washington, DC: Offices of Inspector General of the Departments of State and Defense.

International Crisis Group (2003a), *Afghanistan: Judicial Reform and Transitional Justice*, Asia Report no. 45.

—— (2003b), *Disarmament and Reintegration in Afghanistan*, Asia Report no. 65.

—— (2006a), *Countering Afghanistan's Insurgency: No Quick Fixes*, Asia Report no. 123.

—— (2006b), *Pakistan's Tribal Areas: Appeasing the Militants*, Asia Report no. 125.

Jandora, John J. (2005), 'Factoring Culture', *Joint Force Quarterly*, no. 39, 4th quarter.

Jelsma, Martin *et al.* (2006), *Losing Ground Drug Control and War in Afghanistan*, Debate Papers no. 15 (December), Amsterdam: Transnational Institute.

Johnson, Thomas H. and M. Chris Mason (2007), 'Understanding the Taliban and Insurgency in Afghanistan', *Orbis*, winter.

Jones, Seth G. (2006), 'Averting Failure in Afghanistan', *Survival*, no. 1.

Karimi, Farah (2006), *Slagveld Afghanistan*, Amsterdam: Nieuw Amsterdam.

Katzman, Kenneth (2006), *Afghanistan: Post-War Governance, Security, and U.S. Policy*, Washington, DC: Congressional Research Service.

Kemp, Robert (forthcoming), 'Counterinsurgency in Eastern Afghanistan' in *Countering Insurgency and Promoting Democracy*, Washington, DC: Council for Emerging National Security Affairs.

Lister, Sarah and Hamish Nixon (2006), *Provincial Governance Structures in Afghanistan: From Confusion to Vision?*, Kabul: AREU.

Long, Austin (2006), *On 'Other War': Lessons from Five Decades of RAND Counterinsurgency Research*, Santa Monica, CA: Rand.

Maley, William (1998), 'Interpreting the Taliban' in W. Maley (ed.), *Fundamentalism Reborn?*, London: Hurst.

Marzban, Omid (2006), 'The Foreign Makeup of Afghan Suicide Bombers', *Terrorism Monitor*, vol. 3, no. 7 (21 February).

McCaffrey, Barry (2006), *Academic Report: Trip to Afghanistan and Pakistan*, United States Military Academy.

Middlebrook, Peter J. and Sharon M. Miller (2006), *All along the Watch Tower: Bringing Peace to the Afghan–Pakistan Border*, New York: Middlebrook & Miller.

Ministry of Defence of Afghanistan (2002), *Main Principles and Guidelines for the Creation of the New Afghan National Army and for the Collection of Arms*, Kabul.

Naylor, Sean D. (2006), 'A Stronger Taliban Lies Low, Hoping the U.S. Will Leave Afghanistan', *Armed Forces Journal*, no. 2.

Nivat, Anne (2006), *Islamistes: comment ils nous voient*, Paris: Fayard, 2006.

Pirnie, Bruce R. *et al.* (2005), *Beyond Close Air Support: Forging a New Air-Ground Partnership*, Santa Monica, CA: Rand.

Rahmani, Waliullah (2006a), 'Afghan Authorities Apprehend Leaders of Kabul Suicide Cell', *Terrorism Monitor*, vol. 3, no. 39.

—— (2006b), 'Helmand Province and the Afghan Insurgency', *Terrorism Monitor* (Jamestown Foundation), vol. 4, no. 6.

Rashid, Ahmed (1999), 'The Taliban: Exporting Extremism', *Foreign Affairs*, November/December.

—— (2000), *Taliban*, London: IB Tauris.

Rothstein, Hy S. (2006), *Afghanistan and the Troubled Future of Unconventional Warfare*, Annapolis, MD: Naval Institute Press.

Roy, Olivier (1998), 'Has Islamism a Future in Afghanistan?' in W. Maley (ed.), *Fundamentalism Reborn?*, London: Hurst.

—— (2000), *Pakistan and the Taliban*, Paris: CERI, October <http://www.ceri-sciencespo.com/archive/octo00/artor.pdf>.

—— (2002), *Islamic Radicalism in Afghanistan and Pakistan*, Writenet Paper no. 06/2001, Geneva: UNHCR.

Rubin, Barnett R. (2006), *Afghanistan's Uncertain Transition from Turmoil to Normalcy*, CSR no. 12, Washington, DC: The Center For Preventive Action (Council On Foreign Relations).

—— (2007), 'Saving Afghanistan', *Foreign Affairs*, January/February.

Schiewek, Eckart (2006), 'Efforts to Curb Political Violence in Afghanistan' in Pervaiz Iqbal Cheema, Maqsudul Hasan Nuri and Ahmad Rashid Malik (eds), *Political Violence and Terrorism in South Asia*, Islamabad Political Research Institute, pp. 150–71.

Sedra, Mark and Peter Middlebrook (2005), 'Revisioning the International Compact for Afghanistan', *Foreign Policy In Focus*, 2 November.

Senlis Council (2006a), *Afghanistan Five Years Later: The Return of the Taliban*, London.

—— (2006b), *An Assessment of the Hearts and Minds Campaign in Southern Afghanistan*, London.

—— (2006c), *Canada in Kandahar: No Peace to Keep. A Case Study of the Military Coalitions in Southern Afghanistan*, London.

—— (2006d), *Field Notes. Afghanistan Insurgency Assessment. The Signs of an Escalating Crisis. Insurgency in the Provinces of Helmand, Kandahar and Nangarhar*, London.

—— (2006e), *Helmand at War: The Changing Nature of the Insurgency in Southern Afghanistan and its Effects on the Future of the Country*, London.

—— (2007), *Countering the Insurgency in Afghanistan: Losing Friends and Making Enemies*, London.

Shahzad, Syed Saleem (2007), *Pakistan, the Taliban and Dadullah*, Briefing no. 3, Bradford: Pakistan Security Research Unit.

Smith, Ben (2005), *Afghanistan: Where Are We?*, Camberley: Conflict Studies Research Centre, British Defence Academy.

Taber, Robert (1965), *The War of the Flea: A Study of Guerrilla Warfare: Theory and Practice*, New York: L. Stuart.

Tahir, Muhammad (2007), 'Iranian Involvement in Afghanistan', *Terrorism Monitor* (Jamestown Foundation), vol. 5, no. 1 (18 January).

Trives, Sébastien (2006), 'Afghanistan: réduire l'insurrection. Le cas du Sud-Est', *Politique étrangère*, no. 1.

van der Schriek, Daan (2005), 'Recent Developments in Waziristan',

Terrorism Monitor (Jamestown Foundation), vol. 3, no. 5.

Weinbaum, Marvin G. (2004), *Nation Building in Afghanistan: Impediments, Lessons, and Prospects*, paper prepared for a conference on 'Nation-Building: Beyond Afghanistan and Iraq', sponsored by The School of Advanced International Studies, 13 April 2004.

Wright, Joanna (2006a), 'Taliban Insurgency Shows Signs of Enduring Strength', *Jane's Intelligence Review*, October.

—— (2006b), 'The Changing Structure of the Afghan Opium Trade', *Jane's Intelligence Review*, 9 September.

INDEX